SOCIAL JUSTICE AND HUMAN RIGHTS IN ISLAM

SOCIAL JUSTICE AND HUMAN RIGHTS IN ISLAM

N.K. Singh

GYAN PUBLISHING HOUSE
5 Ansari Road, Darya Ganj, New Delhi-110002

SOCIAL JUSTICE AND HUMAN RIGHTS IN ISLAM
(Religion)

ISBN: 81-212-0592-1

Published in 1998 by
Gyan Publishing House,
5, Ansari Road, Darya Ganj
New Delhi-110002

Printed at Mehra Offset Press, Delhi

Contents

Preface

The book, "Social Justice and Human Rights in Islam" is an analytical study of the nature and motivation of social justice and human rights in Islamic perspectives. Social justice is one of the most important constitutional principles which has been confirmed both in the *Qur'an* and in the *Sunna.* According to the *Qur'an:* "When you judge among men judge with justice even if it hurts one's own interest or the interest of next ones." Prophet Muhammad was also deeply concerned with it and the *Hadith* attests to this. He emphatically warned of the disastrous consequences of injustice, discrimination and inequality before law for an individual or a community. The concept of social justice, as formulated in Islam, is comprehensive and encompasses all aspects of human life which governs all kinds of relations in life.

The present title has been studied in seven chapters. Chapter one is an introductory description of the meaning and importance of justice in Islamic scriptures. The word, 'justice' is God's attribute and it stands firm for it. According to the *Qur'an*, justice is a witness to God. Islamic society constitutes a balanced human community where each individual must feel that he forms with the others a compact and solid unity, based on common objectives and its activity must be organised under the aegis of a just arbitration which can assure work to everyone according to their capabilities and merits, and an equal chance to all. The wealth of *Ummah* (Islamic community) must be evenly distributed to all members according to the need.

Chapter two deals with the Islamic philosophy of human rights and the fundamental freedom of the individual and the society. In Islamic view, 'God, in fact, is supreme and man exists solely to serve Him'. It may appear from this that man exists solely to serve Him'. He has no rights, only duties. Since within the totality of Islam, man's duty to God embraces both his duty to society and to every other individual, paradoxically the rights of each are protected by the obligations of all under divine law. As the state itself is equally subject to this same law, it is also compelled to protect the rights of the individuals. By stressing the equality of all men before God, by emphasizing his dignity and freedom for submission to all save God alone, by making the state answerable before God and thus protecting the individual from oppression at its hands. Islam set high standards in human rights to which the Universal Declaration of Human Rights in 1948 can be seen as a basic corollary or extension of the programme laid down in the *Qur'an*. The *Qur'an* provides powerful integrating force which man needs today.

Chapter three deals with the nature and methods of Islamic concept of social justice. Islam has one universal theory which covers the universe, life and humanity. A knowledge of universal theory is necessary to the faith of Islam, because it enables us to understand its principles and beliefs and to relate the particular to the general. We have examined the universal theory which takes its rise from the nature of Islamic thought about the world, life and humanity. We have studied also the fundamental outlines of social justice in Islam which embraces all sides of life and all aspects of freedom. Islam refuses to admit that life can be reckoned in terms of a mouthful of bread, the appetites of every individual in order to remove their fears of destitution. On the other side, it also forbids unbridled luxury in possessions and desires which produces social divisions and classes. It prescribes the claims of the poor upon the wealth of the rich according to their needs and to the best interest of society, so that social life may be full, just and productive.

Chapter four confines to a brief examination of the evolution of Islamic civil society in western perspectives. Western philosophy of social evolution is that man has come to regard material progress as the highest achievement of life, whereas that a careful consideration it will be found that material development only aids the 'consciousness of man' which has no creative power of its own. Actually, spiritual power is the prime mover of human consciousness. The first task of the Prophet was to unite two scattered philosophies, material and spiritual, into one philosophy of the evolution of civil society.

Chapter five throws light on the social foundation of justice in Islam. Islam establishes its regulation of social justice within the limits of its universal theory. Islam legislates for mutual responsibility in society in all shapes and forms. These forms take its emergence from the basic principle that there is an all-embracing identity of purpose between the individual and society and that life in its fullness is all interrelated. So, Islam lays down a complete liberty for the individual within limits which will not injure him and will not favour society at its expense.

Chapter six describes a historical reality of the theory of social contract in Islam. The first contract between God on the one side and the people and their ruler on the other side has been introduced for the maintenance of true religion. It was upheld by the state in return for the protection and favour of Almighty God. The second contract is between ruler and subjects to preserve and protect the natural rights of subjects in return for their loyal support of the prince.

The last chapter of this book lays emphasis on the revival of true Islamic form of life in modern and post-modern world. It is not sufficient to say that Islam should have been a living force in the past and it has produced a second and well constructed society in the time of the Prophet and in the age of the Caliphate. Since that time, there have been immense changes in life: mental, economic, political and social. There have been material changes on the Earth and in its power relative to man. All these points have been carefully discussed in this chapter.

In completing this book, I have consulted various books and journals. I am thankful to all those authors and scholars whose matter has been utilised in this study. I am also thankful to my Muslim friends and scholars who inspired me in producing the true picture of Islamic socio-religious values in modern global perspectives.

N.K. Singh

1

Introduction

Rights and justice are the most important socio-political values or constitutional principles which Islam has confirmed, both in the *Qur'an* and in the *Sunnah.* The word 'Justice' is Allah's attribute and to stand firm for it, according to the *Qur'an,* is to be a witness to Allah. The *Qur'an* says:

> "O ye who believe stand out firmly for justice, as witnesses to Allah even as against yourselves, or your parents, or your kin, and whether it be (against) rich or poor, for Allah can best protect both. Follow not the lusts (of your hearts,), lest ye swerve, and if ye di-stort (justice) or decline to do justice, Verily Allah is well acquainted with all that ye do." (*The Qur'an* 4:135)

The *Qur'an* is replete with such exhortations. It enjoins persons: When you judge among men, judge with justice even if it hurts one's own interest or the interests of near ones. (al-*Qur'an* 5:58). Faith that is blended with injustice is not acceptable to Allah and the *Qur'an* proclaims:

> "Those who have faith and mix not with injustice, for them is peace and they are the ones rightly guided."

Muslims are, thus, not only exhorted but persistently urged by the *Qur'an* to establish justice:

> "Allah commands justice and doing good and giving to kinfolks and forbids indecencsy and abomination and wickedness." (*The Qur'an* 16:90).

Justice in Islam acquires a place of such paramount importance that being just is a necessary criterion for the pious and the Allah-fearing. Describing the basic characteristic of a Muslim the *Qur'an* says:

> "O ye, who believe, be upright for Allah, bearers of witness with justice and let not hatred of others make you swerve from justice. Be just, this is nearer to piety and fear Allah,

for Allah is aware of what we do.'' (*al-Qur'an* 5:8).

The *Qur'an* not only enjoins the rendering of justice among the Muslims but also commands dispensing it between Muslims and non-Muslims: ''And do not let hatred of any dissaude you from dealing justly. Deal justly for it is closer to piety, and godliness.'' (*al-Qur'an* 5:9).

The *Qur'an* while exhorting justice also suggests severe punishment for injustice as a corrective measure:

> The indictment shall be upon those who oppress people and those who commit injustice and wrong-doing on earth shall be severely punished. (*al-Qur'an* 42:42).

Here, the retribution of injustice signifies or alludes to authority and the state capable of enforcing laws, which implies that the Islamic concept of justice is restricted not merely to the field of ethics but also pertains to the rule of government.

Prophet Muhammad, too, was deeply concerned with justice and the *Hadith* attests to this. In several *Hadith* he specifically ordered carrying of justice and avoidance of oppression. The Prophet emphatically warned of the disastrous consequence of injustice, discrimination and inequality before law for an individual or a community. He said:

> ''Communities before you strayed because when the rich committed theft they were set free, but when the poor committed theft the law was enforced to them. By Allah, if Fatima, daughter of Muhammad committed theft, Muhammad would certainly cut her hand.''[1]

The Concept of Justice

The concept of justice as formulated in Islam is comprehensive and encompasses all aspects of human life. It governs all kinds of relations in life including those between the ruler and the ruled, between husband and wife, between parents and children and between individuals in their private relationships.

Hence, as stated earlier, it is not only an ethical value but an essential principle of government in Islam. Again like other constitutional principles, it lacks full elaboration. These, however, constitute some of the theoretical and conceptual aspects of justice in Islam.

Its practical application is denoted by the institution of *qadi*. The lexicographical meaning of the term *qadi* is execution.[2] It signifies a process of settlement of dispute or its elimination through an explanation of the rights of the genuine claimant by exposing falsehood by arbitration in the language of *fiqh*. It is defined as a command or order according to *shari'ah* values as to what is just and righteous. *Ad-Sarakhsi* described *qada* as the best form of worship and held that there is nothing more obligatory than a just decision.[3] Thus the exercise of the *qada* is a vital principle of religion. It is regarded as a *fard al-Kifaya*-a religious obligation.

The *qada* of Islam includes both the judicial process and the arbitration process of common law. For the judicial process as defined by Peltason is a set of inter-related procedures and rules for deciding disputes and adjusting conflicts by an authoritative person or persons whose decisions are obeyed.[4] The arbitration process as defined by Aiyhah serves the function of assisting in arriving at an equitable solution.[5] The person incharge or *qada* of the person empowered to adjudicate claims and disputes between persons is a *qadi* or a judge.

In medieval literature, the *qadi* is a person who is appointed by the ruler to determine the disputed rights and liabilities of the litigants, civil or criminal, and to adjudicate in the matters of marriage, divorce, maintenance and inheritance, to look after the interests of orphans and to manage public trusts.[6]

The judicial administration in Islam consists of the application of the sacred principles and justice is administered in the name of Allah. The exercise of *qada,* therefore, considered to be one of the noble acts of devotion. For these reasons jurists such as Imam Shafi'i provided that a Muslim who feels himself specially capable of exercising the functions of a judge should solicit those functions. It was sinful to refuse a judicial position.[7]

The right of appointing a *qadi* rests with the ruler. The appointment of a *qadi* is actually the delegation of the ruler's judicial power to another person capable of rendering it. The appointing authority must see that a highly competent and eligible person alone is selected for the office of the *qadi*. The Prophet enjoined:

"He, who confers a post on someone in preference to a better qualified person betrays the trust placed in him by Allah, the Prophet and the Muslim community."[8]

The terms laid down by medieval jurists including *al-Mawardi* for the appointment of the *qadi,* he must be a Muslim, sane, wise, just and honest. He must be fully conversant with the knowledge of *usul al-fiqh*, the principles of laws, must be able to decide disputes according to the tenets of *the Shariah's* must be free from physical disabilities such as blindness, deafness, loss of mental capacity, should be a male and capable of doing *ijtihad* in order to deduce and enunciate *fatwas* to questions of law posed to him.[9]

Women's competence to be appointed as *qadi* is a controversial question among the different schools of Islamic law. According to Imam Malik, Imam Shafi'i and Imam Hanbal, a woman is incompetent to hold the post of a *qadi.*[10] Imam Abi Hanifa holds that a woman can be appointed to act as a *qadi* only in those matters wherein the evidence of a woman is held admissible in law, i.e. all matters other than those of punishment and retáliation, *hudud* and *qisas.*[11]

The opinion that woman is incompetent to be a *qadi* draws its support from the notion that *qada* is a part of *imam* for which a woman is not considered eligible. The ruling that a *qadi* should be a *mujtahid* is also debatable one. According to Imam Shafi'i, it is absolutely necessary that a *qadi* be a *mujtahid.* For Imam Abu Hanifa:

"a *qadi* who is also a *mujtahid* is commendable while a *ghair mujtahid* can also be validly appointed as a *qadi.*"

In medieval times, there seems to be a dilution of the rule that a *qadi* should be from the *ahl al-Ihtihad*, hence later it was established that a *qadi;* who is also a *mujtahid* is preferable but not indispensable. What is essentially required of him is an in-depth knowledge of the provisions of *fiqh.* In the opinion of Imam Abu Halifa:

"the appointment of a *qadi* should not exceed one year, after which the state should ask him to quit and acquire learning lest he, under the pressure of administering justice, may become slack in his knowledge of law."[12]

If a *qadi* proves to be unjust after his appointment, he deserves dismissal. Other reasons for which a *qadi* can be dismissed from his office are blindness, deafness, loss of reason and apostasy. The *qadi* may on his own, resign from his office.[13]

The jurisdiction of a *qadi* may be either general or restricted, i.e., *tanfidh-al tafwid.* In *tanfidh,* there is a provision for the settling of disputes either by arbitration on lawful terms between the disputing parties or by enforcing liabilities by judgement. Originally, this was the only duty of a *qadi* but as time passed on other duties also were added to his jurisdiction. These included control over the insane and their property by reason of madness, infancy or insolvency and enforcement of rights and obligations in their favour.

The *qadi* also had the charge of the execution of the testamentary conditions of wills, if lawful giving in marriage of unmarried and widowed women, provided they deserved it. Imam Abu Hanifa, however, denied that this was a duty of a *qadi*, holding that women are themselves capable of deciding the question of their marriage.[14]

The *qadi* had the duty of ordering for specific legal penalties when complaints were made. Securing the welfare of the district by preventing encroachment on roadways and other public places was included in his jurisdiction as well. When no one was in charge of the collection of *sadaqa* the *qadi* was entitled to collect and expend them for proper objects, since it comes within the fold of religious matter.

However, according to some Imams, the *qadi* is not required to be concerned about it for *sadaqa* comes under the jurisdiction of the treasury and must be left to the ruler.[15] A *qadi* of restricted jurisdiction is allowed to decide cases on admission but not on evidence, or in cases of debt but not of marriage, or he may have general jurisdiction over a restricted area.[16]

The main function of the *qadi*, however, is related to the administration of justice. In this regard, he performs the duties relating to fixation of the date for hearing in the suits filed, to pass an *ex-parte* order in default of the appearance of the plantiff or his witness, to review the decided cases for correction of error and to do all relative duties regarding the administration of justice.

During the process of *qada,* the *qadi* was to administer justice with a consideration of compromise or settlement between the parties. While deciding the cases before him, a *qadi* has to bear in mind both the commandments of Allah and the teachings of the Prophet. When no *Qur'anic* injunction and no *Hadith* applicable to the issue are found, the *qadi* has to rely on the *ijma* of the companions. If the *qadi* is not a *mujtahid* he must seek a *fatwa* and decide in accordance with it. He has to enter into judgement according to the proof furnished by the parties with equal treatment given to both the parties.

The court of a *qadi* was normally held at the mosque, but he was permitted to operate from his own house. Ibn Asakir records that the Caliph Uthman had constructed a special building for the court of justice with the name *Dar al-Qada.* According to Shafi'i, the *qadi* should hold session at a place accessible to and convenient for the concerned parties. The Hanafis asserted that the mosque was the best suited place, since, the rendering of justice was considered to be an act of devotion.[17]

Because of the religious character of the institution of *qadi,* the *qadis* were called upon to legitimize and consecrate the investiture of the new Caliph. The *qadis* were also called upon to legitimize through legal advice, the deposition of a ruler through a palace revolution. The *qadi* also performed acts alien to judicial functions such as legitimising an administrative act or modifying certain regulations with his advice.

On account of these varied functions of the *qadi*, Tyan observes that no rational classification directs the enumeration of the various judicial function. Apparently, there seems to be no distinction between the *qadi's* acts as a judge of the cases and his judicial acts outside those cases. The medieval jurists have noted this distinction: they distinguish ''judgement''-- *al-hukm al-qawli al qada* and ''command or action'-- *al hukm al fi'li* of the judge.

Judicial and arbitration processes come under *al-hukm al-qawli al qada*, while the marriage of a minor who has no guardian, the division of real estate, or in the words of Tyan, the action whose purpose is to settle certain rights but which does not imply a conflict, constitutes *fi'l.*[18] It is related that the *qadis* were entitled to maintenance and other expenses. He was not entitled to receive any presents or gifts except from the state.

In the Maliki practice of appointment of a *qadi,* such conditions were laid down that the appointee will not accept salary, will not be compelled to pass an illegal order and would in no way be approached on behalf of anyone. Justice was administered *gratis* and there was no stamp or court fee leviable in judicial proceedings.[19]

The Judicial Tribunal

Generally, the judicial tribunal in Islam is composed of a single judge--the *qadi.* The ruler cannot, says Kharshi, appoint two *qadis* to pass judgement concurrently on the same matter. It is possible to appoint two *qadis* for the same town, with each *qadi* having his separate jurisdiction, within a certain district, but both of them could not be appointed to pass judgement at the same time. Ibn al Jawzi reports of an earlier precedent wherein Ubayed Allah bin al-Anbari and Umar ib Amir were appointed joint judges in Basara, they sat together as a bench and combined in hearing and deciding.[20]

The basis of the institution of the *qadi* consilium *shura* is contributed to the system of committee of jurists established by Caliph Umar at Medina. The advice of the consilium was, however, not binding and the decision always remained in the hands of the qadi. The system of the appointment of reliable witnesses *shuhud udud* was also recorded in the history of Islamic judiciary. The *shuhud udud* played the role of assessors and protected the validity of legal acts and assisted the *qadi* in serving as witnesses. They were personally appointed by the *qadi* and were relieved in the *qadi's* removal or dismissal from the office.[21]

Apart from *shuhud udud* other officials connected with the court were court clerk-interpreters and assistants entrusted with the maintenance of order during the court's session. The officials entrusted with supplementary judicial functions were termed *a'wan* or legal assistants. The *katib* recorded the full written statements of the parties in the suits along with defence statements and connected matters. The *muzzak* investigated the character of the *shuhud* and also that of the ordinary witnesses. The *qasam or qasim* supervised the division and apportioning of goods, and the *amir al-hukm* took into custody the assets of legally incompetent persons, orphans and absentees while *khazin diwan al-khan* was entrusted with the safekeeping of the court archives. *Wakils* were the lawyers or attorneys who appeared or prepared for appearance on behalf of the parties in the courts.[22] *Wilaya* literally means to be the incharge of something; to have power, authority or command over something.

In Islam, the Caliph is a substitute law-giver and all powers necessary for its rule are centred in him. The exercise of *qada* was to have been the personal task of the Caliphs, but they entrusted others with it because they were busy with general politics and pre-occupied with *jihad*. The delegation of power precisely meant representation. The idea of delegation/ representation is an important principle in Muslim law. Yet, it has been misunderstood by some scholars. For instance, Tyan remarks that the *qadi* is the delegate/ representative of the ruler and by virtue of the fact he lacks autonomy.

The *qadi* appointed by the Caliph could further delegate powers to a third person who in turn could sub-delegate his powers to another and this process could proceed in a chain. In other words, Tyan uses the hierarchical organisation of the judicial personages to support his thesis that the *qadi* lacks autonomy and that he is a subordinate of central authority.[23] The distribution and re-distribution of power was expedient to make the judiciary effective and easily accessible to all.

The survey of source material brought for the existence of two definite stands of thought: one asserting the independence of judiciary in Islam, and the other contending that judiciary in Islam is not free from political interference. The first group comprises the majority of Muslims and can be said to represent the standard Muslim point of view.

Muhammad Hamidullah, a representative of the first group, writes that what the Prophet enunciated for the administration of justice was equality of persons before law. Law is the same for the rich as well as poor. Even the Caliph could be sued before the *qadi*. To make the point clear, he cites the instance wherein the Prophet towards the end of his life publicly announced that anyone having a claim against him should come forward. A man claimed few *dirhams* which were paid him then and there. Caliphs 'Umar and 'Ali' writes Hamidullah, presented themselves and gave their accounts before the *qadi* during their respective caliphates.[24]

It follows, therefore, that the judiciary was absolutely free from outside control or interference, that the ruler could not prevent the decision of the *qadi* from coming into force, as long as the decision of the *qadi* was not openly in conflict with the tenets of Islam.

Rahman, writing on the same issue says that no person in an Islamic state, not even the elected head, can be above the law and he is as much subject to the *hudud* as anyone else. Rahman cites the incident that Abd al-Rahman bin Tariq, a *qadi* of Spain, during the reign of Abd al-Rahman al-Muawiya, gave a ruling against one Habib, a personal friend of the Caliph. Habib complained to the Caliph, who ordered the *qadi* to reconsider the case. Ibn Tariq replied, writes Rahman, that his office, just as that of the Caliph derived its authority from the Prophet, hence his duty, therefore, was to follow the example of the Prophet and administer justice impartially to both the strong and the weak, and had his decree established.[25]

The latter view is largely held and supported by the orientalists. N.J. Coulson states that Islamic legal theory and practice lacks powerful and independent judiciary. Coulson quoting Tyan writes that a *qadi* was merely the legal secretary of the political authority.[26] While investigating the cause of reluctance of many a personage to accept judicial office, Coulson concluded that their reluctance was essentially due to the dependence of the *qadi's* upon political authority.[27]

The doctrine of *wilaya* which defined the scope and nature of the *qadi's* jurisdiction affected the decisions given and actions taken by the *qadi*. He cites the incident wherein the governor of Egypt Abd al-Aziz bin Marwan, who got the decision of his *qadi*

Abbas bin Said reversed. According to Coulson the whole spirit of the religious law is fundamentally opposed to the notion of an independent judiciary fearlessly defining the limits of the power of the state over the individual and powerful enough to give effect to its decisions.[28]

The doctrine of separation of power was first formulated by John Adams who set forth in Article XXX of the Massachusett Constitution of 1780 that "in the government of this commonwealth, the legislative department shall never exercise the executive and judicial powers, or either of them, the executive shall never exercise the legislative and judicial power or either of them, the judiciary shall never exercise the legislative and executive power or either of them."[29]

Adam's proposition meant that the executive, legislative and judical institutions should have autonomous constituencies. The doctrine of separation of powers as it is understood from its definition is inapplicable in an Islamic state. For, an Islamic state is an ideological state-sovereignty of Allah is its starting point. Allah alone is the real law-giver and the authority of absolute legislation is vested in Him. He alone is the source of judicial, legislative and executive authority.

Islamic political system is based on the foundation of the vice-regency of man, under which the Muslims have been given limited popular sovereignty. The Muslims through *baya* delegate their authority to the Caliph. The Caliph thus possesses the overall authority in a limited sense. Through the doctrine of *wilaya*, he can further delegate his authority to other persons.

In a secular state, the doctrine of separation of power is implemented for checking absolute power, that is to create checks and counterchecks on the people at the helm of affairs. In the Islamic state, in ideal circumstances, the question of absolute authority does not arise at all. Right at the apex, the authority is a restrained one.

In addition to this, the Muslims in Islamic state are endowed with a right to political action. The underlying principle of Islamic state is religion. Hence any violation of law is not a violation of a state regulation but an act against the divine commandment, thus a sin. It is on account of the religious and ideological basis that the Islamic state does not require a disconnection of the judicial process from the political system. The fact that contextual reality is far from ideal reality hardly requires emphasis here.

The Concept of Social Justice

Justice is neither only the very foundation of the true Muslim society such as it was, and such as it ought to be, nor is it only one of the five pillars of Islam as symbolized by the *zakat*- that part of income due to the State annually-nor all the related legal provisions. It is not solely one of the attributes of Allah revealed in the *Qur'an*: "He who holds the scales in balance (on the last day)" (5:18), nor is it simply that element present in hundreds of Islamic laws concerning *ibadat* or acts of devotion, even though these acts are a valid criteria. Justice in Islam is much more than the sum of all these things. It is the foundation upon which dogma *(aqida)* is built, and it is directly bound to the sphere of faith *(iman)* itself. In the *Qur'an*, we read:

> "Hast thou observed him who belieth religion ? That is he who repelleth the orphan, and urgeth not the feeding of the needy."

> And in a Hadith of the Prophet:

> 'No, he does not believe in Allah, nor in Last Judgement, he who eats his full at night whilst his neighbour is raked with hunger.'

It appears from this that *adl* or social justice, is brought to full completion by social solidarity, and that both are firmly attached to *iman*, the basis of *aqida* itself.

But where the bond which ties *adl* to the foundation of dogma-that is, faith-seems most apparent, is in the examination of belief in the Last Judgement. What, in fact, would this Judgement Day mean without faith in the Resurrection, in the accounting of deeds-*hissab* in retribution and in punishment: without faith in Allah, in His scriptures and in His Prophets?

To believe in this Day of Judgement, therefore, is to believe in the finality revealed to us by the scriptures and the chosen prophets, in other words, the Resurrection, the Last Judgement or the accounting of deeds whereby each one shall be punished or rewarded according to his deeds, in conformity with the rules of divine justice, or even of human justice, in so far as it requires and aspires to fulfil the human justice, in so far as it requires and aspires to fulfil the divine justice.

For this reason that the Islamic doctrine held by distinguished scholars such as *Zamakhchari* and *Qadi Abdel Djbbar* has given the concept of free will-without which neither retribution nor the punishment of Allah would make any sense but would be seen rather as injustices-the name theory of justice, on the understanding that in this case it is a matter of divine justice.

Since the man who repels the orphan and does not readily encourage feeding of the poor is really the negator of religion, and since the man satiated, forgetting his starving neighbour, is really denying food and the Last Judgement which itself constitutes divine justices, we can affirm that all societies calling themselves Islamic, yet which do not realise this justice, have nothing to do with Islam, and even less to do with faith, other than in name.

Having adduced this philosophical or ideological evidence by way of introduction-which in these days of ideological confrontation may not seem entirely inappropriate-let us now try to give some examples of this social justice in Islam. We shall look at it from two aspects:

> ''formal and spiritual, and also on the plane of behaviour--*suluk* and of goals--*maqassid*--which are sought by the legislator, bearing in mind that the social justice which was the mark of Islamic civilization during its days of splendour remains as much in the letter as in the spirit, a far off work, offering to those who wish to realise it, a vast field of theoretical moral codes and objectives yet to be attained.''

Let us first recall that Islam regards the son of Adam, honoured by the Creator as his vice-regent on earth, as a being endowed not only with a body, but also with a spirit, limited certainly by certain physical constraints in the manner of other living creatures, but possessing dignity and spiritual, moral and social dimensions. For this reason, man cannot survive on a purely material and economic plane of life.

As far as it is possible to define it from the law, Islamic society constitutes a balanced, humane community, where each individual must feel that he forms with the others a compact and solid unity, based on fraternity, social solidarity and equality of rights and duties, This society must work towards a common objective. Its activity must be organised under the aegis of a just arbitration which can assure work to everyone according to his capability and merit, and an equal chance to all. The wealth of the *Ummah*-the Islamic community--must be evenly distributed to all members according to need, taking into account the solidarity which binds them.

Islam has fully defined matters relating to income and expenditure under various heads. It has instigated rights and duties, but it has also exhorted man to generosity in the highest sense-*badhl*, to financial sacrifice (*tadhya)* to the purification of wealth by the *zakat-tazkia,* all directed to the achievement of social justice. In all, it maintains a double objective-to educate souls and preserve the interests of the community *(jama'a)*. When educative methods prove ineffectual, Islam exercises coercive redress-*zair*.

Further, where methods of religious persuasion no longer work on the conscience, when neither the exhortations of the preacher (*w'adh*) nor the counselling of the *murchid*-director of conscience-bear fruit, it brings forth the whip of the *Qadi* (judge) or the sword of the supreme authority of the State.

Social justice, thus, based on economic justice in Islam has been able to guarantee certain standards to all members of the *Ummah*, be they capable or incapable of performing any work, be they poor, weak, widowed or children. It includes among the weak, both Muslims and *Dhimmis*-those, who live in an Islamic country but do not profess Islam. Animals, too, are included among the weak. However, the social justice of Islam has neither approved nor encouraged poverty engendered by laziness or inertia.

Islam absolutely forbids begging. The *mushtassib*-commissioner in charge of economic affairs-has the authority to command a beggar physically capable of work, to do so. If the beggar refuses, the responsible commissioner should employ coercive means until the beggar ceases to hold out his hand. Islam neither encourages parasites, malingering under the protection of *zaouias* or hospices, nor living on charity, regardless of who may be dispensing it.

Justice for Livelihood

The Islamic principle is that man must earn his living by work. Approximately five hundred verses of the *Qur'an* extol the expense of energy in useful work. The Prophet has glorified labour in several of the *Hadith*. It is necessary to understand by *amal* as much the work of a man in his personal enterprise, agricultural, industrial, or commercial and other forms of profit and production, as the work carried out by salaried workers such as civil servants, industrial workers and other employees.

There are a number of *Hadith* devoted to the protection of wages for workers, dealing with taxes, remuneration itself and the need for rapid payment. The Prophet adds to this subject:

> "He who willingly works and does not have shelter, must be given shelter. If he is single, then he must be given a wife. If he does not have a camel let him claim one."

Shaikh Abu Zahra commenting on this subject further states:

> "All this evidently is to be accounted for by the *beit-al-mal* of the Muslim state, that is to say, the public treasury."

These benefits to the worker are productive of many advantages which will in the last analysis benefit the whole of the Muslim community. They imply free housing, transport and also marriage, with the costs to be borne where necessary by the State. Family allowances in the time of the Prophet and Abu Bakr were paid in favour of the husband, wife and children. Under the Caliph Omar, the amount of the allowance was augmented according to the age of the children and continued until they were of age. They were not only granted to the so-called legitimate progeny but equally to illegitimate children. This provision was perpetuated under the Caliphs Othman and Ali and well into the succeeding period.

The spirit of Islam guarantees the well-being of workers. It guarantees the same tranquillity even to animals. The Imam

Ahmad said that it is incumbent upon the *muhtassib* to forbid persons possessing animals to use them in work which they cannot accomplish. The French author Peltier, in his translation of Boukhary, was led to examine these various aspects of solidarity and of social justice in Islam, as well as the guarantees offered to workers by our religion. He is not alone in expressing his admiration of the system. Little of this exists in the Muslim world today. Even so as a model or ideal, the Islamic concept of social justice has a degree of perfection still to be attained even in the most highly developed non-Muslim states.

Islam has given emphasis in favour of employees and workers since the time of the Prophet. It has promised with equal guarantees to families without sufficient resources at their disposal. The Prophet said, ''He who leaves after his death dependents deprived of support or very young children, his affair is my concern. I become a guardian.'' In other words, the State assumes responsibility.

Justice and Social Solidarity

The domain of social justice or social solidarity is extended to the protection of several categories of the weak *(ajaza)* and needy. The aged, the *Dhimmis*-non-Muslims-are amongst those allowed the advantages of social benefits. A celebrated instance from the time of the Caliph Omar illustrates this. Addressing an old Jew, he said:

> ''We have not been fair in our treatment of you, since we have exhausted your youth and abandoned you when you aged.''

Omar immediately invited him to his home, and there gave him his own food and had the treasury bestow a pension on him to the end of his days. The same measures were passed in favour of the poor, the needy, the sick, the blind, the crippled, displaced persons and prisoners, as well as orphans, the weak and illegitimate children as already mentioned.

The concept of social justice was expressed further in quite unique ways. An example may be found in the *waqf* or *zabadi*, instituted to cover the damages caused by the children of slaves, so that they might avoid the pecuniary sanctions or corporal punishment that their parents or masters could otherwise inflict upon them. Provision was also made whereby the public treasury would intervene to help the insolvent debtor pay his debts, and aid was given to poor travellers who found themselves far from home.

Other implementations were devoted to psychiatric hospitals where the sick were given therapy with music and popular comedy, a field where modern psychotherapy has proved the value of methods being used to great effect so many centuries ago. Justice and social solidarity however are not confined to the material side of life.

Social justice goes one step nearer to attaining solidarity by stipulating the need for love, a necessary part of the Islamic community which must present itself as a single body, a compact edifice, It is this which embodies the idea of humanitarian justice. Though the spirit of class and race still prevails in our own days, Islám established equality between all men. This equality is proclaimed in the Qur'an:

> 'The noblest among you in the sight of Allah are the most Allah-fearing.'' And in the Hadith of the Prophet: ''Muslims are all equal, just as the teeth of a comb.''

This principle is repeated in several other *hadith* or deeds of the Prophet and his companions. A brief reference to some of these will illustrate the point. On the equality of race and ethnic origin, there is the example of the Prophet's rebuke to his companion Abu Dharr Al-Ghifari. Abu Dharr had mocked Bilal I'Abyssin, evoking, ''the colour of his mother'. The Prophet said to him:

> ''O Abu Dharr, you are still a man belonging to pagan (*jahilyya*) times. Lift your head and look. Then know that you are hardly superior to a man of colour, be it black or red unless you surpass him in deeds.''

In the legal domain, it is established that the Prophet submitted himself truly voluntarily when it came to the execution of corporal punishment, as the occasion in the mosque when the Prophet was in the process of joining the ranks of the faithful for prayer. Someone claimed that the Prophet had hurt him by knocking him over. Muhammad immediately offered him the right to avenge himself upon his person if he so wished.

A somewhat similar instance was the intervention of Usama lbn Zaid in a case concerning a theft by a woman of the Banu Makhum. The chiefs of this large and powerful tribe asked Usama Ibn Zaid to intervene with the Prophet, who held him in great esteem, since the honour of the tribe would be at stake if the woman were to be subjected to corporal punishment. The Prophet came in, angrily admonishing:

> "Would you intervene in the punishments set forth by Allah?"
>
> Then, he turned to the Muslims declaring:
>
> "what has been the downfall of nations before you is that when a thief of noble origin was caught, he was allowed to go free without punishment, whereas the thief of humble origin was submitted to punishment. I swear by all the oaths of Allah that if Fatima, daughter of Muhammad, committed a theft, I would have her hand cut off."

It was thus that the Prophet applied the rites of justice and equality even to himself, and to his family where necessary, demonstrating the truth of the concept that there is no distinction of class or caste in Islam.

The Caliph, Omar behaved in like manner with regard to his son Abdel Rahman when he applied the famous principle, "From where do your possessions come?" (*min ayna laka hadha?).* He made even the greatest of the Prophet's companions submit to this law-men like Khalid Ibn-Walied, 'Amr Ibn al' As, Sayad Ibn Abi Waqqas, Abu Horaira and many others.

This form of justice is not limited to the conduct of Muslims only among themselves. Islam makes it an obligation for Muslims in their dealings with the faithful of other religions, and there are many instances of its practical implementation in the early history of Islam, as for example in Omar's resolution of the dispute between a Copt and the son of Amr Ibn al'As, Governor of Egypt, and his own appearance before the *Qadi* Choreih with a Jew.

It would scarcely by possible to find a more perfect model of the just ruler than Omar II, Ibn' Abdel' Aziz, whether democratic or revolutionary, at any time in history.

Means of Attaining Social Justice

What are the sources of revenue sufficient to cover all the expenditure demanded by these and many other measures of social justice? To answer this we must formulate some idea of economic justice which is the pre-requisite and complement of social justice; the two cannot be separated.

Alongside charitable institutions like the *awqaf*-holy foundations-which often went as far as protecting animals, many individual contributions imposed by the religious law for the good of the community, such as maintenance for close relatives, expiation of *kaffarat*, funds left by will and testament, or *wasiyya* and other measures designed to reinforce social solidarity, there existed the *Beit-al-mal* or public treasury. This was the chief means of financing social welfare and drew revenues from a number of sources, the most important of which was the *Zakat*-purification dues.

Zakat constitutes the principal base upon which the social structure of Islam is built. It is neither alms nor charity, but an obligatory due. He who consciously refuses to pay this tithe is considered a renegade and runs the risk of mortal punishment. The war of the *ridda*-apostasy-when the Caliph Abu Bakr declared war on the recalcitrants who wanted the Muslims to return to the days of paganism and destroy the Islamic community, evidences the extremity of the punishment.

There is an element of piety in the *Zakat,* since, it is act of devotion-*ibada*-which brings the human being closer to his Creator. It is an act of solidarity with society and educates the soul, teaching it to conquer selfishness and to practise self-sacrifice and generosity. For the spirit it constitutes a source of joy and of peace, and for the conscience procures the satisfaction of having fulfilled its duty to Allah. For all these reasons, the *Zakat* is different from anything which may appear to have a superficial resemblance to it in the modern world. It is not simply a tax which may be avoided by cheating the government fiscal system in one way or another.

Another source of revenue which feeds the *Beit-al-mal* is derived from what Ibn Hazm describes as expenditure due besides the *Zakat*. In this connection, Ibn Hazm has commented upon a *hadith* stressed by Ali which states:

> ''Allah makes it an obligation for the rich of a country to provide for the needs of their poor. Authority must compel them when the resources of the *Zakat* is insufficient.''

Ibn Hazm and other jurists have proclaimed that when a man dies of starvation, the people in whose house, he has died should consider themselves collectively responsible for his death and should, in consequence, pay the *diya* or price of blood. Scholars learned in the *Hadith* have indicated how the Prophet enumerated the superfluous possessions that a Muslim should give to one who has only the bare minimum.

After this enumeration, the companions of the Prophet began to perceive that fundamentally, no person has the right to possess anything superfluous to his needs. Caliph Omar in a public address also said:

> ''If I was to live longer, I would take the possessions that the rich have in excess and give them to the poor. No man is more worthy than another to be in possession of wealth. And following this, I would raise those who are last to the ranks of the first.''

It emerges from this, that the just man in authority must intervene to stop arbitrariness and iniquity. He must ensure justice and equity. When he finds that there are enormous disparities in the heart of the community, and that luxury and wealth exist alongside poverty and misery, he must guarantee economic justice and therefore social justice.

Further way of realising social justice in the Islamic point of view is that of public ownership, that is ownership by the *Ummah* or community. It consists in suppressing large-scale ownership in general, when it exists, by returning property to the State. This is the situation most frequently encountered.

The objective of Islamic law, though in principle it respects and protects individual ownership, is to establish justice, by preventing wealth from accumulating in the hands of an oligarchic plutocracy who live in opulence and luxury, circulating money solely among its members, whilst the majority of people exist in hunger, destitution and contempt. The poor will not be slow, in these circumstances, to form an army of malcontents capable of threatening the stability of the community, of weakening and undermining it. Allah has prescribed that our community be strong and flourishing.

Islam abominates the fact of poor in its bosom. The Prophet said:

> "I am in the hands of Allah with regard to poverty and infidelity-*Kufr*-poverty is tantamount to infidelity."

The Prophet sequestered *hama* -a piece of land at Medina called Naqui' to serve as pasture land for horses belonging to the Muslims, which was to be shared by all Muslims. For the same purpose Omar put aside a piece of land at Rabdha. The proprietors of this land came to him complaining, "O, Prince of Believers! This land belongs to us! We have fought for it during the *jahilyya*. It belonged to us even when we entered the Islamic religion. Why then have you sequestered it?" 'Omar, after reflecting for a moment, replied, "All goods belong to Allah! People are the creatures of Allah! If I were not obliged to do certain things to remain in the path of Allah, I would not have sequstered a single span of the land." The word *huma*, to sequester, denotes the act of taking a certain area of land which was private property and making it over as a possession of the community, for the benefit of those members of the community in need.

This objective seems clear and incontestable when we read the instructions given by Omar to the agent in charge of land sequestered at Rabdha. He specified that the pasture be " for those who were in need"-*muhtadyin*. And we can read in several histories, that he had no wish to hear about the beasts of Ibn Affan or Ibn Awf who were wealthy, since if they were to lose their livestock they would still have the time to go to their watering places and gather grain, whilst the wretched poor man, having lost his herd, had no recourse but to come to him with his children crying, "O Prince of Believers."

To the argument that such a man in distress had the right to ask help from the State, since he had a right to part of the *Beit-al-mal*, Caliph Omar enjoined, "Should I abandon them to their sad fate: could you anymore lose your own father? To supply them with grazing is easier for me than to give them gold or money. Yes, I know that this land belongs to its owners, that they fought for it in the *jahilyya* and that they owned it when they came into Islam. I know they think I am unjust in this matter, but it is to try to walk in the way of the Lord that I have done all this.'' Omar's action put into practice the *Hadith* of the Prophet:

> ''Men are united by three things: water, pasture and fire.''

His conduct is consistent with the principle:

> ''One should suffer a small ill to avoid a major harm.''

There is a further example of the same kind also stemming from the Caliphate of Omar. It was suggested to Omar that he distribute the regions conquered in Iraq and Syria and give them to the people. He refused, and made these regions the property of the State justifying his action in the following words:

> ''If we were to divide these lands, nothing would remain for those who come after you. What would they say, these Muslims, when they saw the land already distributed, inherited and possessed?''

The idea is unthinkable. What then would be left of these Syrian and Iraqi lands for the orphans and widows of these countries?'' The story further relates that Ibn Djabel, who with the Imam Ali was among those who agreed with Omar, suggested to the latter, ''If you distribute these lands, their harvests will be in the hands of these particular people, but after their death all will be concentrated in the hands of a single man or a single woman.'' Instead of dividing these immense areas between a limited group of the Prophet's companions and forming a new caste of big property owners. Omar and certain others preferred to establish, as Al-A'wzal says, a greater number of small *fellahs* and villagers in village groups, allowing them to run their own affairs, and act on their own initiative.

In this way they would be enabled to till the earth profitably, and pay the taxes which would be due to the State. They were fully aware that no Muslim would be able to buy the land whether by agreement or coercion, since all agreed that the possessions thus acquired could neither become an object of sale, nor of inheritance. The greatly mourned Shaikh Abu Zhara writing on this subject deduced that Omar had made his judgements on three grounds, all of them concerned to promote the general good. His intention was to prevent the creation of large landed estates, since the lands of Iraq and Syria together accounted for many thousand *feddans*, and if divided between ten thousand people they would inevitably create a class of large landowners. To benefit the State and the progress of *jihad* by the land tax--*kharadj*--these lands would bring in, both of which would be pleasing to Allah; to supply further State revenue for the benefit of the needy.

It is beyond question that Caliph Omar based his judgement on the interests of the *Ummah*, when he might very easily have taken advantage of certain other precedents of the time of the Prophet. Since, in the first two instances quoted, Islam put large-scale individual ownership at the disposal of common interest, and in the third prevented the development of large scale ownership after the property had actually fallen into the hands of the State, it is established beyond doubt that Islam prohibits the development of private ownership wherever the acquisition or monopoly of wealth threatens to create properties on a large scale. Commenting on these Shaikh Abu Zhara wrote:

> "The utterances of the Prophet *(Hadith)* proving that *ihtihar* is unlawful *(haram)* are numerous. No matter what form this acquisitive aggrandisement assumes, it is unlawful since it constitutes a *habs* by stopping the circulation of goods, whether food, clothing or other things. *Ihtihar*, therefore, prevents the weak from gaining access to agricultural property and from working the land. In fact, where there are great landed proprietors, it is they who buy all the land which might be put for sale. The small farmers cannot fight against them to acquire this land. It is then the duty of authority to intervene."

The uncompromising attitude of Shaikh Abu Zahra is well known. He stood by his beliefs and was never obsequous to those in power. He was not the kind of man who changed his opinion with each change in government. The lines above were not written out of opportunism or fear since he always resisted all pressures. His firm stand often caused him problems yet, he did not change, and such was his position to the end of his days.

We have touched briefly on the concept of social justice in Islam, examining its literary tradition, its spirit, its finality and the way in which it was realised during the golden age of Islam. We have even examined the content of economic justice upon which it is built. Indeed, the first is conditioned by the second, since it supplies the means by which social justice is translated into concrete form. This idea of complementarity may be compared to that of Kant, who wrote:

> "Understanding is composed of two complementary elements: concept and sensations. The concepts without the sensations are empty. Sensations without concepts are blind: they have neither goal nor significance."

In the context of our subject, social justice is the concept and economic justice its terms, its substance, the condition without which it cannot be applied. How otherwise can Islam go forward and proclaim that the right of the individual is tied to the right of the community, that general interest takes precedence over particular interest and that the good of the *Ummah* comes before the good of each person?

Our religion has realised all this without leaving the individual suffocated, harmed or crushed by the mass of society. How, otherwise, can it go forward and claim that Islam is at the same time a religion, a State and a perfect social order? Sayyid Qutb wrote on this subject:

> "According to modern terminology, Islam means a system of organisation-*nidham*-fulfilled by the idea of dogma-*aqida*-at the level of conscience, by ethics at the level of behaviour-*suluq*-and finally by that of divine law-*Shari'ah*-at the social level."

The complementary roles of social and economic justice were protected by the State, which watched over their application. They were enriched and furthered by a network of beneficent popular institutions, like an immense carpet worked by open and outstretched hands working side by side, capable of protecting each man who might be a victim of adversity or in danger of perishing. And all this was the work of a law-giver who persisted in efforts for its application. Has there ever existed, does there exist even today, anything to rival the conceptual order of Islam such as it was applied in times past? At that time of Omar Ibn Abdel Aziz, not only were there no beggars, poor or needy, but no evidence could be found of people liable to receive the benefit of the *zakat* even thought the legal definition of the *massakin* - needy - is, "those who do not have the means to feed themselves for one year." An African Governor under the same Caliph said one day:

> "We have to go from door to door to find someone who will accept the *zakat*."

Can social justice, in its essence, attain a higher degree of development? Call it what you will, the essential is that it should have suppressed tyranny, exploitation and slavery; that it be general; that it guarantee dignity and freedom of man; that it protect spiritual values and that the religion of Allah should predominate. Call it what you will, 'social justice' with Sayyid Qutb, or 'social solidarity' which Abu Zahra, or *ishtirakyya* - 'socialism'--with Dr. Muhammed Al-Mubarak who wrote:

> "To say that there is no socialism in Islam is to be ignorant of the nature of socialism, and to demonstrate in addition an inability to understand the teachings and objectives of 'Islam; to prove that one has no acquaintance with Islamic laws pertaining to the subject. Call it, if you like, the socialism of Islam, as does Mustafa Siba'i, or Islamic socialism' as does Hassan Al - Banna; give it any other name you can think of, provided that the word chosen contains real substance; for without this, it would be nothing more than a slogan."

The essential is not to be found in names, or in forms, or in slogans. The essential is the content, the substance. The essential is that it should actually exist, this social justice, just as it did during the golden age of Islam, and enriched now by the addition of new substance, which must, above all else, conform to the general interest, that is to the interest of the *Ummah*, without stiffling the individual.

It should also take into account the experiences, good or bad, of other nations making use of the criterion of rational effort - *ijtihad* - and its rules for amelioration and perfection. And then let this social justice be designated by whatever name one cares to choose, even that of 'socialism', since, it is this name that the young prefer in our days, provided that it had conferred upon it the original meaning, and that it is anything but *shirk-* infidelity, *shirac*-stumbling blocks, or *ishrak*-idolatry. It will signify, quite simply, *el ishtirak*-a community of effort and of fruits. In the major capitals of the developed world, there are beggars and poor wretches who can be described as beggars.

In the European and American press, we read that men have died on the streets from cold or hunger, or even worse evils. What makes one stop and think is not the high number of such cases-and according to the paper they are relatively high, but the very fact of their existence at all. Does this mean to say that the situation in this respect is better in the Islamic world than in Europe or America? Sadly, we are forced to admit that our situation is much worse; we cannot even establish any comparison.

Even in the richest of the Muslim countries (and perhaps more so in these than elsewhere), we see the existence of the most atrocious poverty alongside the most scandalous opulence together with all the tragedy invitable in such stimulation. In our community it is no longer just a matter of the kind of cases which surprise journalists, as in Europe and America; there is a gulf, a bottomless chasm, between the social justice defined by Islam and the situation of Muslims today. "Where justice reigns there also reigns the law of Allah." Such was the opinion of Ibn Al-Qayyim Al-Jauzyya. In the same vein Sayyid Qtub wrote:

> "In this world which is called 'the Islamic world', you look and then you see a social reality which is not pleasing. Then you open your eyes and ascertain that there are social institutions which do not guarantee justice."

This is the same point of view as that expressed by Dr. Muhammad Faruk al-Nabhan, Professor at the Kuwaiti University of Law and Islamic Teachings, at the IXth Seminar on Islamic Thought which took place at Tlemcen, where he condensed all these reflections in a few words:

> "To begin with, we have to recognize that reality for the Islamic peoples is gloomy, dismal and a long way from the justice and even the spirit of Islam. We have to recognize that social injustice imposes itself on us in a form which contradicts all religious and human values."

Concepts of Human Rights

Concepts analogous to human rights have certain precursors in the Islamic heritage of philosophy and theology, but human rights lack precise equivalents in medieval *fiqh* (jurisprudence). In *fiqh* the category *haqq al-ad*, the right of the individual Muslim, was used to distinguish cases in which legal actions against a wrongdoer were left to the discretion of the injured party or parties from other cases belonging to the category of the right of Allah, *haqq* Allah, in which prosecution was mandatory and was to be undertaken by the government.

One settled *fiqh* principle corresponding to a modern right was the right of the owners of property to seek legal right against interference with their property. Rather than constructing doctrines or proposing institutions designed to curb the powers of the ruler or to protect the individual from the ruler's oppression, Islamic legal thought long concentrated on defining the theoretical duties of believers, including rulers, vis-a-vis Allah.

According to the prevailing perspective, rulers had the obligation to rule according to *shari`ah* law; their subjects were to obey them unless ordered to do something constituting a sin. The development of institutions that could place real curbs on rulers' despotism or make them accountable to those whose rule was neglected. Rebellion was commonly proposed as the remedy for tyranny.

To deal with the practical problems of protecting rights and freedoms, Muslim intellectuals and statesmen began to adopt the principles of European constitutionalism in the nineteenth century. In the latter half of the twentieth century, after the common acceptance of the principles of constitutionalism, the related question of the compatibility of international human rights principles with Islamic doctrine was raised.

The strongest influence on Muslim's ideas came from French concepts and legal principles developed during the Enlightenment and the French Revolution. These included the first great statement of modern human rights, the 1789 Declaration des Droits de I'Homme et du Citoyen, and the 1791 French Constitution, as well as concepts of public liberties.

In the areas of the Muslim world ruled by Britain, which lacked a written constitution expressly guaranteeing specified rights, the models were democratic freedom as developed in the common law tradition and Britain's system of parliamentary government.

Many nineteenth-century officials, diplomats, and writers from Muslim countries played roles in disseminating European ideas of constitutionalism and public liberties. They included the Egyptian Shaikh Rifa an Raff al-Tahtawi (1801-1891), an al-Azhar scholar who studied at French legal and political institutions in Paris from 1826 to 1831. He prepared a report on concepts of political rights, the rule of law, liberty, equality, and the ideas of the Enlightenment, and translated the French Constitution into Arabic; in 1839 his report was translated into Turkish.

Persian diplomat Mirza Malkom Khan (1833-1908), who educated in Paris and had lived in Turkey, later becoming Persian ambassador to Great Britain, wrote extensively on European concepts of government, the rule of law, and liberty, claiming that these could be reconciled with Islam. In the Ottoman realm the literary figure Namik Keman (1840-1888) was prominent in disseminating ideas of rights and freedom and the notion of their compatibility with Islam.

Constitutionalism and Rights

In the nineteenth century early clashes between inherited Islamic doctrines and modern norms regarding rights came on the question of the equality of Muslims and non-Muslims before the law. The issue was joined as European powers pressed for the elimination of the disabilities traditionally placed on non-Muslims.

A fundamental pact announced in Tunisia in 1857 under European pressure guaranteed equality for all before the law and in taxation as well as complete security for all inhabitants irrespective of religion, nationality, or race. Tunisia was the first Muslim country to promulgate a constitution, doing so in 1861 and affirming the rights established in the pact; however, the constitution was suspended by the French Protectorate (1881-1956).

In Tunisia as in many other Muslim countries, the independence struggle against European domination accentuated people's consciousness of the importance of rights and democratic freedom. After independence, the 1956 Tunisian Constitution stated that the republican form of government was the best guarantee of "human rights."

The most important early reforms in the direction of realizing rights were undertaken in the Ottoman Empire, which had many non-Muslim subjects and which, owing to its military and economic vulnerability, was also exposed to pressures from European powers. The *hatt-i-serif* of 1839, reinforced by the *hatt-i humayun* of 1856, was part of a series of modernizing reforms in the Tanzimat period that aimed to establish the security of life, honour, and property, fair and public trials, and equality before the law for all Ottoman subjects irrespective of religion. The principle of non-discrimination based on language and race was added by the *hatt-i-humayun.* In 1840 the new penal code affirmed the equality of all Ottoman subjects before the law. [*See* Tanzimat.]

By mid-century, reformist pressures prompted the adoption of the 1876 Ottoman Constitution, which contained a section on *hukuk-i-umumiye*, or public liberties, of Ottoman subjects, providing for equality regardless of religion, free exercise of religions other than Islam and freedom of worship, inviolability of personal freedom of worship, and guarantees against arbitrary intrusions, extortion, arrest, or other unlawful violations of person, residence, or property.

There were also provisions for freedom of the press, association, and education. This constitution was suspended in practice and not revived until after the Young Turk Revolution in 1908, a central goal of which was reviving the constitution and establishing the equality of all Ottoman citizens. The Young Turk's reforms expanded constitutional rights protection, prohibited arrests and searches except by established legal procedures, abolished special or extraordinary courts, and guaranteed press freedom. Turkey's second republic saw in 1861 the promulgation of a constitution that undertook in its preamble to ensure and guarantee ''human rights and liberties'' and made men and women equal (Article 12).

In the area of free exercise of religion, conditions were imposed to safeguard the policy of secularism adopted by Mustafa Kemal Ataturk (1881-1938), the first President of the Turkish Republic. Article 2 of the 1982 Turkish Constitution proclaimed Turkey to be a law-state that respects human rights.

In Republican Turkey the energetic pursuit of Kemalist seculariam, beginning in 1925, led to the repression of various Islamic groups, especially dervish orders. In Soviet Central Asia the atheistic policies of the Soviet Union curbed the religious freedoms of the Muslim populace until the collapse of the Soviet state in 1991.

Suppression of Islam and denial of religious freedom also occurred under the Marxist regimes that ruled Albania from 1945 to 1991 and Afghanistan from 1978 to 1982. Elsewhere in the twentieth century regimes with secular orientations often indulged in harsh persecutions of Islamic fundamentalists.

Popular agitation against the despotism of the Qajar Shah culminated in Persia's first constitution in 1906-1907. Persia's Shi'i clerics were divided about the religious legitimacy of constitutionalism and its attendant rights provisions. The Supplementary Constitutional Law of 1907 included Islamic qualifications of two rights provisions; publications were said to be free except where heretical or harmful to Islam (Article 21) and the study and teaching of science, education, and art were to be free except as prohibited by religious law (Article 18). Moreover, ministers in the government wre required to be Persian Muslims (Article 58). However, the country's inhabitants were to enjoy equal rights before the law (Article 8).

After the 1978-1979 Islamic Revolution in Iran, official spokesmen invoked Islam as the reason for the clerical regime's hostility to international human rights, which they often dismissed as products of an alien, western cultural tradition; however, Iran did not repudiate its ratification of the International Covenant on Civil and Political Rights.

The 1979 Iranian Constitution in Article 20 expressly provided that all citizens enjoyed human, political, economic, social, and cultural rights according to Islamic standards; Article 4 provided that Islamic principles prevailed over those in the constitution. Notwithstanding the reference in Article 20 to economic, social, and cultural rights, the concern seemed to be with using Islamic criteria to curb civil and political rights-many of the latter being expressly limited by Islamic criteria (see Articles 21, 24, 26, 27, 28 and 168). The principle of equality and equal protection for women and religious minorities were breached in many ways.

In the name of implementing Islamic criminal justice, the regime irnored principles of criminal procedure designed to protect the rights of the accused both before and during trial, as well as prohibition of cruel and inhuman punishment. Religious minorities and individuals and groups opposed to clerical rule or the regime's religious ideology were excluded from the political process and were often subject to harsh persecution.

Islamic and Western concepts were combined in the Afghan Constitution produced between 1921 and 1924. For example, all inhabitants were to be equal before the government without distinction of religion and sect, and it was provided that all Afghans would be equal before the *Shari`ah* and the laws of the State. Nonetheless, Hindus and Jews (the only recognized non-Muslim communities) were required to pay the *jizyah,* the poll-tax traditionally imposed on *dhimmis* (protected non-Muslims), and to wear distinctive emblems. [*See* Dhimmi; Jizyah.]

By the end of the twentieth century all Muslim countries had adopted constitutions containing some or all of the rights principles set forth in international human rights law. The 1989 Algerian Constitution was noteworthy for its guarantee of equality before the law regardless of gender (Article 28), fundamental liberties and human rights (Article 31), and human rights advocacy (Article 32). Like most Muslim countries, however, Algeria retained Islamic personal status rules and constitutional provisions according Islam a privileged status, perpetuating the ambiguous relationship between religious and constitutional norms.

Fiqh survived longest as the official law of the land in Saudi Arabia. However, changes inaugurated in 1922 suggested that the country might be moving gradually towards a governmental system that would accord at least limited recognition to rights and constitutionalism, albeit subject to Islamic criteria. The principle that Islam entails on human rights was adopted in the Basic Law of Government promulgated by the Saudi Arabian regime in 1922; Article 26 provided that "the State protects human rights in accordance with the Islamic *Shari`ah.*"

What the *Shari`ah* limits on rights would entail was not defined. The basic law provided for many citizen entitlements in the area of social welfare, but only a few rights in the political or civil area were recognized. These included the provision that no one should be arrested, imprisoned, or have his action restricted except as provided by law (Article 36); that homes should not be entered or searched save in cases specified by statutes (Article 37); that communications should not be confiscated, delayed, read or listene to except in cases defined by statutes (Article 40); and that private property must be protected and could only be taken for the public interest and with fair compensation (Article 17).

Women's Rights

One of the areas where the clash between inherited Islamic principles and international human rights norms was most acute was that of women's rights. Although conservatives propounded the nation that full equality for women violated Islamic precepts, feminists argued that it was patriarchal attitudes and inadequate study of the Islamic sources that led to the notion that Islam required keeping women in a subordinate position.

Already in the late nineteenth century liberal writers like the Egyptian Qasim Amin (1865-1908) had propounded the thesis that certain problems facing Middle Eastern societies-despotism, moral degeneration, and the degraded status of women-were not intrinsic to Islam but were the products of corrupting influences and social customs. While not advocating full equality for women, Amin demanded that women's rights should be enhanced. He also linked the cause of women's freedom to the realization of freedom and rights for citizens in general. Feminists such as the Egyptian Huda Sharawi (1882-1947) became prominent advocates of women's rights and emancipation.

One of the boldest attempts to reconcile Islam with full equality for women was offered by al-Rahir al-Haddad, a Tunisian graduate of al-Zaytunah, who in 1930 published *Imra'atuna fi al shari'ah wa-al-mujtama* (Our Women in the *Shari`ah* and Society), which propounded the idea that Islam had envisaged a progressive emancipation of women; he advocated the reform of Islamic laws to eliminate obstacles to male-female equality in the domestic as well as the public sphere. For the boldness of its thesis the book was condemned with particular vehemence by conservatives and its author denounced as a heretic.

Unequivocal support for full equality for women came from Kemal Ataturk, who in the wake of the Turkish war of independence proclaimed that women had the right to be equal; he subsequently took measures to remove the disabilities imposed by Turkish custom and Islamic law-without attempting to reconcile his reforms with Islamic precepts.

In the Arab world, the most dramatic reforms was embodied in the Tunisian Law of Personal Status of 1956 promulgated by President Habib Bourguiba. Presented as an Islamic law, the code undertook bold reforms improving women's status, such as abolishing polygamy and establishing equal rights for men and women in divorce.

Into the late twentieth century Muslim countries preserved laws that discriminated against women and denied them full civil and political rights, often in the face of constitutional provisions mandating the equality of all citizens. In general, laws afforded women considerable equality outside the family; it was in the area of personal status that discriminatory features taken from *fiqh* were retained. Saudi Arabia was notable for its reliance on Islam to justify its refusal to grant women rights and freedoms widely enjoyed elsewhere in the Muslim world.

Few Muslim countries ratified the 1979 Convention on the elimination of all forms of discrimination against women, and those that chose to ractify did so subject to reservations regarding various central provisions. The reservation made by Bangladesh, Egypt, Libya, and Russia were specifically justified by their need to adhere to Islamic law.

Human Rights Movements

Independent, non-governmental organizations founded for the defence of human rights have spearheaded campaigns to improve respect for human rights in Muslim countries. One of the earliest Muslim human rights organizations was established by Moroccans in December, 1933 in the Spanish-controlled enclave of Tetouan as an affiliate of a Spanish human rights organization.

A human rights group with Islamic affiliations, the Iranian Committee for the Defence of Freedom and Human Rights, was formed with the participation of several religious figures; it aimed primarily at achieving democratization and the elimination of torture and in camera political trials. A central participant was Mehdi Bazaragan (b. 1907), a proponent of Islamic liberalism who went on to become Iran's first prime minister immediately after the Islamic Revolution. He and his associates later suffered persecution when their stance on human rights put them at odds with the central regime.

Human rights organizations in which educated professionals were prominent proliferated throughout the Muslim world in the 1980s in the face of daunting obstacles and dangers. One of the most important was the Arab Organization for Human Rights, which, like the overwhelming majority of independent human rights organizations, espoused the human rights programmes.

Muslim States and International Human Rights Law

It was in the aftermath of World War II that the modern international formulations of human rights were produced, setting standards that became incorporated in public international law. Muslim countries were among the founding members of the United Nations, whose 1945 Charter called for respect for human rights and fundamental freedoms; all Muslim countries eventually joined the UN.

Aspects of the Universal Declaration of Human Rights, passed by the General Assembly in 1948 provoked criticism for representatives of Muslim countries, although in the end only Saudi Arabia failed to support its passage.

Muslim nations different greatly in their willingness to ratify the human rights conventions subsequently drafted under UN auspices. Muslims sometimes charged that international rights norms had a Western or Judeo-Christian bias that precluded their acceptance in the Muslim milieu.

In terms of the compatibility of international rights norms and Islamic law, the alleged conflicts centred around civil and political rights; problems of the compatibility of Islam with economic, social, and cultural rights were rarely raised. The principles of freedom of religion-notably the right to convert from Islam to another faith-and the full equality of persons regardless of sex or religion seemed to pose particular problems.

The Charter of the Organization of the Islamic Conference (OIC), an international organization founded 1973 to which all Muslim countries belong, indicated in its preamble that the members were ''reaffirming their commitment to the UN Charter and fundamental human rights.'' In 1980, however, the OIC issued the Cairo Declaration on Human Rights in Islam, which diverged significantly from international human rights standards; it was not made clear how this declaration was to be reconciled with the conflicting obligations undertaken by OIC members in ratifying international human rights covenant or in their individual constitutional rights provisions, which in many cases corresponded to the international norms.

Like the many other self-proclaimed "Islamic" human rights schemes that proliferated from the 1960s onward, the OIC declaration extensively borrowed terms and concepts from the International Bill of Human Rights, presenting a hybrid mixture of elements taken from Islamic and international law. The OIC declaration asserted that ''fundamental rights and universal freedom in Islam are an integral part of the Islamic religion,'' but proceeded to insert 'Islamic' qualification and conditions on the rights and freedom guaranteed under international law-in conflict with international human rights theory, which does not permit religious criteria to override rights. Representative provisions included the rule in Article 24 that all the rights and freedoms stipulated in the declaration were subject to the *Shari`ah,* without defining what limits this would entail.

There was no provision for equal rights for all persons regardless of sex or religion. Instead, Article I stated that "all human beings are equal in terms of basic human dignity and basic obligations and responsibilities (not 'right'), without any discrimination on the grounds of race, colour, language, sex, religious belief, political affiliation, social status or other considerations." Article 6 further provided that "woman is equal to man in human dignity" ['not rights'], but it imposed on the husband the responsibility for the support and welfare of the family. In contrast, Article 13 provided that men and women were entitled to fair wages "without discrimination." Article 5 provided that on the right to marry there should be "no restrictions stemming from race, colour or nationality," but did not prohibit restrictions based on religion.

The provisions regarding religion did not aim at neutrality : Article 2 stated that Islam was the religion of unspoiled nature and prohibited "any form of compulsion on man or to exploit his poverty or ignorance in order to convert him to another religion or to atheism." Article 9 called for the State to ensure the means to acquire education "so as to enable man to be acquainted with the religion of Islam."

The favoured treatment of Islam carried over to freedom of speech, with Article 22 (a) stating that expressing opinion freely was allowed "in such manner as would not be contrary to the principles of the *Shari'ah.* Article 22 (c) barred the exploitation or misuse of information "in such a way as may violate sanctities and the dignity of Prophets, undermine moral and ethical values or disintegrate, corrupt or harm society or weaken its faith." Article 18 stipulated a right to privacy in the conduct of private affairs, in the home, in the family, and regarding property and relationships. Article 15 set forth "rights of ownership to property acquired in a legitimate way, barring expropriation except for the public interest and upon payment of immediate and fair compensation."

Noteworthy by their absence were provisions calling for the observance of democratic principles in political systems and guarantees of freedom of religion, freedom of association, freedom of the press, and equality and equal protection of the law.

Although torture was prohibited in Article 20, there were no provisions explicitly endorsing international rights norms in the area of criminal procedure-only the vague assurance in Article 19 that the defendant would be entitled to "a fair trial in which he shall be given all the guarantees of defence." Since Article 25 stated that the *Shari'ah* "is the only source of reference of the explanation or clarification of any of the articles of this Declaration."

"The possibility was left open that a trial would be deemed 'fair' as long which were historically underdeveloped in the area of criminal procedure. There was no principle of legality *per se*. The provision in Article 19 that there should be no crime or punishment except as provided for in the *shari`ah* seemed to open the door to the application of ta'zir (discretionary) penalties, as well as rules regarding *hadd* crimes. Article 2 prohibited taking away life except for a reason prescribed by the *Shari'ah*. Reflecting the third world setting in which Muslim nations elaborate their position on rights, Article II prohibited colonialism and stated that "peoples suffering from colonialism have the full right to freedom and self-determination."

In sum, the OIC Declaration suggested that the official approach of Muslim countries to civil and political rights was distinguishable from that of non-Muslim countries by reason of their reliance on *Shari'ah* rules.

Governments and individuals throughout the Muslim world continue to take many positions on human rights that are by self-designation 'Islamic.' Given the variety of approaches and principles involved, it is evident that Muslim opinion remains divided on the relationship between international human rights principles and the Islamic legal heritage, and on the compatibility of the two.

In conclusion, one cannot but view the future with some apprehension. If Muslims persist in their acceptance of the absence of social justice among them, if they continue to separate worship in the mosque from the social justice to be observed in lands where the spirit of Islam is to be sown, and to separate the places of prayer from business and industry; if they uphold the hypocrisy of a worship without soul, showing themselves " mean towards those who needs help,'' then woe betide them in this world, and woe betide them in the Hereafter, even if they are not among those whom the *Qur'an* says ''neglect their prayers.''

References

1. *Sahih Bukhari,* trans, Muhammad Muhsin Khan, New Delhi, Kitab Bhavan, 1984, Vol. 8, p. 512.
2. Elias, *Arabic-English Dictionary.*
3. ''Al-Sarakhsi, al-Mabsut,'' cited by Tanzil ur-Rahman, ''Adab al -Qadi,'' *Islamic Studies,* 1966, p. 200.
4. *International Encyclopaedia of Social Sciences*, ''Judicial Process,'' by J.W. Paltason.
5. P.S. Atiyah, ''From Principles to Pragmatism,'' *Iowa International Review*, 1954, p. 1249.
6. Tanzil ur-Rahman, ''Adab al-Qadi,'' *Islamic Studies*, 1966, p. 201.
7. A.A. Qadiri, *Justice in Historical Islam*, Pakistan, 1969, p. 3.
8. Al-Bayhaqi, *Sunan Kubra*, Vol. 7, p. 1, quoted in Rahman, p. 201.
9. Al-Mawardi, *Akkam al Sultaniya,* 2nd edn., Cairo, 1966, pp. 61- 62.
10. Hidya, trans, Hamilton, Lahore, 1957, p. 334. It is held that rules of jurisdiction are derived from rules of evidence. According to Imam Shafi'i the evidence of women is not admissible on account of their defect of understanding, their want of memory and governing incapacity.
11. *Ibid.,* p. 341. This according to Imam Abu Hanifa, is in conformity with the rule that evidence of women is admissible. It is inadmissible in cases of punishment and retaliation.
12. *Etawa-i-Alamgiri,* trans. S.A. Mir Ali, Lucknow, Nawal Kishore, 1932, Vol. 5, p. 119.
13. *Ibid.,* p. 107.
14. *Ibid.,* p. 21.
15. Al-Mawardi, *Ahkam*, p. 17.
16. *Ibid.,* p. 21
17. Muhammad Hamidullah, ''Administration of Justice in Early Islam,'' *Islamic Culture* (1937), p. 170.
18. E. Tyan, ''Judicial Organization,'' in *Law in the Middle East*, eds., Majid Khadduri and Leibesny (Washington, D.C. 1955), p. 261.
19. Al-kindi, *Kitab al wulat wa-la quat*, p. 673 quoted in *Qadiri*, p. 483.
20. Muhammad Hamidullah, *op. cit.*, p. 169.
21. Al-kindi, *Kitab al wulat*, p. 361.
22. *Ibid.*
23. E. Tyan, op. cit., p. 240.
24. Muhammad Hamidullah, ''The Government of the Holy Prophet,''

Islamic Review, 1942.
25. Rahman, "Adab," p. 204.
26. N.J. Coulson, "The State and Individual in Islamic Law," *International Law Quarterly*, 1957, p. 57.
27. N.J. Coulson, "Doctrine and Practice in Islamic Law" BSOZS, 1956.
28. *Ibid.*
29. *International Encyclopaedia of Social Sciences,* Vol. V, "Constitutional Law."

2

Islamic Concepts of Human Rights

Anyone who undertakes to speak of 'Islam and Humanity' in an age in which, the universal respect for and observance of human rights and fundamental freedoms for all, without distinction as to race, sex, language, or religion, has been highlighted by the Charter of the United Nations (Art. 55), followed by the Declaration of Human Rights of 10th December, 1948 and by the two Covenants that have been subsequently drawn up on social and cultural rights and on civil and political rights, ought to provide the contextual framework of human rights as understood both in the West and in Islam.

In this way, we will throw into better relief those aspects of human rights as conceived by Islam which may be radically different from those normally associated with a modern approach. At the conclusion of the Second World War, when thought was again turned to the orderly functioning and reconstruction of the international community of mankind, the primary purpose which inspired the founding fathers of the United Nations was undoubtedly 'to save succeeding generations from the scourge of war, to maintain international peace and security.'

But the indispensable means for the realisation of that purpose in their thinking could only be the recovery of the individual from the super-incumbent weight that had been imposed on his freedom, initiative and growth by totalitarian regimes. Hence, the emphasis in the United Nations Charter on 'Human Rights and Fundamental Freedoms.'

The full extent of that crisis which had brought about a disruption in the soul-life of the modern man had never been fully appreciated by those publicists who in the mid-twentieth century had set out to make a general survey of the political, economic, social, cultural or humanitarian implications of human rights and fundamental freedoms that had to be guaranteed to the people of United Nations, since, the unhappy predicament of modern man had not as then been fully comprehended.

The forces of modern history have been virtually at war with the harmony of human life. This generation which has been actually involved in the chaos and the crises that have overtaken human civilization is not able to appreciate the extent to which the individual had been made subservient to the authority of totalitarian states that have emerged in the wake of mass society. Ortega de Gessa in *The Revolt of the Masses* speaks of the characteristics of such societies.

In the welter of contending voices that are even now being heard from the protagonists of the philosophy of enlightenment, and the pioneers of secularist liberalism and Marxist socialism, we have not as yet been able adequately to appreciate the extent of the disruption that has taken place in the contemporary value system.

On the one hand, thanks to the technological and scientific revolution of our times, the social environment of modern man, on a world-wide scale, has become much more integrated, in the sense that the days of isolated civilizations and localised cultures are gone never to return. There was a time when diverse cultures and civilizations could coexist and grow side by side without interaction or interference one with the other. Now, largely due to the application and transport, modern man, no matter where he may be, is involved in the total life of humanity as never before.

On the other hand, although the overall external shell in which the snail of humanity is living has been woven into a more or less homogeneous pattern through the interplay of all those factors which go to define the social and cultural environment of modern man, the springs of modern man's actions are ruled by the most contradictory philosophies of life.

There is, to begin with, the religion of love and universal brotherhood brought to us by the Prophets of universal religions and a great deal of our life, at least in Asia and Africa, is lived as though religious norms even today were the decisive criteria in evaluating the worth of man's activities.

Then there is the philosophy of life founded upon the secularist approach which, in the name of liberalism, places a high degree of emphasis on the value of the dignity and freedom of the individual and upon the gospel of tolerance, mutual discussion and debate as a means of organising political institutions with a view to securing the development of human personality.

This approach had been countered by the challenge from the Marxist socialists who are prepared to surrender the value of human individuality at the altar of new gods who must be worshipped in the temple of dialectical materialism. Their claim for social justice, security and a planned social order as prime movers of social change in the requisite direction are well known.

The arrogance of race and of power, the worship of the cult of saviours and of heroes who applaud the military virtues of conquest, total discipline and blind obedience, seem to triumph precisely because of the confusion in thinking which is reflected by this western secularistic approach to life. Modern man is so completely caught up in this confusion that he is prepared to sell his soul to anyone who offers him the chance to enjoy what he considers to be the good things of life--the ability to 'eat, drink and be merry.'

Islam and Humanity

There is a fundamental difference in the perspectives from which Islam and the West each view the matter of human rights. The Western perspective may by and large be called anthropocentric in the sense that man is regarded as constituting the measure of everything since he is the starting point of all thinking and action. The perspective of Islam on the other hand is theocentric-God conscious.

Here, the Absolute is paramount and man exists only to serve his Maker, the Supreme Power and presence which alone sustains his moral, mental and spiritual make-up, secures the realisation of his aspirations and makes possible his transcendence. It is this which constitutes the decisive distinction between the two attitudes.

The Western tradition of liberty is evidenced by the most notable of its charters of rights: the Bill of Rights consequent on the

English Revolution of 1689, the Bill of Rights promulgated by the State of Virginia in June 1776, the Declaration of Independence issued by the thirteen American States Constitution of 1789. The Declaration of Rights of Men and Citizenship issued by the Constituent Assembly of France in 1789, and later incorporated word by word in the Revolutionary Constitution of 1791 and again more recently in our own time in the Soviet Constitution of 1939, are in the same tradition.

Here, the rights of man are seen in a setting which has no reference to his relationship with God, but are posited as his inalienable birthright. The student of growth of Western civilization and culture notices throughout that the emphasis is on human rights within the framework of an anthropocentric perspective of human destiny. Each time the assertion of human rights is made it, it is done only to secure their recognition from some secular authority such as the state itself or its ruling power.

In marked contrast to this approach the strategy of Islam is to emphasize the supreme importance of our respect for human rights and fundamental freedom as an aspect of the quality of religious consciousness that it claims to foster in the heart, mind and soul of its followers. The perspective is 'theocentric' through and through. Man has first to believe in the cardinal doctrine:

"There is no God but God and Muhammad is His Prophet."

Before he can hope to do good deeds, the emphasis in the Holy *Qur'an* is on securing the transformation of the quality of man's consciousness. Man is asked to live and work in full awareness that he must show obedience to the Will of God.

Islam in its turn affirms the grand tradition of the development of the institution of universal religions, which tradition, according to the Holy *Qur'an*, was consummated in the mission of the last Prophet by means of the revealed word communicated to him by process of divine revelation.

It seems at first sight, that there are no human rights or freedoms admissible to man in the sense in which modern man's thought, belief and practice understand them; in essence, the believer has only obligations or duties to God since he is called upon to obey the Divine Law, and such human rights as he is made to acknowledge stem from his primary duty to obey God.

Yet paradoxically, in these duties lie all the rights and freedoms. Man acknowledges the rights of his fellow men because this is a duty imposed on him by the religious law to obey God and the Prophet and those who are constituted as authority to conduct the affairs of state.

In everything that a believer does his primary nexus is with His Maker, and it is through Him that he acknowledge his relationship with the rest of his fellow men as even with the rest of the creation. In the words of the *Qur'an*:

"Man has been created only to serve God."

And further he alone is acceptable who has acquired nearness to God.

This distinction between the attitudes of Western man and a Muslim is implicit in the Qur'anic view of life which divides its functions into *haqooqullah*-obligations to God-and *haqooqunnas or haqooqulabad*--obligations to society. The former category embraces matters like prayers, the need for ritual purity of mind and body, etc., primarily the personal concerns of the individual; the latter category has a social aspect.

In both cases the foundation for 'righteous action' whether on the individual or social plane is no other than the quality of consciousness or *niyyat* which directs all man's actions to the sole purpose of obeying the will of his maker, in order to please his ever-watchful Lord and Master, who sees even the innermost thoughts and motivations that impel him to act.

He is eventually to return to his Maker and will have to render an account of what he did with the opportunities with which life provided him to do that which was demanded of him by the Divine Law, and his accountability is absolute which constitutes the sanction which Islam provides to secure the believer's obedience to the demands that the Divine Law makes upon him.

The *haqooqunnas* is obligations to society, in the last resort and come within the scope of the jurisdiction or authority of the state in Islam, and relate largely to what in our own time are treated by Western thinkers as constituting secular affairs and secular dealings or relationships between man and man.

It was in relation to this aspect of enforcing obligations to society that the first four rightly guided *Caliphs*, in view of the nascent stage through which the *Ummat* in the early days of Islam had to pass, were forced to keep 'a mild form of patriarchal watch whenever necessary and even interpreted the religious injunctions in their application to new conditions of life in consultation with their companions.' But by doing this they did not claim 'spiritual leadership' of the community.

Indeed *haqooqullah* and *haqooqunnas* were as binding on the Caliphs themselves as on any other believer who was a member of the community. The Caliph was himself accountable directly to *God* no more and no less than the humblest citizen of the realm, and obedience to the Caliph so long as he conducted the affairs of the community according to the Book of God and the Practice of the Prophet was based on the divine injunction:

> "Obey God, obey the Prophet and those who are acting as constituted authority from amongst you."

This accountability, in the last resort, was owed to the Maker, and the believer knew that even if he erred in disobeying the order of the Caliph and escaped the punishment prescribed for such disobedience, he would eventually be punished on the day of judgment when his accounts would be audited with merciless severity in respect of those aspects of his conduct which injured the rights of others. This is the sense in which though man has no rights within a theocentric perspective, only duties to his Maker, these duties in their turn give rise to all the rights, including those contained within the modern understanding of human rights.

This mode of approach to the problem of human rights has the obvious advantage of dispensing with the need to provide and implement separate procedures for giving effect to human rights since, within the religious context of Islam, no one escapes the penalty for violating the rights of others, and state power is only an earthly agent of the divine power acting by virtue of delegated authority to enforce the Divine Law.

The ruler himself, if he betrays his trust, will also be punished. Since, both are bound by the Divine Law, there can, in the strict theory of the Islamic law, be no conflict between the state authority and the individual.

This view is fully reflected in the very first address given by the First Caliph of Islam when elected to his office as Head of the Muslim State which had been founded by the Prophet:

> "My fellow men! I call God to witness, I never had any wish to hold this office; never aspired to possess it. Neither in secret nor in the open did I every pray for it. I have agreed to bear this burden lest mischief might raise its head. Else, there is no pleasure in leadership. On the other hand, the burden placed on my shoulders in such as I feel I have not the inherent strength to bear, and so cannot fulfill my duties except with Divine help. You have made me your leader, although I am in no way superior to you. Co-operate with me when I go right; correct me when I err; obey me so long as I follow the commandments of God and His Prophet; but turn away from me when I deviate."

Even he who is called upon to handle the affairs of the state is within the grip of Divine Law, and cannot claim any special privileges or prerogatives or immunities.

The affairs of the people are to be run for the benefit of the people as a whole. No Caliph had any special privilege attached to his person. As Abdul Latif points out, he was at best only first amongst equals. When food and clothing had to be rationed in Medina he had but to receive his share just as any other ordinary citizen; every man and every woman had the right to question him on any matter touching the affairs of state; he must appear, as did not Caliphs Umar and Hazarat Ali, before subordinate judges appointed by them, to answer charges against them. The same author goes on to add:

> "the economic system of life formulated by the *Qu'ran*, laying a special emphasis on the uplifting of the economically depressed, under which a state levy was to be collected from the rich for the relief of the poor, was rigidly enforced by the state. The exchequer of the state was considered to be the treasury of the people; the surplus, if any, accruing at the end of the year came back to the people in the form of annuities distributed on the basis of individual needs."

The Quranic injunctions governing the status of women, as independent economic units functioning in their own individual right, were scrupulously respected and upheld. Similarly, security of life and property and freedom of conscience were guaranteed to non-Muslim minorities who were styled Dhimmis. The Dhimmis were protected by the Prophet of God. The Prophet had proclaimed, 'I shall myself be the complainant against him greater than he can bear or deprive him of anything that belongs to him.' Indeed so mindful was he of their welfare that a few moments before he expired, the thought of the Dhimmi came to him. He is reported to have said:

> "Any Muslim who kills a Dhimmi has not the slightest chance of catching even the faintest smell of Heaven. Protect them; they are my Dhimmi."

In a moment of like remembrance, Caliph Umar, as he lay assassinated, exclaimed, 'To him who will be Caliph after me, I commend my wish and testament-Dhimmi are protected by Allah and the Prophet. Respect the Covenants entered into with them, and when necessary, fight for their interests and do not place on them a burden or responsibility which they cannot bear.

Indeed, Islam went further in catering for the welfare of the human race by securing the consent of the believers to certain basic principles guaranteeing its preservation in times of war. These are the principles of justice and moderation laid down by Caliph Abu Bakr for the guidance of the first expedition into Syria:

> "Be just; break not your plighted faith; mutilate none; slay neither children, old men nor women; injure not the date-palm nor burn it with fire, nor cut down any fruit-bearing tree; slay neither flocks nor herds nor camels, except for food; per chance you may come across men who have retired into monasteries, leave them and their works in peace."

The foregoing illustration is typical of the emphasis on what man is not to do, yet the rights of others are implied even when the principles are formulated as prohibitions on the believers.

On the more positive side, the Prophet's last *Khutba* (congregational address) on the occasion of his final pilgrimage provides the earliest declaration ever made in the history of mankind of what might be called the obligations that were imposed upon believers:

> "Then the apostle continued his pilgrimage and showed the men the rites and taught them the customs of their hajj. He made a speech in which he made things clear. He praised and glorified

God, then he said, 'O men, listen to my words, I do not know whether I shall ever meet you in this place again after this year. Your blood and your property are sacrosanct until you meet your Lord, as this day and this month are Holy. You will surely meet your Lord and He will ask you of your works. He who has a pledge let him return it to him who entrusted him with it; all usury is abolished, but you have your capital. Wrong not and you shall not be wronged. God has decreed that there is to be no usury and the usury of Abbas b. Abdul Muttalib is abolished, all of it. All bloodshed in the pagan period is to be left unavenged. The first claim on blood I abolish is that of b. Rabia b. al-Harithb. Abdul Muttalib (who was fostered among the b. Layth and whom Hudhay killed). It is the first bloodshed in the pagan period which I deal with. You have rights over your wives and they have rights over you. Your have the right that they should not defile your bed and that they should not behave with open unseemliness. If they do, God allows you to put them in separate rooms and to beat them but not with severity. If they refrain from these things they have the right to their food and clothing with kindness. Lay injunctions on women kindly, for they are prisoners with you having no control of their persons. You have taken them only as a trust from God (*bi amanatillah*) and you have the enjoyment of their persons by the words of God, so understand my words, men, for I have told you. I have left with you something which if you will never fall into error-a plain indication, the Book of God and the Practice of His Prophet, so give good heed to what I say. Know that every Muslim is a Muslim's brother, and that the Muslims are brethren. It is only lawful to take from a brother what he gives you willingly, so wrong not yourselves."

The International Charter of Human Rights

Talking about the sum and substance of the various human rights and the fundamental freedoms which have been incorporated in the Universal Declaration of Human Rights of 1948, Syed Abdul Latif sums up the position as follows:

"The twin aim of this Declaration is one the one hand to equip the individual to live a free life considered successively as (i) physical organism; (ii) a moral personality; (iii) a worker; (iv) an intelligent being and (v) a member of a community and of a

> polity, and on the other to help the individual so equipped to make his contribution to international amity or the peace of the world..For the student of the Qur'an not one word in the preamble or in the objective of the Charter, and not a single article in the text of the Universal Declaration of Human Rights, will seem unfamiliar."

Under a creed which places man next to God, and brushes aside distinctions of race, colour and birth, and calls upon all mankind to live together as a family of God or as a 'fold' every member of which shall be a shepherd or keeper unto every other and be accountable for its welfare,' the Universal Declaration of Human Rights must follow as a basic corollary, or an extension of the Quranic programme. But a mere declaration of them will not carry humanity far. Several questions call for attention from the Quranic point of view.

The questions he raises concern first the impulse underlying the Charter of the United Nations, and the Universal Declaration of Human Rights adopted in pursuance thereof. Is the scheme in the interest of or for the good of humanity as a whole, or is it a practice to serve the interest of a particular country or group of countries? Secondly, looking at the list of rights covered by the Universal Declaration, he asks if it is possible for any country claiming to be civilized at the present hour to say with confidence that all the rights are observed by it, or that it may serve as a pattern for the rest.

It is obvious that the initiative for implementing them must come from the government or legislature of each country. Is the system of political life in every country such as may place in high office the type of men who may have the urge and the high-mindedness to respect the Declaration and implement its provisions? Lastly, he considers the world order which is the aim of the two documents, and which argues a common purpose acceptable to all the countries of the world. As things stand, the world is divided, broadly speaking, into two camps-the Soviet and the American.

A world arrangement, whatever its form, will be possible only on the basis of some sort of reconciliation between the two contending ideologies, or by building a half-way house for mutual cooperation. Is such a reconciliation possible? He surveys possible answers to these disturbing questions, and records as his opinion that there is a vast discrepancy between the provision of these rights contained in the Universal Declaration and the actual practices of the people of the modern West. In the words of Professor Hitti:

> "Unfortunately during the last decade or two, in particular, the impact of the West has not been entirely for good. There is a striking contrast between the humanitarian ideas professed by Western missionaries, teachers, and preachers, and the disregard of human values by European and American politicians, and warriors; a disparity between word and deed; and over-emphasis on economic and nationalist values."

The behaviours of the so-called advanced nations during the last two wars waged on a scale unknown in history; the ability of Western man let loose those diabolic forces which are the product of his science and his machine and which now threaten the world with destruction; their intervention in the Near East, particularly in the handling to the Palestine problem by American, England, France, and other nations, all these have worked together to disillusion this man of the near-East who has been trying to establish an intellectual rapprochement with the West. It is these actions of the West which alienate him and shake his belief in the character of Western man and his morality on both the private and the public levels.

Islamic Viewpoint

It is within the context of such evaluations of the negative impact in any practical terms of the Universal Declaration of Human Rights that we can point the excellence of the strategy with which Islam has enjoined upon its members the obligation to acknowledge and implement human rights. Islam is primarily interested in securing for its believers 'right belief and right conduct,' but in accordance with its teachings the conduct is never right unless it is based on right belief and is consciously willed.

Islam is an enemy of all mechanical actions. One cannot in Islam perform prayers without forming conscious intention to pray; one cannot give *zakat* (alms) without consciously intending to do so; one cannot fast without forming conscious intention to fast; you cannot go on pilgrimage and perform the prescribed rites without being aware of their significance and without the formation of conscious intention to do so. This 'conscious intention' is the core of the matter and the Prophet said that the *niyyat* (intention) of the *momin* (believer) to do the deed, in obedience to the Law of God, was better than mere external conformity with the terms of the conduct prescribed by such law (*Al-niyyatul Momin Khairun Minal Amalhi*).

Since, it is in the inwardnes of his being that such a conscious willing intention can be formed, Islam takes good care to insist that its primary purpose is to produce the *Saliheen* (righteous people), the *Muttaqis* (self-controlled people) and the *Sadiqeen* (people who adhere to truth). It is the transformation of the old Adam in man into an expression of the Divine that forms the essence, if not the quintessence, of the strategy of Islam.

The Western world believes that mechanical conformity to the pattern of conduct, prescribed by the law of the state or by some such authority, is sufficient to secure public order and universal peace. In other words, its procedure is to attempt to influence from outside the inner condition of man believing that social, political economic and other institutions are capable of influencing the individual character. It is submitted that this is a fallacious approach; only slaves can be thus handled, not free people.

Islam, on the other hand, begins by inviting man to accept the paramountcy of the power of the Lord, his own servitude and bondage to the will of his Master who is the Sovereign Ruler of the universe; in the last resort it redeems him by prescribing norms of behaviours by which he is to regulate his life. In the words of Professor D. De Santillana:

> "We may agree with the Muslim jurists when they teach that the fundamental rule of law is liberty...God has set a bound to human activity in order to make legitimate liberty possible for all; without the 'bounds of God,' liberty would degenerate into licence, destroying the perpetrator himself along with the social fabric."

This 'bound' is precisely what is called law, which restrains human action within certain limits, forbidding some acts enjoining others, and restraining the primitive liberty of man so as to make it as beneficial as possible either to the individual or to society. Whatever their form, these rules tend to the same end and have the same purpose, that is, the public weal (*maslahah*). Accordingly, law, divine in its origin, human in its subject-matter, has no other end but the welfare of man, even if this end may not at first sight be apparent; for God can do nothing which does not express the wisdom and mercy of which He is the Supreme source. The Qur'an itself provides clear justification for such a thesis:

> "In the name of Allah, the Beneficent, the Merciful. Nay, I swear by this city-and thou art an indweller of this city-and the begetter and that which he begat, we verily have created man in affliction: thinketh he that none hath power over him? And he saith: I have destroyed vast Wealth" thinketh he that none beholdeth him? Did we not assign unto the parting of the mountain ways? But he hath not attempted the Ascent-Ah, what will convey unto thee what the Ascentis! It is to free a slave, and to feed in the day of hunger an orphan near of kin, or some poor wretch in misery, and to be of those who believe and exhort one another to perseverance and exhort one another to pity. Their place will be on the right hand. But those who disbelieve our revelations, their place will be on the left hand. Fire will be an awning over them."

The title of the *surah* is *Al-Balad* or 'the City,' and it represents the condensed essence of the wisdom upon what may be called the subject of civic rights in the context of the development of monotheistic religion. By the word 'City', by which the verse begins, is meant Mecca. The *surah* is in the nature of a 'charter of freedom' give to man after the prayer of Ibrahim for the foundation of a city by one of his descendants-the Prophet of Islam-had been answered.

It draws attention to the evolution of religion and man from Ibrahim to Muhammad-the entire period of Semitic civilization-and Mecca as its place of birth and completion.

Man has been created to face difficulties, and to help him confront these trials with fortitude he has been reminded that there is some 'power' that is an overseer of his deeds, namely his Lord and Master who sees him through and through. The *surah* goes on to recount the grace of God to man evidenced by the conferment of powers of sight and of speech.

Furthermore, man has been shown two conspicuous ways and now the choice is his, either to elect to negotiate the way of truth or of falsehood to choose the good or evil deed. Of these two possible choices the path of righteousness consists in siding with the truth and of doing good deeds. This is the uphill or higher way, and the highest deed available to the believer is to 'free a slave'. This constitutes not only physical freedom, but moral, mental and spiritual freedom, as much from other human beings as from one's lower self. It is this freedom from necessity that 'freeing the slave' expresses. This amounts to securing the emancipation of man from virtually all manners of servitude.

It imposes on man a whole range of social duties-freeing the slave, feeding the orphan, caring for 'the poor wretch in misery'-and these duties which confer corresponding rights on all. Over and above these are the duties to believe, and exhort one another to patience and to mercy. Man must believe in the 'Unseen', he must believe in 'all the Prophets' in 'the Angels', in all the 'revealed books' including those that have preceded the Qur'an. Man's ultimate return is to God who is his Creator, and his liability to render account is absolute.

While facing the tests and trials of life, a believer is called upon to be 'patient and to pray' and to show 'compassion and mercy to others'. Those who can adhere to this way of life and exercise their power of choice in conformity with the tenets of the Divine Law are declared to be the 'people of the right hand' and those who disbelieve are characterised as the 'people of the left hand.' It is this distinction which is vital.

Islam presents man with a charter of human liberty within a religious framework which emphasizes the necessity of his being aware of his responsibility and accountability. In the earlier forms of religious belief and practice, the injunctions prescribed to regulate man's conduct were conched as 'absolute commandments', as for instances in the Ten Commandments give by Moses.

In those cases the obedience of the believer was complete if he conducted himself in accordance with the law; at worst even mechanical conformity was enough. But the *Qur'an* is also the *furqan*. That is to say it is book that makes exercise of discretion and discrimination possible for man, in that it outlines for him the possible courses of conduct that are open to him as a free agent and invites him to choose the difficult uphill way; to choose the right side with truth and to stand steadfastly against all odds.

Islam makes the believer his brother's keeper, particularly if the brother is helpless, uncared for or unprotected. It extends the sphere of his responsibility by commissioning him to believe, because without proper belief there is no proper conduct. He is, therefore, asked to base his conduct on right belief taught through the revealed Word of God contained in the *Qur'an*. He is also invited to be a missionary in the cause of Islam, to become a diligent crusader in the cause of inviting his fellow men to the way of patience, to show fortitude and compassion so long as his earthly life lasts.

Should he do all this, he is rightly guided and will be duly rewarded by the grant of Eternal Life; real life as opposed to this life which is only the seed-bed of the Hereafter. That life which is to come is better and eternal; this life exists only to provide the opportunity to win the reward of that life. If he uses this to its full advantage, not only will the believer achieve success here and now, but will also gain the reward of Eternal Life in the Hereafter. If the life of man is to be located in the conceptual framework which results from close study of the Holy Book, the position of man in the scheme of things must be viewed not as though he were a finished product, but rather as an evolving being, in a state of transition.

Broadly speaking, man is to be regarded as one who is here on the earth to spend his time as though it constituted a transitional phase which will one day be brought to an end by the most certain of all events, namely, his death. During this interim phase he cannot, on his own, hope to know the path he should pursue in order to enable himself to reach higher levels of his being.

Just as it is inconceivable, seeing the rose bush embedded in manure and covered in thorns, to imagine the beauty of the rose it will one day produce, it is equally impossible to envisage the final phase of man's evolution in which he is destined to reach his highest fulfillment and expression. As the gardener prunes the rose to encourage yet more beautiful blooms, so process of *taqwa* in the life of the believer.

Instead of abandoning himself completely to the animal impulses within him he must learn to acquire self-control-so that the energy available within him does not exhaust itself on the animal plane of his existence, but is transmuted into higher forms of being capable of surviving the ravages of death and of enjoying the reward of higher, better and eternal life.

Human rights conceived from the anthropocentric perspective are treated by Western thinkers as thought they were no more than an expedient mode of protecting the individual from the assaults that are likely to be made upon him by the authority of the state's coercive power-by the unjust laws that may be imposed by the power of the brute majority to deny man the possibility of self-development.

Islam, on the other hand, formulates, defines and protects these very rights by inducing in the believers the disposition to obey the law of God, the practice of his Last Prophet, and to show obedience to those constituted authorities within the realm who themselves are bound to obey the law of God and the practice of the Prophet and conduct man's affairs accordingly.

Furthermore affirmation of those rights is to enable man not only to secure the establishment of those conditions in terms of which the development of man as an individual on the earth may be possible, but also to enable man to so conduct himself inwardly as well as outwardly, that he may be able to obey the Divine Law, that only his Maker is qualified to impose on him. By accepting to live in bondage to this Divine Law, man learns to be free.

Islam terminates the era of revealed religions, declares man free by telling him that no other Prophet hereafter would come, indicates the straight road to be traversed by him, and in the Holy Book provides sufficient guidance to enable him to choose. It is now for him to choose. Depending on the choice he makes, the road he takes will lead him either to Heaven or to Hell.

It is quite impossible within the scope of this chapter to do full justice to all aspects of our subject. But before concluding, there is a question which must be answered. The question so frequently asked by Western scholars is why Islam has insisted so strongly on rewards and punishments? Why the emphasis on Heaven and Hell. The answer to their question turns on the interpretation of freedom.

Islam, a religion of mature minds, gave man complete freedom in the conduct of his life for the first time in history. To this freedom were annexed the consequences of his choice. Given the particular nature of man, true freedom lies only in obedience to God's law; only when he disobeys this law and submits to the rule of the lower passions that stem from his animal nature is man condemned to bondage. It is with this in mind that the *Qur'an* asks, "have you seen that person who has taken his lower patience as his gods?"

In disobeying God man acts counter to his own nature and reduces himself to slavery. It is too his obedience to God which itself ensures that he shall retain the capacity to be free and responsible. Heaven and Hell are not locations, but merely names for the states of man's being:

> he makes heaven or hell for himself by the way he conducts his life. Rewards and punishments are not imposed from outside but follow as natural consequences of what a man does with his life here below.

God is not some kind of policeman who enforces the law, but His Prophet sent down to help humanity is the warner and guide. He, through the revelation from God, has told us what we must do if we wish to avoid the many pitfalls along the way and make the most of the opportunities which life on earth offers. According to Islam, human action has an objective quality inherent in it, and it is this which overtakes man either as punishment if his conduct be bad, or as reward if it be good.

Solution of Human Confrontation

How can we best sum up the contribution Islam can make to the world today? In a lecture delivered by Arnold Toynbee in 1948, under the title "Islam--the West and the Future," he observed that Islam could provide the solution to two of the main problems of the present day, famely those of racial discrimination and of alcoholism. But these are no more than symptoms of a far deeper malaise.

There is neither spiritual nor practical reason why Islam should confine itself to the solution of these issues rather than to other far more deeply-rooted problems now confronting mankind. The mission of Islam is to face all such problems and to offer a solution by showing mankind the true path he should follow to gain salvation in this world and the next.

Let us determine the solution by first of all defining the need. What is mankind's greatest need today? How can Islam meet this need? According to Holy Revelations the basic issue in man's life has been, and will be till the Day of Judgment, the question of worship. Who is to be worshipped and how is He to be worshipped? Let us deal with the first question:

> ''who is to be worshipped? Writers and thinkers in the West during the Age of Enlightenment and the Age of Materialism in the 18th and 19th centuries when these ideas were first raised, sought to solve the problem by making it disappear.''

Their advice was 'Forget about this issue, it is of no concern whatsoever; live life and enjoy it, if you choose, do not worship anything at all?' By freeing man from the bondage of religion they thought to offer him an unprecedented opportunity of finding happiness on this earth. But their thinking was based on two major illusions. The first illusion was the belief that humanity would attain happiness, and would experience constructive development when it rejected religion.

Indeed the West has progressed tremendously, both technologically and scientifically, since it rejected religion. This very progress fostered the illusion in the hearts of men. They forgot that religion in itself was not the force that held them back, but their own interpretation which, since the Middle Ages in Europe, had obstructed their progress.

However, they overlooked a more important factor--that the scientific and technological progress achieved by Europe after neglecting its religion was not the first, nor even the fundamental, ingredient of life. It cannot by itself establish a sound human life.

Only now is the West coming increasingly to realise this, as they recognize that the absence of spiritual values is the main reason behind the anxiety, confusion, madness, suicide, many other psychological and nervous disorders, and the feeling of perplexity and illusion among youth, all of which constitute a threat to the security, peace and welfare of humanity, despite all the material progress achieved during the last two centuries.

The second illusion is the related thought that man can do without worship altogether. This naive illusion is not borne out by our knowledge of man's history from his earliest known origins up to the present time. Whether in the ancient or the modern world 'worship' in some form or the other has never ceased to exist in man's life.

When man says to himself 'I will worship nothing whatsoever', he does not, as he imagines, rid himself of the problem of worship. He merely changes the object of worship, and proclaims himself or his interests as the God to be worshipped and to govern his whole life. Worship is not confined to the offering of prayers, devotions or the submission of offerings, as people appear sometimes to imagine when talking of the subject.

This is a matter of form only. Worship itself is essentially obedience and acquiescence to a certain Being, and the belief that it is our duty to obey that Being. Worship in this sense is an integral part of every man's entirety and existence because it is a component part of himself. Within this context there can be no one who does not worship even man's entirety and existence because it is a component part of himself. Within this context there can be no one who does not worship even though he claims otherwise.

Man is an instinctive worshipper whether or not he chooses or is aware of it. It is only in the nature of the worshipped deity or the way he is worshipped that one man differs from another. Either he worships God, or he worships some other deity or deities by whatever name. His worship of God is either true or deviant, and no sensible man would make false deities the object of his worship.

Having established this fact, the *Qur'an* proceeds to the other part of the question, namely the explanation of the right way to worship God. It stipulates the uniformity of worship just as it stresses the Unity of God. The correct worship of God is represented in two integral indivisible aspects, namely the maintenance of the rites of worshipping God to the exclusion of any other, and the following of God's revelation in establishing a point of reference for guidance in life. To pray or present offerings to an idol, an object, or a person, is corruptive of religion as well as of worship. The same corruption results from the adoption of a non-godly attitude and practice in life.

There must be unity between man's worship and his attitude towards life. The deity addressed by man in his prayer and devotions is the same deity addressed while studying, earning a living, attempting to better conditions on earth, eating, drinking, copulating, as well as while communicating with his family, with other individuals, with other societies, peoples and states, whether in peace time or during war. Say:

> "Lo! my worship and my sacrifice, and my living and my dying, are for Allah, Lord of the Worlds" (VI. 163).

In all that he does, the constant reiteration of God's name in his heart had the practical effect of recalling to him God's commands, so that he may obey them. In Islam God's commands deal with all such matters and indicate the permitted as well as the prohibited.

When this happens somethings of considerable significance occurs in man's life. To being with man will be giving due worship to His Creator. Man would never appreciate God as he truly should if he worshipped Him in prayer once during the day and considered this to be the end of it. God says:

> "I created the Jinn and humankind only that they might worship Me" (LI:56).

Meaning by this the wide range of worship which comprises prayer and devotions, living and dying. To do otherwise would be to worship two deities, one in the holy shrine through prayer and devotions, the other (or others, though eventually they culminate into one), through obedience in affairs of everyday life. Allah hath said:

> "Choose not two gods. There is only one God. So of, he only, be in awe." (al-Nahl XVI:51).

The ability of the human heart to sense the glory of God and His miraculous powers revealed in the creation of a universe which is such a wonderful model of accuracy, order and uniformity, as well as in the creation of all living objects, will or should lead man to worship this Almighty God in due veneration of His glory and power.

This could never occur through a worship that is pursued from moment to moment and relinquished for the remainder of man's day-to-day living. Regardless of God's reward for this worship, a sense of duty demands that it should be followed as a means of paying others what is due to them.

> Lo! Allah commandeth you that ye restore deposits to their owners. (IV. 58), and who except this Omnipotent God serves disinterested and constant worship?

Yet of His Mercy God is bounteous to those who give Him His due, namely worship in its wider or uniformly comprehensive sense, for He will reward them by eternal life in paradise, and secure their future after death, which, since it is the longer period of man's life, is the worthier to be preserved.

The uniformity of worship during man's span of life influences many important aspects of his living. It gives him first of all an inner security which is nowhere to be found outside the frame of faith. It cannot be obtained either through drugs, drinks, narcotics, leisure or sensual pleasure. All these confirm the state of mind which man wants to evade, but they neither remove nor cure it. Security emanates from faith and the mention of God's name.

As the *Qur'an* puts it:

> ''those who believe, and whose hearts find satisfaction in the remembrance of God: for without doubt in the remembrance of God do hearts find satisfaction.''

This security is not a placid resignation to events. Rather, it is the search for the good life wherever it is to be found; the *Jihad* under God's name to instal God's justice in the world; the opposition to all forms of injustice abhorrent to God; the search for knowledge and instruction. In all these activities the believer will rely on God because everything is moved by an returns back to Him.

The believer, moreover, is confident that God promises only goodness to him, and this is why no anxiety overshadows the earning of a living, the pursuit of study, the *Jihad*, and the establishment of a civilization, a fact that was once apparent in the early Muslim period.

Until recently, there were writers who acclaimed the present age as the 'age of anxiety', calling it the age of creative anxiety. But they came to realise that it was now more in the nature of a poisonous drug even though taken in the smallest doses. They also realised that the impetuous frantic activity was neither a real nor creative activity. It was only symptomatic of an illness that would soon lead to other consequences, causing man to lose his sense of security and psychological balance. Other writers have said that anxiety is a necessary accompaniment of civilization however damaging or beneficial.

This interpretation lacks scientific precision, since, anxiety goes hand in hand only with a civilization thriving on materialism and neglecting the spirit. This type of civilization lacks the basis for inspiring a true sense of security, and it is this civilization which is responsible for tearing the human soul between two deities, the other who dominates the realities of day-to-day life. This latter deity who accompanies man is more often than not a tough and ruthless one who does not inspire security and stability in his worshippers.

As history shows this was once a flourishing civilization that sensed no pangs of fatal concern because it was secure in the name of God. Uniformity of worship brings together many aspects of man both within his inner self or in his life generally, which present-day deviations have, without justification, torn as under.

It brings together spirit and matter, body and soul. It brings together religion and science, piety and material development, religion and life. Finally, it brings together this life and the Hereafter.

Let us look briefly at each of these unities brought about by Islam. Soul and body or spirit and matter are both or genuine authenticity in the human make-up.

> " Behold, thy Lord said to the angels: I am about to create man from clay. When I have fashioned him (in due proportion) and breathed into him of My Spirit, fall you down in obeisance unto him."

They were brought together inseparably at the birth of man, and the whole of his history is a living confirmation of this fact. But in periods of *Jahiliyyah*, there is always a tendency to set them apart by directing each on a separate course of its own, and by the exaggeration of one at the expense of the other.

Some pre-Islamic periods emphasised the spirit as the real essence of man and despised the body as an impure object unworthy of veneration. Such an object was entitled only to degrading and tortuous acts. The material aspect of life was also despised as it was nearest to the body, to clay. Other pre-Islamic periods exaggerated the body and sensual pleasure. They considered the body to be the real thing, and the soul only a beautiful shadow that lacked substance. They saw it as a secondary object in man's life or as an inhibitor.

As a result these years of history dedicated a great deal of their interest to material produce and construction and almost completely neglected the spiritual make-up of man. Both attitudes base themselves on a false premise, namely that there is a deep-rooted contradiction between body and soul that can be only conciliated by suppressing one in favour of the other. One either suppresses the body to free the soul, or suppresses the soul in order to attain material emancipation.

But, in reality, in neither case does suppression lead to goodness. The suppression and devitalization of the body runs counter to instinct, resulting in the obstruction of man's energy, material and cultural retardation, poverty, misery, depression, pessimism and despair.

Alternatively, the suppression and blackening of the soul lead to inner worries that can never be satisfied even by the deepest immersion in earthly pleasures which necessarily result in conflict between individuals, communities, states and peoples. These are signs that something counter-instinctive has occurred; the result is a loss of equilibrium in man's life.

Islam, on the other hand, provides the balanced alternative which harmonises soul and body and disposes of any contradiction and conflict between them. Islam never accepted the idea of an irreconciliable situation between these two entities.

It is true that the body and the soul are two different elements but they are integrated in man. Their lack of cohesion is not caused by their mutual existence in the human-being, but by the domination of one by the other, and the consequent loss of the instinctive equilibrium which God bestowed on him:

> "O Man! What has seduced thee from Thy Lord Most Beneficent? Him who created thee, fashioned thee in due proportion, and gave thee a just bias." (V:7).

Moderation or equilibrium lies at the basis of God's creation. But man in his ignorance disturbs this equilibrium. As a result disturbance occurs in the soul well as in the actualities of life, as is testified by events. This idea is expounded in *L' Homme Cet Inconnu* by the scientist-physician Alexis Karel. He indicates:

> "out serious ignorance of the nature of man as well as our neglect of his spiritual aspect, and our setting up of economic, social and political systems based on ignorance, lie at the root of our scientific and cultural progress."

And it is Islam which restores to man the balance and moderation with which he is endowed by God. It puts into effect a simple and realistic though far-reaching measure, namely an invitation to the soul and body to take part in the whole of life.

Prayer is not only a spiritual hymn, it is also a set of movements performed by the body through standing, kneeling and prostration, combined with a conscious mental concentration on the verses recited in prayer. Food, drink and sex on the other hand are not pure body movements, but also represent spiritual aspirations made permissible by mentioning God's name, and performed in strict observance of what is lawful and what is forbidden. In this way, such acts invariably lie between these two poles and is thus included in the integrating system which brings together soul and body, spirit and matter, earth and sky.

A similar split occurred between religion and science. Man has an instinctive disposition to worship, yet he too has an instinctive disposition to worship, yet he too has an instinctive disposition to know the secrets of the material world around him, and to subject these to his power. Both dispositions are instinctive and authentic; both are innate. No necessary contradiction, split or conflict exists between them.

Divine Revelation provided no grounds for it, but man's errors have created conflict and dispute between them. This dichotomy occurred in Europe at the beginning or the Renaissance when the Church opposed science and scholars, and threatened to bury, torture and kill people of science such as Copernicus, Galileo and Jordan Bruno.

As time passed, the gap widened and the conflict deepened, until the mere mention of God's name in scientific research was tantamount in the ordinary European's sense to a violation of the spirit of that research and an unwarranted attempt to integrate two irreconciliable attitudes. As Darwin put it:

> "The interpretation of evolution with reference to Providence is an introduction of a metaphysical element into a purely mechanical situation."

This misinterpretation of the nature of the relationship between the two subjects could not help but disturb man's balance and security. It aroused conflict in man's inner self between two genuine elements each requiring satisfaction. When one feels that the satisfaction of one's spiritual needs lies outside the frame-work of science, and that the satisfaction of scientific needs lies beyond the reach of religion, and if at the same time feels that these needs proceed in two separate and diverging directions, one ends by worshipping two irreconciliable deities, each demanding from his worshipper a differing attitude, behaviour and point of view.

For the time being, there is no choice other than to worship the two. Again, man is torn apart, whether consciously or unconsciously. His anxiety is reinforced, and when, as frequently happens, he is forced to choose between them, he succumbs to the deity of science as being more able to satisfy his immediate needs, and abandons the deity of religion as belonging to a world altogether less real and tangible whose existence in any case, he doubts.

Islam in its simplicity eliminates this contradiction again by means of a realistic and simple procedure. The God who man worships in his prayers is the same God who gave man knowledge for the first time, and the same God who invites man still to learning and knowledge.

> "He taught Adam the nature of all things" (p. 31).
> Read in the name of the Lord who createth.
> Createth man from a clot.
> Read; And thy Lord is the Most Bounteous, who teacheth by the pen. Teacheth man that which he knew not." (XCVI. 1-5).

God invites man to contemplate the secrets of the universe:

> "Behold in the creation of the Heavens and the Earth; in the alteration of the night and the day; in the sailings of the ships through the ocean for the profit of mankind; in the rain which God sends down from the skies, and the life which he gives

therewith. To an Earth that is dead, in the beasts of all kinds that he scatters through the Earth, in the change of the winds, and the clouds which they trail like their slaves between the sky and the earth; (here) indeed are signs for a people that are wise." (II.164).

God taught that He was all that is between the sky and the earth:

"And hath made of service to you whatsoever is in the Heavens and whatsoever is in the Earth." (XLV. 13).

In order to exploit what is in the Heavens and on Earth by his physical and mental efforts, all that man has to do is to learn the universal law by which God administers this universe:

"It is He who has made the Earth manageable for you, so traverse ye through its tracts and enjoy of the substance which He furnishes (But unto Him is the resurrection)."

Thus will come the unity of orientation through the Oneness of God.

Human knowledge is not stolen from God despite His will as in the Greek myth of Prometheus. It is a divine gift bestowed on man. Man does not need to disobey God in order to learn. It is God who instructed mankind to learn and to seek knowledge. The Prophet says:

"The quest of knowledge is an obligation."

Man should not have any sense of guilt when he exploits the resources of the Heavens and Earth for his benefit, nor should he think that he is doing so in rebellion against a Divine Will which seeks to crush and oppress him in the way the relationship between man and God is portrayed in the Greek myth. It is God who harnessed the resources of this universe for the benefit of man and instructed man to settle on the earth.

"It is He who produced you from the earth and settled you therein."

There is thus no need for man to feel that he is worshipping two opposed gods, each one with conflicting demands on him. In all that man does there is only one God. When man seeks knowledge Allah demands him not to use the fruit of this knowledge in wrongful tyranny over the earth. Man does not feel that he is surrendering to God only out of ignorance of inability, as Julian Huxley claimed in *Man in the Modern World.* According to Huxley:

> "when man gains knowledge and control over his environment, he rebels against God, making a god of himself."

On the contrary, the more man learns the nearer he becomes to God and to the fear of God.

> "The erudite among his bondsmen fear God alone." (XXXV:28).

Man prays to God of give him more knowledge:

> "Oh My Lord. Advance me in knowledge." (Taha 114).

Thus even when he is seeking knowledge, man is in his heart always thinking of Allah. He will conduct his life in exploiting the fruits of science for righteous ends with the same assurance and confidence he has in Allah when he offers Him his prayers. In this way, Islam establishes a unity between religion and science and learning, as between religion and life.

In Europe life was excluded from the sphere of religion through particular circumstances which were not inherent in religion itself. Western man thought of religion as a spiritual relation between man and God, and of life as human endeavour with no relation to God. This is invented by the West, and not revealed by God. It is inconceivable that such a concept could be supported by the words ascribed to the Messiah:

> "Render therefore unto Caesar the things which be Caesar's and unto God the things which be God's."

This is contradictory to the entire concept of religion according to which Allah is the Lord of the heavens and the earth, and Caesar and all men must surrender to the judgment of Allah.

These words should be seen as an instruction by the Messiah to his followers not to declare war against Caesar, but to pay the taxes, he required, till the establishment of a state that would enforce what Allah had revealed, and would subject Caesar himself to he judgment of Allah. There is a similar case in Islam.

Allah told the Muslims in Mecca before the establishment of the Muslim State:

> "Withhold your hands establish worship and pay the poor due." (IV. 77).

No Muslim has understood from this instruction that religion is only a spiritual relation between man and Allah, and that the daily affairs of life should be administered by Caesar or other non-believers in the way they choose. This instruction was for a period of time only, and was followed by the establishment of Muslim society and the Muslim state, thus making life in its entirety subject to the judgment of Allah. This was accompanied by the revelation of detailed legislation governing all aspects of life.

As a result of this wrong interpretation of the scope of religion in the West, life increasingly moved away from religion, until in modern times it was finally excluded completely from its ambit. Politics followed the principles of Machiavelli who justified lying, deception, hypocrisy, dishonesty, killing, murder, fraudulence and trickery, all of which were forbidden in Islam.

Economy was based on the usurious system which is also forbidden in Islam. Social relations were based on social hypocrisy and the hideous isolation of individuals described by Aldous Huxley in *Texts and Pretexts,* where every man had become an island in itself without any connection with other islands scattered in the ocean of life.

Karel considers that the contravention of innate laws cannot take place without severe punishment, as these laws are as crucial as the Law of Nature itself. The chaos and turmoil now rampant all over the world is the heavy price man has paid for the contravention of the innate laws created by Allah. It is Allah and not man who knows human nature.

How ignorant man is of his nature, as Karel again so rightly observes. Though he has learnt a great deal about the universe surrounding him, his ignorance of himself is profound, since, he sees himself only through his passions and desires. Allah alone knows the innate human nature; He knows what is suitable for it and what is not. He has revealed this religion to guide the life of man as well as his relation with Allah. In a simple yet far-reaching way, Islam establishes the connection between religion and life, and extends this to embrace the hereafter.

Islam presents the true concept of religion. Religion is faith and laws; a faith governing spiritual relations with God, and laws administering the affairs of life in the name of God. In both cases, we are seeking the same God, we worship one God. The *Shari'ah* as revealed encompasses the whole range of human activity, as well as international relations whether in peace or in war. Thus, politics becomes Islamic politics; economics becomes Islamic economics, social relations become Islamic relations and relations between the two sexes will be organised according to Islam, thought and art become Islamic activities. Islam embraces the whole of life.

Allah who revealed the *Shari'ah* knows that in man's life there are permanent elements, and others that develop and change. Allah does not want these latter to be petrified or stunted in their growth, therefore, he enacts in his *Shari'ah* comprehensive and constant principles which, without themselves altering, allow for the process of continuous change through the right interpretation of these laws in their detailed application to new circumstances. This had been the endeavour of Muslim scholars throughout history.

In this way, a constant interconnection is maintained between religion and life. Life will neither be petrified in one form, nor will its development contravene the scope of religion. As Khalifah Omar Ben Abdel Aziz said:

> "The more new problems people have, the more new rules they will find."

It is through this fusion that unity of this life and the hereafter will be achieved. The dichotomy between religion and life led to a separation in the awareness of people of this life and the hereafter. In pursuit of these separate ends they developed two completely unconnected sets of actions, one bearing no relation to the other.

Islam establishes a unity between this life and the hereafter and considers them as a continuous process. Together they constitute one path, the beginning of which is this life and its end the hereafter.

> "But seek, with the (wealth) which God has bestowed on thee, the home of the Hereafter, not forget thy portion in this world". (XXVIII. 77), and "Say who hath produced for His servants and the things, clean and pure, (which he hath provided) for sustenance? Say they are, in the life of the world, for those who believe, (and) purely for them on the Day of Judgment."

In Islam, there is not a single deed which is concerned exclusively with worldly life or with the Hereafter; its purpose is always twofold. Offering prayers, for example, which people may think of as a deed motivated solely by concern for the hereafter, also has its purpose in the worldly life. As God says in the Qur'an,

> "Prayer restrains from shameful and unjust deeds." (XXiX. 45).

Prayer is intended to be offered in the worldly life, and be rewarded in the hereafter. Even the relationship between the sexes, which might be thought of as an exclusively worldly affair, is linked in the consciousness of Muslims with the hereafter. Muhammad said: "You will be rewarded by Allah for copulation with your wives." He was asked: "We do that to satisfy our desire how can we be rewarded for it?" Muhammad replied: "If you satisfy your desires in a forbidden way, wouldn't you be punished for it?" They answered:"Yes we would." Muhammad then said: "If you then satisfy your desire in a permissible way, you must be rewarded."

The result is that this world and the hereafter are interconnected in the awareness of the Muslim individual. In everything he does he commits himself to act in accordance with the revealed Will of Allah. While he conducts his worldly affairs in this life, he will be looking forward to God's reward in the hereafter.

This full integration in the structure of Islam is clearly expressed in a way which has roused the interest of many Orientalists writing about Islam. The English Orientalist Gibb says,

> "The kind of society that a community builds for itself depends fundamentally upon its beliefs as to the nature and purpose of the universe and the place of the human soul within it."

This is a familiar enough doctrine and is reiterated from Christian pulpits week after week. But Islam is possibly the only religion which has constantly and consistently aimed to build up a society on this principle. The prime instrument of this purpose was law.

The Canadian Orientalist Wilfred Cantwell Smith remarks:

> "Observers have noted the paramount position of the community in Islam. Less thought has been devoted to its significance in Islamic history, which is that community in motion. it is well known that Muslim society has a remarkable solidarity, that the loyalty and cohesion of its members are intense. Many have

recognised that the community is not only a social group but a religious body; that the 'church and state' are one, to use the inappropriate language of the West.''

We would go much further, as has been said, in interpreting this. Yet to stress these facts, to insist upon the centrality of society, is not deny but to interpret our initial emphasis on religion as personal. The community is based on, as it is integrated to, individual faith. Not only is Muslim society held together (as other societies) by common loyalties and traditions, and by a very carefully worked out system of values and of beliefs. Not only is it the product of a superb ideal. It pulsates with the vitality of a profoundly held and deeply personal conviction, a religious conviction that is warm and meaningful for the individual member.

We may say that this society, this community, is the expression of a religious ideal, using 'religious' in the personal sense earlier proposed. As a creed or theological system may be expression in an intellectual form of a personal faith-as is often the case, particularly with Christians-so a social order and its activities are the expression in a practised form of a Muslim's personal faith.

Singularity of the Creator

This integration, which is an expression of the unity of worship and the Oneness of God, is most precious in Islam. It is the real meaning of *Shahadah:*

''No God but Allah.''

It is the most precious gift that Islam can give to humanity in this age; a humanity perplexed, confused and suffering from anxiety through its loss of the unifying element, whether in its theoretical concepts or in its actual behaviour. It seems uncertain in Toynbee's discussion of the possible future contribution of Islam to new manifestations of religion, whether he was aware of this meaning or not.

Whatever the case may be, this meaning does not present ' a new face of religion' as Toynbee and others thought. It is the true meaning of religion revealed by God to mankind. It is the true meaning which materialised in Islam fourteen centuries ago, and was formulated in a concrete way over a long period and in large areas of the world.

Islam provides us with guidance throughout life from cradle to grave, answering their innate questions that consciously or unconsciously press on man in his journey through this world. What exactly is man? What is his role on the earth? What are the limits of his energies? From where have we come? To where will we go after death? For what purpose do we live? How should we organise our life? These are the questions which demand answers. If no convincing and decisive answer is provided, and if that answer is not that right one, it will undoubtedly affect man's psychological stability and his behaviour.

Man will be in a state of crisis. The present world situation is the most obvious example of the extent of this crisis: no further evidence is needed than modern man's present behaviours. What is man? A simple question, yet how difficult for contemporary mankind to answer, and how far their answer from the truth. Is man really an animal as Darwin suggested, or is he a human being? Is he a God as portrayed by Julian Huxley? Does man stand alone as his own creator, as suggested by a book with the title *Man Makes Himself*? Is he a slave as conceived by other doctrines and theories, and if so, a slave to what?

To an exploiting class as suggested by the materialistic theory of history; to his own body and desires; or to the machine as he came to be under technological progress? What are the potentials of man? What are the limits of reason? Is he able by it alone to understand and explain all things? What is his attitude towards those things which he cannot understand or explain? Should he ignore them, or surrender to them reluctantly? Where does man go after death? Is the end of man's limited life on this earth the end of everything, or is there some form of continuation? What is the purpose of human life? Is it to obtain as much material enjoyment as possible, or is there some other objective, and of what kind? Is it to control nature, or to control others? (Or is it perhaps to co-operate with them?) And to what use should this control be put? To enslave others? To destroy? Or merely to assert ourselves?

On the other hand we desire to control others that we may co-operate with them, the same question arises; to what end will we co-operate? the questions are endless. How should man live? Who will decide the question for him? Philosopher, politicians, dictators, the masses, youths, elders? Or should each man decide for himself as

Sartre's existentialist philosophy suggests? Clearly the answers to all these questions and more will determine man's behaviours and the kind of life he will lead on earth.

Contemporary mankind whether in the East or the West has provided a variety of answers. For the most part, they are wrong and misleading. The result is the present unprecedented turmoil and chaos, and the misery the vast majority of mankind is suffering from, despite the technological and scientific progress which was theoretically to provide humanity with spiritual happiness in addition to material prosperity.

The Role for Man

Islam provides humanity with the right guidance for its journey, and right answers to its persistent questions. Thus assured, man is enabled to set out to achieve his objectives in complete harmony of aspiration, thought, and feeling. Man in Islam is simply man. He is neither God nor animal-the two extremes argued by Huxley and Darwin respectively. His role is to be a Vice-regent on earth; to inhabit it in accordance with the will of Allah. Allah has bestowed on man the talents and abilities necessary for this role. Among them is the ability to learn, the ability to know and distinguish between the path or righteousness and the path of evil, and the ability to choose and pursue one of them. It is because of this ability that man's actions acquire moral value. Man cannot, and should not live without moral values.

There is no single human action which does not fall within the scope of morality. We cannot say that morality has no bearing on politics, science or sexual relations. The only acts that have no relation to morality are the acts of an animal:

> "for an animal there is no choice. Man on the contrary had two alternative courses of action open to him, and he is able to follow one of the two. As a result, all his actions have moral value. If he opts out of the moral choice, behaving like an animal, he will pay the price of his action in misery and perplexity."

We came to be by the will of Allah. We will in the end return to Allah. On the day of resurrection, Allah will question us as to what we did in our worldly life. Those who followed the course of

Allah and the way revealed by Him, will later see the paradise of Allah. Disbelievers will end up in Hell:

> "And if as is sure come to you guidance from Me, whosoever follows my guidance, on them shall be no fear, nor shall they grieve, But those who reject faith and belie our signs, they shall be companions of the fire, and shall abide therein." (II: 38-39).

The duty of man of earth is to worship Allah:

> "I have only created jinns and men, that they may serve Me." (LI:56).

The worship meant is the comprehensive worship already indicated, including not only specific acts of worship but everything that man does, Say:

> "Truly my prayer and my service of sacrifice, my life and my death, are (all) for God, the Cherisher of the world. No partner hath He." (VI: 163-164).

If fulfilled in accordance with Allah's purpose, every act becomes an act of worship. The course humanity should pursue is the course of Allah, since Allah is Lord and man is not; He is the Creator and man is not; Allah is Omniscient and man is not. Wherever man creates laws for himself, he sustains harm and introduces disorder and confusion into his life.

Man can only be truly free and truly equal, when he worships Allah alone, complying only with His *Shari'ah.* All man-made slogans of freedom and equality will remain illusions with no substance in reality, as long as some men remain the legislators or others.

Such a state of affairs would be consistent with the materialist theory of history. He who owns will be he who rules, while all other people will be his slaves. Feudalists become the rulers and peasants are condemned to servitude; capitalists rule and workers are the slaves; Communism rules, and all people become slaves of the state and are subject to it as their only source for sustenance.

But when Allah is ruler through compliance with *Shari'ah,* all people, the rulers and the ruled, will be in the servitude of Allah alone, equal in their servitude to Allah, therefore equal in freedom vis-a-vis each other, since all are bound by *Shari'ah* which has not been made by any of them, and none can alter it to defend his own interests at the expense of others.

When man finds this type of guidance on his journey, he will immediately discover the landmarks of the path ahead of him, and will follow this path. His soul then will not be thrown into confusion; his mind will not suffer bewilderment; his footsteps will be firm and steady.

Man should not demean himself. He is a being greatly honoured by Allah, and should not be humiliated or lose his dignity:

> "We have honoured the sons of Adam; provided them with transport on land and sea; given them for sustenance things good and pure; and conferred on them special favours above a great part of our creation." (XVII:70).

On the other hand, man should not imagine himself greater than he is and out of arrogance turn his back on the worship of God:

> "Nay, but man doth transgress all bounds. In that he looketh upon himself as self-sufficient. Verily, to the Lord is the return (of all)." (XCVI: 6-8).

Man should not feel that life is an unrepeatable opportunity, a feeling that leads inevitably to over-indulgence in sensual pleasures. Rather he should avail himself of the reasonable share permitted by Allah, and realise that the excessive pleasure he is seeking without permission from Allah, and realise that the excessive pleasure he is seeking without permission from Allah is not good in itself. Allah did not prohibit this excess in order to torture man, but lest it might discourage him from attaining his ultimate aim, and degrade him from human dignity to the level of an animal.

Moreover, every excessive pleasure that man abandons in his worldly life in obedience to Allah, will be compensated for man if old and his return back to Allah. Man should play his role on this earth with clear vision and awareness. He should not build the world of matter while undermining the spiritual world, neither should he create material facilities as ends in themselves, neglecting the ultimate aims of human existence, which will only be attained by establishing divine justice on Earth, and will only be attained by establishing divine justice on Earth, and will only be fulfilled by belief in Allah and by following His course.

It is by presenting this concept to humanity, after providing a true meaning of divinity and worship, the Islam gives humanity the guidance it needs instead of the present fumbling in the dark. We return now to a point raised earlier, namely the question of stability and change in human life.

Darwinism has had a immense influence over Western thought. It has suggested that there are no permanent elements in human life, or in any form of life, throughout the entire universe. To regard any value system such as morality or religion as permanent is, therefore, an unscientific way of thinking and a restriction on human life that should be eliminated.

When we think about it outside the context of local and particular conditions in Europe, and the ensuing conflicts between science, religion, learning and other human activities, we realise that it is the extremist rejection of the permanent values in human life that is unscientific, and that it is this which needs a careful scientific examination unconnected with emotional or historical factors.

The economic, political and social aspects of people's lives do change owing to the constant interaction between human reason and the Universe. This reaction constantly generates more knowledge of the mysteries of the Universe; knowledge which is put to use in harnessing its resources in the service of man. This is true. But what has this to do with constant values in human life? What has this to do, for example, with worshipping Allah?

The necessity of this worship is derived from the fact that Allah is the Creator and the Organiser of this Universe with all therein, including mankind. How does man's discovery of the properties of matter, splitting the atom and its molecule, or sending a rocket to the moon, stars or other planets change this necessary relationship?

The story of Prometheus and his rebellion against God when man learned more about the Universe and harnessed its resources, is a myth and not science. We should note, in the age of science, be dominanted by unscientific stories. To say that man knows himself and his requirements better than Allah is also an emotional statement which lacks the scientific spirit of enquiry.

This is a result of the situation in mediaeval Europe, when the clergy tyrannized on Earth in the name of God in a way that led people to abandon the God of the church in whose name tyranny was practised, and to invent another God-call it Nature or any other name-who had no church, no priests, and who put people under no kind of obligation.

These circumstances were peculiar to Europe and not universal realities or scientific facts. How can we, in the age of science, cling to a concept derived from a specific historical and geographical base, and turn it into a permanent and universal reality on which our life should be based?

The existence of values in the life of man is objective and derived from the fact that he has more than one course open to him; is able to choose and commit himself to a certain course. How this changed by man's discovery of the secrets of the Universe, or by his harnessing its resources?

The abolition of moral values from the life of man-which means a regression to the level of animals or machines-is based on an unscientific concept, presupposing absolute passivity on the part of man. This is true whether we are talking of the psychic determinism preached by Freud and psycho-analysis, or the economic determinism on which the materialist philosophy of history was based. Freud, for example, has not offered a shred of scientific evidence to proved the existence of the Oedipus complex on which his psychological determinism was based.

In the light of the economic determinism propounded by Marx, England should have been the first country in Europe to experience Communism. England is still not a communist state, while the biggest communist blocks in the world, Russia and China, have moved from feudalism to Communism.

The claim that moral values are not permanent, and that they should keep pace with material development, is based on a supposition incapable of scientific testing or proof, namely that innate entity of man develops with material development. There is no evidence of this. We talk, for food, water, clothes, shelter, sex, ownership of property and self-assertion, and we can say with all certainty that the forms of the these things have developed greatly with the passage of time.

However, who can say in a truly scientific sense, that their substance has changed as Well? Moral values are concerned with substance, not form. Though, the forms of human activity change, the moral values related to this activity are not changeable; they continue to determine, by virtue of their permanency, all the variable forms of human activity from one generation to another.

The permanency of values does not prevent change in form, nor do changes in form require any change in essence. Contemporary humanity went astray when it removed many things from the realm of permanence and pushed them into the realm of evolution without any valid scientific basis.

The most flagrant example of this was placing the issues of religion and morality within and evolutionary context and claiming that man's behaviour had nothing to do with morality. An illustration of this is the assertion that man's sexual behaviour remains outside the scope of morality since it is a purely biological function.

A strange claim, and stranger still to attribute it to the evolutionary process. Sex as a biological relation unrelated to morality had been for millions of years a fact in the world of animals. What kind of evolution is it which takes man millions of years back to the state of an animal and no more? What scientific spirit is this, Darwinism or other, upon which such a concept and its resulting behaviour can be based?

Islam provides us with a decisive judgment on this topic. It teaches us that human life should develop constantly -scientifically, politically, economically and socially but that in its continuous development it should not abandon the constant values derived from the permanent and unchanging facts related to Allah, in his creation of the Universe, life and man. Life based on this concept will be balanced in its movement. It will not become fixed at any one point, not will it set out irrationally on the path to its own destruction.

By providing humanity with these three major concepts-the unity of divinity and of worship, guidance throughout the human journey, the resolution of what is permanent and what is changeable in human life-Islam gives humanity a radical solution to the chief problem now leading to the disorder and confusion we are witnessing. Having fulfilled its primary mission by re-establishing the right concepts, Islam goes on to provide practical solutions to the problems of every day living. Unfortunately, there is no time to deal with these in detail in the present chapter. The hope is that as here, and elsewhere within this book, a clear model of that solution has been indicated.

3

Nature of Social Justice

It is not possible to give the right analyses of the nature and methods of Islamic social justice until we have first examined the general lines of Islamic theory on the subject of the Universe, life, and mankind. Social justice is only a branch of the great science to which all Islamic studies must run back. The faith of Islam, which deals with the whole field of human life, does not treat the different aspects of the life in the mass, nor yet does it split up the field into a number of unrelated parts.

Islam has one universal theory which covers the Universe and life and humanity, a theory in which are integrated all the different questions. In this Islam sums up all its beliefs, its laws and statutes, and its modes of worship and of work. The treatment of all these matters emanates from this one universal and comprehensive theory, so that each question is not dealt with on an individual basis, nor is every problem with its needs treated in isolation from all other problems.

A knowledge of this universal theory is necessary to the faith of Islam, because it enables the student to understand its principles and beliefs and to relate the particular to the general It empowers him to study with pleasure and with understanding its characteristics and its aims. While on the other hand, the fact that the basis is religious guarantees that the theory will be both coherent and comprehensive, and not compartmentalized.

No theory of life can be of profit unless it comprehends all the departments and all the aims of human life. So, the best method of studying Islam is to start by understanding its universal theory before going on to study its views on politics or economics or the relationship between communities and individuals. For such questions as these are but issues arising out of that universal theory and they cannot be truly or deeply understood except in the light of it.

The true Muslim philosophy is not to be sought in Ibn Sina[1] or Ibn-Rushid,[2] such men as these who alone are known as the Muslim philosophers. For the philosophy which they teach is no more than a shadow of the Greek philosophy, and has no relation to the true Islamic philosophy. The faith of Islam has a native universal philosophy which is to be sought only in its own familiar authorities:

> "the Qur'an and the traditions, the life of its Prophet and his every day customs."

These are the authorities in which the student must go deep to find the universal Islamic theory from which come all the Muslim teachings and laws, its modes of worship and work. Islam as a faith has laid down the nature of the relation between the Creator and His creation, the nature of man's relation to the universe and to the world, and of man's relation to his own soul; it has laid down the relation between the individual and society, between different societies and mankind as a whole, and the relation between one nation and another.

All these teachings are the expression in different aspects of the one universal, comprehensive theory which relates to one another all the separate aspects all of which together is Islamic philosophy. The detailed study of this philosophy is no part of this present work. Here, we shall confine ourselves to the examination of one specific subject, to the full completion of which may Allah's help be vouchsafed. So, here we shall merely outline the main headings of the general scheme, in order to facilitate our study of social justice in Islam.

The Creator and His Creation

Man lived for long ages without achieving a comprehensive theory of his Creator and the Universe, or of the Universe, life and mankind. That is to say, 'man had never reached the point of working out such a universal and comprehensive theory until the birth of Islam. The relation between the Creator and His creation is to be found in the power of the World, the Active Will from which all creation came."[3]

There is no mediating power of any kind between the Creator and His creation, but from His universal and absolute Will proceed all existing things in due and proper order; and by that universal, absolute, and active Will all things are sustained, ordered, and energized. "He manages the affair, sets the signs in order."[4] "He grasps the Heavens that they fall not upon the Earth, save by His permission."[5] It is necessary for the sun not to overtake the moon, nor the night to outrun the day; but each in its circle they revolve."[6] " Blessed be He in whose hand is the kingship; and He over all things hath power."[7]

So all creation, issuing as it does from one absolute universal active Will forms an all-embracing unity in which each individual part is in harmonious order with the remainder. And thus, too, every form of existence embodies a principle which relates it to this perfect and comprehensive order. "He it is who hath created seven Heavens, one above the other, thou canst not see any oversight in the creation of the Merciful. Look again; canst thou see any flaw? Look again and again, thy sight will turn back, dim and wearied out."[8] " And He set up upon it mountain peaks above it, and blessed it, and arranged its various kinds of food in it."[9] "He it is who hath created death and life to try you, to test which of you is the best in deeds."[10] "Allah it is who sends the winds to stir up the clouds, and He spreads it in the Heavens as He wills, and breaks it up; so you see the rain coming out of the midst of it; and when He causes it to fall on which of His servants He wills, behold they rejoice."[11]

Accordingly, it is obvious that all creation must have a fundamental connection with the creative purpose and that the Will from which all creation finally proceeds, and by which it is continually sustained and ordered, is related to creation itself; thus only can that Will give to creation a coherence and a completed meaning. Thus, then, all creation is a unity comprising different parts; it has a common origin, a common providence and purpose, because it was deliberately produced by a single, absolute, and comprehensive Will.

It was suitable, adapted, and ready for the appearance of life in the general sense, and for the appearance of man, the highest form of life, in particular. So, the universe cannot be hostile to life or to man; nor can 'Nature' in our modern phrase be held to be antagonistic to man, opposed to him, or striving against him.

Rather she is a friend whose purposes are one with those of life and of mankind. And the task of lifting beings is not to contend with Nature, for they have grown up in her bosom, and she and they together form a part of the single Universe which proceeds from the single will.

Basically, man lives in a purely friendly environment, among the powers of a friendly Universe. So Allah, when He created the Earth, set up upon it mountain peaks above it, and blessed it, and arranged its various kinds of food in it. ''And He cast upon the Earth mountain peaks, lest it sway with you.''[12] ''And the Earth--He established it for mankind.''[13] ''He it is who hath laid the Earth low for you, so walk ye about in its regions, and eat of its provision.''[14] ''He hath created for you what is in the earth, all of it.[15] So, the Heavens with their stars are a part of creation; they are connected with the other parts, and everything that is in them and in the Earth is friendly, cooperative, and interrelated with all the remaining parts. ''And He decked out the lower Heavens with lamps.''[16] ''Did we not make the Earth a flat expanse, and the mountains as tent--pegs? We created you in pairs, and We appointed your sleep to be a rest. We made the night for a covering, and We made the day for a livelihood. We built about you seven firm Heavens, and We set a lamp ablazing. We sent down from the rain-clouds copious waters to bring forth grain, and vegetation, and luxurious gardens.''[17]

And further, the Creator does not place the living beings and men in this world, without giving them also His kindly care and constant attention, for His perfect Will is constant throughout all the world, constant, too, over every individual part of the Universe at all times. ''There is no beast on the earth but its provision is a charge upon Allah he knows its lair and its resting place.''[18] ''We have created man, and We know what he whispers to himself. We are nearer to him than his jugular vein.''[19] ''Your Lord said, 'Call upon Me, and I shall answer you.'[20] ''And do not kill your children because of poverty; We shall provide for you and for them.''[21] And so on.

Because, then, the Universe is a unity emanating from a single Will; because man is himself a part of the World, dependent upon and related to all the other parts; and because individuals are as atoms, dependent upon and related to the world, therefore, they must have the same dependence upon, and relation of, one another. So, the Islamic belief is that humanity is an essential unity; its scattered elements must be brought together, its diversity must give place to uniformity, its variety of creeds must in the end be brought into one. For thus and only thus can man be made ready to be at one with the essential unity of creation. " O ye people, We have created you male and female, and We have made you races and tribes, that you might know one another."[22]

There can be no permanent system in human life until this integration and unification has taken place. This step is a prerequisite for true and complete human life, so that the rule of force may be done away once for all, and so that those who have wandered from the true path may be brought back to it. "The recompense of those who make war against Allah and His Messenger, exerting themselves to cause corruption in the Earth, is that they be killed or crucified, or that their hands and feet on opposite sides be cut off, or that they be banished from the land."[23] " If two parties of the Believers fight, then make peace between them; if one of them oppresses the other, then fight the oppressing party until it returns to the affair of Allah; if it returns, then make a just peace between them, and act fairly."[24] "And if Allah had not resisted one party of the people by means of others, the land would have grown corrupt."[25]

Accordingly, the fundamental matter is this interdependence and solidarity of mankind, and whoever has lost sight of this principle must be brought back to it by any means. For the first great divine law of existence is to identify the desires of individuals and of societies; and such mutual responsibility among all is in the end the sole aid of our unified world and of its Creator.

When we come to consider man as a race and as an individual, there is the same comprehensive unity to be observed; man's faculties which are so diverse in appearance are essentially one in purpose. Thus in this respect also man is comparable to the world in its entirety, since its power too is a unity, though diverse in appearance.

Man lived through long ages without arriving at any comprehensive theory of human and universal powers; he continued to differentiate between spiritual and material powers, he denied one of these in order to strengthen the other, or he admitted the existence of both in a state of opposition and antagonism. He organized his life on the basis that such an opposition between these two types of power was natural, and that the superiority of one was only to be gained at the expense of the other. He held that such superiority on the one side and inferiority on the other was inevitable, because, as he believed, such opposition was inherent in the nature of the world and of man.

Christianity at time shows examples of this theory of opposition, because it was by such a theory that it was led to libertarianism on the one hand and austerity on the other, accordingly as these two alternated in its life. For Christianity the salvation of the soul is to be gained by humiliating the body, by punishing it, or even by destroying it, or at the least by neglecting it and turning away from indulgence.

In Christianity and in other similar faiths, this is the cardinal principle on which are built up their systems of belief to it can be traced their doctrines on life and its purpose, on the duties of the individual on the one hand and of society on the other, and on man and the different powers and abilities which attach to his existence.

Thus, the struggle between the two types of powers--spiritual and material--continued, with men continually uncertain and perplexed, and without any definite assurance as to the true solution. Then came Islam, bringing with it a new, comprehensive, and coherent theory in which there was neither this tension nor this opposition, neither hostility nor antagonism. Islam gave clarity to all powers and abilities, it gave an identity of purpose to all desires and inclinations and leanings, it gave a coherence to all men's efforts.

In all these Islam saw one embracing unity which took in the Universe, the soul, and all human life. Its aim was to unite Earth and Heaven in one world; to join the present world and the world to come in one faith; to link spirit and body in one humanity; to correlate worship and work in one life. It sought to bring all these into one path--the path which led to Allah.

In the same way, the world is a unity, composed of things which are seen and otherwise sensually perceived, and of things which are unseen and imperceptible. Life is a unity, made up of material abilities and spiritual powers, between which no separation can ever be made without a resultant disorder and confusion. And similarly human personality is a unity of spiritual desires which rise toward Heaven, and bodily appetites which cling on Earth. No separation can be made between these aspects of personality, because Heaven and Earth are one, because in the world there is a unity of things, seen and things unseen, and because in religion there is a unity of this world and that to come, between daily life and worship.

But beyond all this, there does exist one eternal and unchanging power, which has no beginning and no comprehensible end. To it belongs the government of the world, of mankind, and of life. It is the power of Allah. The human individual in his transience seeks to attain to this power which eternally pervades life, and from it he seeks help in his misfortunes. He strives after it when he is in the mosque at prayer, lifting up his heart to Heaven, and he seeks it no less when he is abroad in the world, busily intent upon his livelihood. So, he seeks to deserve the future life, not only when he fasts and denies himself all manner of pleasurable indulgence, but also when he breaks his fast and enjoys all the good things of life--so long as he does either of these two things with his heart firmly directed towards Allah. And thus the life of the present world, with all its prayer and its work, all its luxuries and its privations, is the only way to the future world, with its Heaven and its hell, its punishment and its reward.

This surely is the true unity between the sundry parts of the Universe and their powers, between all the diverse abilities of life, between man and his soul, between his experiences and dreams. Such a unity it is which can set a lasting harmony between the world and human life, between life and living men, between society and the individual, and between man's spiritual desires and his appetites. In a word, it means a harmony between the world and the faith, between Earth and Heaven.

This harmony is not established in favour of the physical side of man, nor yet in favour of the spiritual side; rather it imparts to both of them an equal freedom, thus bringing both to a healthy position of well-being and growth. Similarly, this harmony is not established in the favour of the individual, or of society; nor in favour of one nation over another, nor in favour of one community over a people.

But each of these is held to have its own rights and its own responsibilities. For the individual and society, the people and the community the nation and all other nations--all are bound by one law which has but one aim, namely, that the freedom of the individual and of society should be equally recognized without any mutual opposition; and that the nations, one and all, should work to gather for the growth and progress of human life and for its orientation towards the Creator of life.

Islam, then, is a faith of the unity of all the powers of the world; and beyond doubt it is a uniting faith. It stands for the unity of gods, and for the unity of all religions in the faith of Allah, and also for the unity of all the Prophets in their testimony to this one faith since the dawn of time.[26]

> ''Verily this community of yours is one, and I am your Lord so worship Me.''[27]

So also Islam stands for the unity of worship and work, of faith and life, of spiritual and material realities, of economic and spiritual values, of the present world and the world to come, of Earth and Heaven.

From this pervasive unity there issue all the Islamic laws and ordinances, all its exhortations and rules, as well as its teachings on political and economic theory, on the balance of credits and debits, and on privileges and responsibilities. Thus in this fundamental principal of unity there are contained all the various rules of life.

While we are examining this universal theory which takes its rise from the nature of Islamic thought about the world and life and humanity, we may study also the fundamental outlines of social justice in Islam. Above all other things it is a comprehensive human justice, and not merely an economic justice; that is to say , it embraces all sides of life and all aspects of freedom. It is concerned alike with the mind and the body, with the heart and the conscience. The values with which this justice deals are not only economic values, nor are they merely material values in general;

rather they are a mixture of moral and spiritual values together. Christianity looks at man only from the stand point of his spiritual desires and seeks to crush down the human instincts in order to encourage those desires.

On the other hand, Communism looks at man only from the stand point of his material needs; it looks not only at human nature, but also at the world and at life from a purely material point of view. But Islam looks at man as forming a unity whose spiritual desires cannot be separated from his bodily appetites, and whose moral needs cannot be divorced from his material needs. It looks at the world and at life with this all-embracing view which permits of no separation or division. In this fact lies the main divergence among Communism, Christianity, and Islam.

Thus, in the Islamic view, life consists of mercy, love, help, and a mutual responsibility between Muslims in particular, and between all human beings in general. Whereas in the Communist view, life is a continual strife and struggle between the classes, a struggle which must end in one class overcoming the other; at which point the Communist dream is realized. Hence, it is patent that Islam is the undying goodness of humanity, embodied in a living faith, working in the world; while Communism is the evil of human nature, limited to a single nation.

Individual and Society

There are, then, these two great facts: the absolute, just, and coherent unity of existence; and the general, mutual responsibility of individuals and societies. On these two facts Islam bases its definition of social justice, having regard to the basis elements of the nature of man, yet not unmindful of human abilities. The *Holy Qur'an* says of man that "Verily, for the love of gain he is violent;"[28] the "love of gain" belongs to his nature and to his native endowment. It says also, describing that greed which is of the nature and constitution of man, that "souls are close to avarice;"[29] it is always near to them. So also there occurs in *the Qur'an* a wonderfully skillful description of this human trait Say: "If it were you who had in your power the treasures of the mercy of my Lord, then you would keep a tight hold for fear of spending; for man is niggardly."[30] But, he is certainly liberal with His mercy in every way; and so, from this liberality of Divine mercy and from that human meanness, it is apparent how great is the extent of avarice in the nature of man if he is left without discipline of exhortation.

Accordingly, when Islam comes to lay down its rules and laws, its counsels and controls, that natural " love of gain" is not overlooked, nor is that deep natural avarice forgotten; selfishness is rebuked, avarice is death with regulations and laws, and the duty laid on man is that of liberality. At the same time, Islam does not overlook the needs and the welfare of society, nor does it forget the great achievements of individuals in life and society in every age and among different nations.

There may sometimes occur that type of social oppression which is inconsistent with justice, when the greed and cupidity of the individual prey upon society; or that same oppression may also take the form of society preying upon the nature and ability of the individual. Such oppression in a sin, not against one individual alone, but against the whole principle of the community.

It is an encroachment upon the freedom of the individual whose natural rights are infringed; but its evil effects do not touch merely the welfare and rights of the one individual; they go beyond him to touch the welfare of the whole community, because it cannot profit to the full from his abilities.

So, the regulations lay down the rights of the community over the powers and abilities of the individual; they also establish limiting boundaries to the freedom, the desires, and the wants of the individual but they must also be ever mindful of the rights of the individual, to give him freedom in his desires and inclinations; and over all there must be the limits which the community must not overstep, and which the individual on his side must not transgress, nor must there be interference with great individual achievements, for life is a matter of mutual help and mutual responsibility according to Islam, and not a constant warfare, to be lived in a spirit of struggle and hostility. Thus, There, must be freedom for individual and general abilities rather than repression, and a restrictive constraint. Everything that is not legally forbidden is perfectly permissible and everything that is not useless is of value.

The individual is to be encouraged by having every freedom in a life which reflects the Divine nature and which gives promise of the highest achievement. This breath of vision in the Islamic view of life, together with the fact it goes beyond merely economic values to those other values on which life depends -- these things make the Islamic faith the more powerful to provide equitable justice in society, and to establish justice in the whole of the human sphere. It also frees Islam from the narrow interpretation of justice as understood by Communism. For justice to the Communist is an equality of wages, in order to prevent economic discrimination; but in recent days when theory has come into opposition with practice, Communism has found itself unable to achieve this equality. Justice in Islam is a human equality, envisaging the adjustment of all values, of which the economic is but one.

In the Islamic view values are so very composite that justice must include all of them; therefore Islam does not demand a compulsory economic equality in the narrow literal sense of the term. This is against nature, and conflicts with the essential fact, which is that of the differing native endowments of individuals. It arrests the development of outstanding ability, and makes it equal to lesser ability; it prevents those who have great gifts from using their gifts to their own advantage and to that of the community, and it discourages the community and the individual from producing such gifts.

There can be profit in disputing the fact that the natural endowments of individuals are not equal. And while we may not be able to see this in the case of mental and spiritual endowments as we can in the sphere of practical life--yet we cannot deny that some individuals are born with endowments of disposition, which as goodness, or perfection, or patience; while others are born with endowments of body, such as sickness, or debility, or weakness. Can we deny that others can earn their living by the pleasantness of their conversation, by their pleasing appearance, or by their agreeable nature; thus the gates of undertaking and accomplishment open before them, the same gates which remain closed in the face of others not similarly endowed.

Accordingly, to deny the existence of outstanding endowments of personality, intellect, and spirit, is a piece of nonsense which cannot explain the existing differences between individuals. So, we must reckon with all these endowments and to all of them we must give the opportunity to produce their greatest results; then from these results we may take that which appears to be of permanent profit to society. we must not close off the outlet for such endowments, or discourage them by making them equal in reward with lesser abilities; we must avoid shackling such gifts and stifling them, and thereby depriving of their fruits the community and the human race alike.

Islam does, of course, acknowledge a fundamental equality of all men, and a fundamental justice among all, but over and above that is leaves the door open for achievement of preminence through hard work, just as it lays in the balance values other than the economic. "Verily the noblest among you in Allah's eyes is the most pious."[31] " Allah will raise up in degrees of honour those of you who believe, and to whom knowledge has been brought."[32] "Wealth and children are an ornament to life in the world, but the things which endure, the works of righteousness are better in thy Lord's eyes--better for reward, and better for hope."[33]

From this it is apparent that there are values other than the merely economic; with these values Islam reckons, and these it brings into relation with the idea of justice in society, since different individuals have different methods of gaining their livelihood. Islam admits the reasonable causes of these differences, as begin differences in strength and in endowment. It does not admit differences which depend on rank and station; such it absolutely denies on economic theory.

Islam, then, does not demand a literal equality of wealth, because the distribution of wealth depends on men's endowments, which are not uniform. Hence absolute justice demands that men's rewards be similarly different, and that some have more than others--so long as human justice is upheld by the provision of equal opportunity for all. Thus rank or upbringing, origin or class should not stand in the way of any individual, nor would anyone be fettered by the chains which shackle enterprise.

Justice must be upheld also by the inclusion of all kinds of values in the reckoning, and by the freedom of the human mind completely from the tyranny of the purely economic values, and by the relegation of these to their true and reasonable place. Economic values must not be given an intrinsically high standing, such as they enjoy in those human societies which lack a certainty of true values, or which give to them too slight an importance; in such conditions money alone becomes the supreme and fundamental value.

In Islam money is not given this value ; Islam refuses to admit that life can be reckoned in terms of a mouthful of bread, the appetite of the body, or a handful of money. Yet at the same time, it demands a competence for every individual, and at times more than a competence, in order to remove the fear of destitution. On the other side it forbids that unbridled luxury in possessions and desires, which produces social divisions and classes. It prescribes the claims of the poor upon the wealth of the rich, according to their needs, and according to the best interests of society, so that social life may be full, just, productive.

This, it is not unmindful of any one of the various aspects of life, material, intellectual religious and worldly; but it organized them all, that they may be related together and thus furnish an all-embracing unity in which it will be difficult to neglect any one of their various integral parts. So, these departments of life become an organized unity, similar to the greater oneness of the Universe, and to that of life, of the nation, and of all mankind.

Spiritual Nature

Islam operates on the inner, spiritual side of human nature, rather than on the external; it is from the depths of the conscience rather than on the surface that it seeks to improve man. But at the same time, it is never unmindful of the practical situation in the realm of wordly life; it does not forget the true nature of the human spirit, nor the things which influence if for good or evil, for better or worse: it has a care both for the aspirations which soar aloft and for the material necessities which are chained to Earth, for human strength which is ever limited and for the perfection which is always absolute. Thus because it has a profound knowledge of the depths of the human spirit. Islam makes use both of laws and of exhortations, it formulates commandments and prohibitions, it lays down limitations and enforces them. But it also encourages the human spirit to rise above such legalistic responsibilities as far as it can.

Life becomes possible and profitable only as we observe the lowest limit of the legal responsibilities of this faith; but even then it still lacks the perfection at which Islam aims, so long as it is not inspired by the promoting of conscience towards self-control, loftiness, and nobility. So, in Islam this prompting of the conscience is complementary to all legal duties; conscience must reinforce these duties, making their performance a pleasure, and thus imparting to human life a value and a nobility which are above the range of compulsion.

When Islam seeks to establish complete social justice, it sets it on a higher level than mere economic justice, and on a more elevated plane than can be attained merely by legislative measures; thus, it establishes a comprehensive human justice, established on two strong foundations: first, the human conscience, working within the spirit of man; and second, a system of religious law, working in the social sphere. These two powers it unites by an appeal to the depths of feeling in the human consciousness. "Verily in that there is a reminder for everyone who has a heart, or who will lend an ear; he is a witness of it."[34] Islam does not overlook the weakness of man, or his need for external compulsion, "*Allah* guides by his power more than by *the Qur'an*."[35]

Anyone who bestows even a passing and casual glance on this religion must perceive the immense effort which it devotes to the reformation of the human spirit in all its aspects and from everyside. And it is not without our subject to take a brief and summary look at this effort. It is designed for the good of society only to the point at which there can be a permanent control by human conscience; it works to guarantee all human society only until the individual becomes aware of his own practical obligations. " Do not play the spy, and do not backbite one another. Would one of you care to eat his dead brother's flesh? You would abhor it."[36] Spying is the worst crime against personal freedom and against the sanctities of the individual, just as backbiting is the worst characteristic which can find a lodgment in the weakness of personality; not only does it render a character incapable of praise, but it robs it eventually of all vital and practical courage.

"O! you who believe, do not go into houses other than your own, until you are received as friends and have greeted the inmates."[37]

Individual sanctities must be respected, because individual honour is the first requisite of social justice. "O! you who have believed, let not one people mock another who are possibly better than themselves. And let not women mock other women who are possibly better than themselves. Do not scoff at one another, nor shame one another with nicknames; it is bad to get the name of evil conduct when you are a believer; and those who do not repent are evil-doers."[38]

Mocking one another and scoffing at one another and calling one another by unpleasant nicknames are things which are forbidden alike by the essential values of personality, by human equality, and by social justice. "And do not walk the Earth in pride; verily you cannot split the Earth, nor can you reach the mountains in height.'[39]

Vanity and arrogance are characteristics which are unpopular in personality; similarly they are in opposition to the instinct for equality and justice and brotherhood. In a word Islam has the highest regard for the saying of its Prophet that " Verily you are of a great character.'[40] Character is the most essential foundation for the building of a firmly based society, for the joining of Earth to Heaven, the temporal to the eternal in the human consciousness with all its finitude and its frailty.

Islam places a great deal of reliance on the human conscience when it is educated; it sets it up as the guardian of the legal processes, to see that they are observed and maintained, and for the observance of the major part of the laws conscience alone is accountable. The giving of evidence, for example a fundamental matter which must be governed by laws, yet which, at the same time, must ensure the rights of men; and the giving of evidence is a question which runs back to the individual conscience and to the dependence of society on the conscience.

As for those who cast imputations upon innocent women, and then do not bring four witnesses in corroboration, flog them with eighty lashes and never again accept evidence from them;

they are those who deal corruptly.[41] And as for those who cast imputations upon their wives, and who have no witness but themselves--let the evidence of one of them be a fourfold testimony in the name of Allah that he is those who speak the truth. And let the fifth testimony be to invoke curse of Allah upon himself if he is of those who lie.

And punishment may be averted from the woman if she testify four times in the name of Allah that the man is of those who lie; and the fifth testimony shall be to invoke the curse of Allah upon herself if he is of those who speak the truth.[42] So too even, where a written agreement is demanded, it must necessarily be witnessed. ''O! you who believe, when one of you contracts a debt to another for a stated time, write it down; let a scribe write it down between you justly; let not the scribe refuse to write as Allah has taught him, but let him write, and let the debtor dissect.''

''Let him fear Allah his Lord, and let him not lessen the amount in any way. If the debtor is a fool, or if he is in weak health, or if he is unable to dictate, then let his kinsman dictate for him, justly. Then have the writing witnessed by two of your men; or if there are not two men, then by one man and two women out of those on whom you agree as euthanasias; so, if one the women should err, the other may remind her.''[43] The duty of witnessing is statutory and a matter of principle: ''Let not witnesses refuse when they are called.''[44] Similarly, the giving of evidence is a statutory responsibility in cases of legal dispute:

> ''And do not conceal evidence; for whoever does so, his heart is guilty.''[45]

Thus, Islam places reliance on the human conscience in matters which go as far as flogging, or stoning, and in matters touching the rights of property. Such a reliance must necessarily ennoble human nature and raise it towards the equality for which it longs and searches.

Islam does not leave the human conscience to its own resources; it allots to it these noble duties, making it the guardian of the observance of the law and of the carrying out of human responsibilities, and at the same time challenging it to rise above what law and responsibility prescribe for it. It has set the fear of

Allah as a sanction on the conscience, and has placed over it the thought of Allah's omniscence, with the aim of ensuring and inspiring its activity. "There is no private talk between three, but, He makes a fourth, nor between five, but He makes a sixth; and whether there be less than that or more, he is always with them wherever they are.

On the Day of Resurrection, he will tell them what they have done. "Verily Allah is aware of all things."[46] "We have created man, and We know that his soul whispers within him; We are nearer to him than his jugular vein. When the two meet and sit, one on the right hand and one on the left, he cannot utter a word without a watcher being beside him, ready."[47] "Verily he knows what is secret and what is hidden."[48]

Islam preached to men in warning, taking into account not only in this world but also in the next every single human action, for which there is no escaping punishment and no avoiding recompense. "We shall set up the balances of justice on the Day of Resurrection, and no soul will be wronged in the slightest degree; even if it is only the weight of a grain of mustard seed. We shall produce it; for We are sufficient as a reckoner."[49] "When the Earth--quakes with a great quaking; when the Earth brings forth what has been buried in it; when man says, 'What is the matter with it?; on that day the Earth shall tell her tidings, because your Lord has inspired her. On that day men shall come forward separately to see their works--whoever has done the weight of an atom of good shall see it; and whoever has done the weight of an atom of evil shall see it.[50]

Thus, runs the constant teaching of Islam, making reverence and piety a sanction upon the conscience and thus it makes the human conscience the means of advancement by making it responsible for the observance of all that the faith lays down in the way of laws and duties.

The Poor Tax

In the two-fold way, Islam proceeded to set the foundations of social justice, and by this means it succeeded in producing a balanced and interrelated human justice. We shall examine some aspects of this justice in another chapter; for the moment it will be sufficient to consider one example of this system of law and custom. I shall choose the subject of the poor--tax and the alms, because it has an intimate connection with the subject of this title.

Islam makes the poor-tax an obligatory claim on the property of the wealthy in favour of the poor. It is a due which the government can exact by the authority of the law and by the power of its administration; but the public conscience has progressively taken over the enforcement of the payment of this due, until such payment has become a natural part of the will of the wealthy.

The poor-tax is one of the pillars of Islam, one of the essentials of the faith. ''Prosperous are the believers who are humble in their prayers, who turn away from idle talk, and who are active in paying the poor-tax.''[51] ''These are the signs of the *Qur'an,* which is a book which makes clear, a guidance and a gospel for the believers, who observe the prayers, who pay the poor-tax and who are certain of the world to come.''

On the other hand, the act of withholding the poor-tax is a form of heresy and of unbelief in the world to come.[52] ''And woe to the heretics who do not pay the poor-tax and do not believe in the world to come.'[53] But payment of the poor-tax is a method of gaining the mercy of Allah:

> ''Observe the prayers, pay the poor-tax, and obey the Messenger; it may be that you will receive mercy.''[54]

Help from Allah comes to those who pay this due and who discharge their obligations to society, this meriting their place in the Earth.

> ''Allah will surely help the man who helps Him; verily, Allah is Powerful, Mighty. Such, if We establish them in the Earth, will observe the prayers, will pay the poor-tax, will urge to do good and will restrain from evil.''[55]

The poor-tax is a human institution of long standing, advocated by the commands of the prophets before Islam; thus, there is no religion devoid of this important social responsibility, ''And make mention in the Book of Ishmael, he was true to this promise, and was a messenger, a prophet; he bade his people pray and pay the poor-tax, and he was acceptable in the eyes of his Lord.''[56] So *the Qur'an* says of Abraham:

> "We gave to him Isaac and Jacob as extra gift; We made them upright men and We made them patterns to guide men by Our bidding. We inspired them to good work, to observe the prayers, and to pay the poor-tax; so, they served Us."[57]

And woe to him who does not discharge this legal obligation. Said the Messenger of Allah:

> "The man to whom Allah has given wealth, and who yet will not pay his poor-tax shall be thus recompensed on the Day of Resurrection; a huge snake with glowing eyes will encircle his neck on the Day of Resurrection, will grasp him by the maxillaries--that is to say, be the jaws--and will say, 'I am your wealth; I am your treasure, Which is a fearful, terrible and awesome picture."

This poor-tax is a due imposed by the force of the law, an amount of money in a specified proportion. But in addition to this, there is the institution of alms-giving which is imposed on the individual conscience without any fixed rate, it is at the discretion of the will and the conscience.

It is the outward sign of charity and brotherly feeling, to both of which Islam attaches supreme importance; it is an attempt to establish the mutual ties of mankind and the responsibilities of society along the lines of an individual perception of what is necessary, and along the lines of a personal conception of charity. It serves two purposes: first, to establish an inner control of the conscience; and second, to foster a belief in the inherent solidarity of mankind.

Islam makes this charity a pure and humane thing, not limited by the bounds of a religious fellowship, so *the Qur'an* says:

> "Allah does not forbid you to act righteously and justly towards those who have not fought against you in the matter of religion, and who have not expelled you from your homes."[58] And the Messenger says: "You will never be Believers until you show charity." They said to him, "O! Messenger of Allah, all of us are charitable." He replied: "It is not a question of your charity to your neighbour, but of your charity to men in general." And thus he sets a lofty

pattern of charity which is pure and universal, to the point of making it a feature of the faith.

He even takes the final step and includes in the scope of charity all living things. Thus, the noble Prophet of Islam said: "Once while a man was travelling, he became violently thirsty, so, finding a well, went down to the water, and drank. When he came up again he noticed a dog panting and licking the dust in an agony of thirst. He said to himself, This dog has the same violent thirst which I had, whereupon he went down again to the water and filled his boot with liquid. Grasping it in his mouth, he climbed out of the well and gave the dog to drink. And Allah the Exalted, gave him praise and pardon." His hearers asked him: "O Messenger of Allah, is there such a reward for us in the case of animals?" He replied: "There is such a reward in the case of every living creature." And again he said: "There was a woman who went to Hell only on account of a cat; she had tied it up, and had not fed it, nor had she even given it to eat of the herbage of the earth."

Such charity is a fundamental part of Islam, as it is one of its characteristic signs; it indicates the religious sincerity and depth of the conscience, and it testifies to the existence of that humane spirit without which, in the Islamic view, there can be no religion.

It is on this basis that Islam establishes the custom of alms--giving and charity; it makes one fond of spending voluntarily and freely, in anticipation of the approval of Allah, of a return from Him in this world, and of a reward for Him in the world to come. Thus too one may escape His anger, His vengeance, and His punishment.

So, the good news is for the humble, those who are obedient to Allah, and who spend of their wealth according to His will. "And give good news to the humble whose hearts are afraid when Allah is mentioned, who are patient in their afflictions, who observe the prayers, and who expend freely of what We have given them."[59] This is a picture to inspire the heart of man, and the same idea appears in another connection, where it is written:

> "Only those believe in our signs who, when they are reminded of them, fall down in adoration and celebrate the praises of their Lord, and are not puffed up. As they leave their beds they call upon their

Lord in fear and in hope, and of what We have given them they expend in alms. No one knows what pleasure is reserved for such, as a reward for what they have been doing."[60]

And the same inspiration is to be found in the beautiful and touching picture of the character of the people of Medina when they received the emigrants and gave them shelter, sharing with them their property and their houses in cheerfulness and gladness of spirit. "As for those who occupied the houses and the faith before them, they loved those who emigrated to them and they found no desire in their hearts for the share which had fallen to the others; they preferred them before themselves, though, there was poverty among them. Those who are preserved from niggardliness of soul shall be prosperous."[61]

This is a picture of human nature in its highest and best aspects; and here is another description which is not inferior to the first, of the kindness, the compassion, and the sympathy of a community of Allah's servants; some authorities hold that the people in question here are Ali and his wife, Fatima, the daughter of the Messenger, and their household.[62] They fulfil their vows, and they fear a Day the evil of which will fly broadcast. For love of God they give food to the poor, the orphan, and the prisoner, saying, 'It is only for the sake of Allah that we give you food; we want from you neither reward nor gratitude. We fear from our Lord a day which will be grim and forbidding.'

So, Allah has preserved them from the evil of that Day, and has given them cheerfulness and joy; He has rewarded them for their endurance with Paradise and silk clothing. There, they recline on courage, and there, they see neither not bitter cold nor extreme hot; near over them is the shade of the garden of Paradise, and hanging low around them are its clusters of fruit. They shall be served round with vessels of silver and goblets of glass, with glasses of silver whose measure they have themselves determined; in these they shall quaff a drink tempered with ginger, drawn from a spring named Salsabil. There pass round among them boys of eternal youth, whom to see is to imagine that they are unstrung pearls, and whom to see is to envisage delight and a great kingdom. They are clothed with garments of green satin and brocade, and they are adorned with bracelets of silver; their Lord has given them to drink a pure draught. Verily, this has come to you as a reward, and thus your life's striving has been recompensed.''[63]

So, the giving of alms is to make a loan to Allah, a loan which is certain to be repaid: '' Who is he who will make a fair loan to Allah, and He will double it for him. For such a one there is a noble reward.''[64] ''Verily, men and women who give alms thus make a loan to Allah, He will double it for them. For such, there is a noble reward.''[65] Or it may be regarded as a profitable and remunerative business:

> ''Verily, those who recite the Book of Allah, who observe the prayers, and who expend in alms of what We have given them, both secretly and openly--such hope for a business that will not fail. So, He may pay them their rewards in full, and may give them increase of His bounty; verily he is forgiving, grateful.''[66]

In either case alms--giving is profitable, and does not involve loss or injury:

> ''That which you expend in alms of your possession is to your own advantage, even though you expend it only for the love of Allah; what you expend in alms of your possessions will be repaid to you in full measure, and you will suffer no injury.''[67]

So, in the next world Paradise is the worthy recompense of those who expend freely in alms:

> ''And hasten to forgiveness from your Lord, and to a Paradise whose width is as that of the Heavens and the Earth, a Paradise prepared for those who are pious; they it is who expend in alms both in prosperity and in adversity, who curb their wrath, and who deal leniently with others. Allah loves those who act well.''[68]

Again, alms--giving is a means of purification for one's character and for one's property; the Messenger of Allah commanded that a portion of their property should be taken from people who have sinned and have acknowledged their sins, and that this should be spent on good causes thus, such people might be purified and cleansed. ''Others have acknowledged their sins;

they have done both, deeds that are good and deeds that are evil; it may be that Allah will relent towards them, for Allah is forgiving and compassionate. Take of their property an alms which will purify and cleanse them, and pray over them; verily your prayers will mean a repose for them, for Allah hears and knows. Have they not learned that He is Allah who received repentance from His servants, and who accepts the alms? Have they not learned that it is Allah who is relenting and compassionate?''[69]

Thus, expenditure on alms is encouraged by repayment according to the compact of Allah, by reverence for Him, and by fear of an evil record; to give alms indicates wisdom and understanding. But to refrain from alms-giving is to nullify what Allah has commanded to be accomplished; it is a form of violating the compact and of dealing corruptly on the Earth. Only those who have insight are reminded, those who fulfil the compact of Allah and who do not violate the agreement. They accomplish what Allah has commanded to be accomplished, they revere their Lord, and they fear an evil record. They endure with patience out of regard for the love of Allah, they observe the prayers, and they expend in alms out of what We have given them, both secretly and openly; they drive away the evil by means of the good.

Such shall have the recompense of the Abode, gardens of pleasure into which they shall enter, they and those of their fathers and their wives and their descendants who have been upright; angels shall come in to them by every gate, saying, ''Peace be upon you for your patient endurance; good is the recompense of the Abode''. But as for those who violate the compact of Allah after coming to an agreement with Him, who nullify what Allah has commanded to be accomplished, and who deal corruptly on the Earth--for them is the curse, and for them there is an evil abode.''[70]

To refrain from expenditure in the way of Allah is destruction:

''Expend freely in the way of Allah, and do not hand yourselves over to destruction.''[71]

The 'destruction' of the individual is to lay oneself open to the punishment of Allah in the world to come, and to the vengeance of others in this world. The 'destruction' of society is the discrimination and the oppression which come in the train of the absence of free expenditure in alms, together with the accompanying discords and hatreds, debility and weakness.

To hinder good works is a form of hostility: "Cast into hell every obstinate unbeliever who hinders good work, who is hostile and contentious."[72] "And do not obey any contemptible swearer, any slanderer who goes about maligning, who hinders good works, who is hostile and guilty."[72] He is hostile to the claims of Allah; to the claims of his own soul as a member of that society.

Charity leads to Paradise, and the charitable man will pass over the hard path which leads thither; the path consists in the setting free of slaves, and in the provision of food in a case of hunger and destitution. "And what has taught you the nature of the 'hard path'? It is to set free slaves, to give food in a day of famine to an orphan who is of your kin, or to a poor man in destitution."[74] But to refrain from charity leads to the Fire, and he who merits it will go thither along with the unbelievers. "What made you go into Hell-fire?" They replied: "We were not among those who prayed, nor were we among those who fed the poor; we plunged into discussion with others, and we scoffed at the Day of Judgment. Until the final account came upon us."[75] "As for those who have been niggardly with what Allah has given them of His bounty, let them not think that it will be well with them; nay it will go ill with them, for on the Day of Resurrection that which they have stingily withheld will be hung about their necks."[76] "As for those who have heaped up for themselves treasures of gold and silver, and who do not expend them in the way of Allah, announce for them a painful punishment. On that day their treasures will be heated in the fire of Hell, and they will be branded with them on their foreheads, their sides, and their backs. These are the treasures which you heaped up for yourselves. So taste now of what you have heaped up."[77]

The treasures which are referred to in this verse are explained in a tradition; "Whoever collects dinars or dirhams, gold in the nugget or silver, and does not pay it over to a creator or expend it freely in the way of Allah -- a treasure, and he will be branded with it on the Day of Resurrection."[78] Treasure, properly understood, is not merely money on which no poor-tax is paid, as some have maintained; all money which is hoarded and which is not paid out for these specified purposes is treasures, even if poor-tax has been paid on it. And the other tradition which indicates that money on which poor-tax has been paid is not treasure, is not in opposition to this tradition; for the latter tradition merely makes the former specific.

Indeed, in the case of men who hoard, punishment sometimes overtakes them in this world as a reward for their niggardliness, and for their hindering of good works. The noble *Qur'an* tells a parable of such in a short story concerning a community which had a walled garden, from the produce of which they used to feed the poor. Then, it occurred to them to be niggardly and to keen the fruit for themselves; but a change of fortune fell upon their garden, and Allah took away their produce, so that the next morning they were regretful. "We have tested them as We tested the owners of the garden when they resolved that they would reap it in the morning, and made no qualification of their resolve. So, while they slept a disaster from your Lord encircled it, and in the morning it lay like a garden already reaped. That morning they called to one another, 'Come early to your field, if you intend to reap', and they went their way, whispering to one another. 'Let no poor man come upon you in the garden today.' So, they went out early with this settled purpose, but when they saw it they said, 'Verily we have erred, and we are cheated of our fruits.'

The most fair-minded of them said, 'Did I not say to you, Will you not give praise to Allah?' They said, 'Praise to our Lord. Verily, we have been evil doers.' So they turned upon one another, blaming one another, and saying, 'Alas for us. Indeed, we have been presumptous; it may be that our Lord will give us something better than this in exchange. Verily, our desire is towards our Lord's.' Such was the punishment; and the punishment of the world to come is yet greater, if only they knew."[79]

The Qur'an summons men to be generous before the opportunity is lost to them. "Say to My servants who have believed that they must observe the prayer and expend freely of what We have given them, both secretly and openly, before there comes a Day on which there will be neither bargain nor friendship.''[80] ''And expend freely of what We have given you, before death comes upon one of you, and he says, 'O! my Lord, Would that my death might be deferred for a short space, so that I might give alms and thus become one of the righteous,' But Allah will not defer the death of any soul when its time is come.''[81] Similarly, *the Qur'an* cautions men against avarice, that they may guard themselves from it, and that they may not be betrayed into it by their desire for wealth and children; for these things are only a trial and temptation for men. ''Your wealth and your children are only a temptation, but Allah has a great reward. So be pious towards Allah as far as you are able, attend and obey. Expend freely in alms; that is better for yourselves. It is those who are protected from avarice of soul who prosper.''[82]

The Prophet makes alms--giving a duty for every Muslim, even though he may have nothing. The explanation of that is this saying of his: ''The giving of alms is a duty for every Muslim. They asked him; 'O Prophet of Allah, what of him who has nothing?' He replied: 'Let him turn his hand to labour, and thus profit himself, and then let him give his alms.' They said, 'And what if he can find nothing to do?' He answered: 'Let him find some unfortunate soul who is in need'; They said: 'Suppose he cannot find such a one?' He replied: 'Then let him do some one a service, or let him restrain someone from evil, and that shall be his alms.'' Thus, all men have an equal opportunity for generosity, each according to his means, and each according to his ability.

Universal Charity

The recipients of charitable expenditure must vary according to varying needs and circumstances; relatives have the prior claim on a man's benefactions, but there are others also who are joined with them, and who are mentioned side by side with relatives in the passages of *the Qur'an* which urge to charity. For charity is a universal emotion, and must take precedence over family consciousness; and indeed the mention of charity in *the Qur'an* is generally linked with that of faith. More than that-- it is an indication of faith, as we have shown. '' Serve Allah, and do not associate any other with Him. Show kindness to parents and relatives, to orphans and to the poor, to the stranger under your protection, whether or not he be a relative, to the companion at your side and to the wayfarer, and to those who are your possession (i.e, such as slaves). Verily Allah does not love any crafty boaster. Those who are niggardly and who urge others to niggardliness, who conceal what Allah has given them of His bounty -- for such unbelievers We have prepared a shameful punishment.''[83] '' They will ask you how they should expend money in alms. Say, what you expend is for benefit of parents, relatives, orphans, the poor and the wayfarer. Whatever good you do, Allah is aware of it.''[84]

Thus, the stranger under a man's protection and the companion are placed alongside the parents and relatives, just as the poor and the wayfarer are grouped with all of them. All have an equal right to alms. And this is so, even in the case of those who have committed some evil deed, as in the occurrence connected with Mistah, a relative of Abu Bakr, who shared in the slanderous story about A'isha, the daughter of Abu Bakr and wife of the Prophet.

Islam ordains that such persons be forgiven, and it forbids that they be punished in this way. Abu Bakr swore that he would cut off the charity which he had been extending to Mistah, for he was exceedingly angry at the calumnies which the latter had been spreading about the character of A'isha. But this verse was revealed to Muhammad: ''As for those of you who have abundance and ample means. Let them not abstain from giving to relatives and the poor and to those who have emigrated in the way of Allah; rather let them pardon and forgive. Do you not wish that Allah should pardon you?''[83] Thus, Islam seeks to raise human instincts to a high and noble level which does honour to human nature in all ages, which makes human nature a proud thing in the past, the present, and the future, as long as Allah wills.

Islam also elevates the conception of charity itself by making it charity for the sake of Allah the Glorious. It depicts charity in this striking picture which has come down through the traditions. ''On the Day of Resurrection Allah will say: ''O! man, I was ill, and you did not visit Me.'' Then man will reply: ''O! my Lord, how could I visit You, since You are Lord of the Worlds.'' Then, Allah will say: ''Did you not know that such and such a servant of Mine was ill, and you did not visit him? If you had visited him, you would have found Me there. "O man, I gave you your food, but you have given Me no food." He will answer: "O my Lord, how could I give You food, seeing that You are Lord of the Worlds?' And Allah will say: "Did you not know that such and such a servant of Mine gave you food, yet you gave him none? Surely if you had given him food, you would have found it with Me." 'O! man, I gave you to drink, but you did not give to Me." Man will say, "O my Lord, how could I give You to drink, seeing that You are the Lord of the Worlds? And Allah will reply: "Such and such a servant of Mine gave you to drink, yet you did not give to him. Had you given him to drink, you would have found it with Me."

Islam also makes alms--giving a matter of the public conscience, thus raising it above the stage where it is merely a mark of the superiority and pre-eminence of the rich over the poor, and thus raising it also above the stage where it may be only a form of hypocrisy arising from ignoble instincts. For if the impulses leading to alms-giving are allowed to deteriorate, or if charity is followed by a sense of obligation on the part of those who receive it, then it becomes an ungracious business which can only injure the soul, the nature, and the conscience, and which can only injure society also by injuring its individual members. There is nothing like attaching a sense of obligation to an act of benevolence for paining people, for humbling them, and rendering them unwilling to accept benevolence. Similarly, there is nothing like hypocrisy in alms--giving for corrupting the conscience and sapping the moral fibre.

Accordingly, Islam labours to elevate the nature both of those who give and of those who receive, and it is this result which it seeks most strenuously to achieve. "Those who expend their wealth freely in the way of Allah are like a grain which produced seven ears with a hundred grains in each ear; so Allah will give a double return to whom He wills, and verily Allah is powerful and aware. Such as expend their wealth in alms in the way of Allah and do not follow this expenditure with obligations or annoyances shall have their reward with their Lord; no fear shall oppress them, nor any sadness rest upon them. Favourable speech and forgiveness are better than alms followed by annoyance; Allah is rich and clement. O! you who have believed, do not make your alms in vain by putting obligation or annoyance upon the recipients, as he does who gives alms for the sake of appearance before the people.

He has no belief in Allah or in the Last Day, and he is like a smooth rock with earth in it; if a heavy rain falls upon it, it is left bare. Such men have no power over what they have stashed, and Allah does not give guidance to people who are unbelievers. But those who expend their wealth in alms out of a desire for the approval of Allah and as a support from themselves are like a garden on a hill; if a heavy rain falls upon it, brings forth its fruit in double measure; and even if no heavy rain falls upon it, yet still there is the dew. Allah is aware of what you do. Would anyone of you like this to happen? Suppose he has a garden of palm trees and vines with perpetual water flowing through it, so that he has all kinds of fruits in it; old age comes upon him, and he has only a weak family; then a fiery whirlwind strikes his garden, so that it is burnt up. In such a way does Allah make the signs clear to you; it may be that you will consider.''[84]

For this reason it is desirable that alms be given in secret and privately to the needy. Thus on the one hand the self-esteem of the recipients is safeguarded, and on the other hand a check is put upon conceit and pride. ''If you give alms in public, that is good; but if you do it secretly and give to the poor, that is better for you.''[85] And there is a tradition of the Prophet in praise of the man who ''Gives his alms, but conceals the fact to the point where his let hand does not know what his right hand is giving.''[86] This is an outstandingly fine picture of the way charity should be kept secret, and should not be accounted as a matter for pride or publicity.

The Sway of Materialism

Islam is aware of the power of the love of material gain, and the power of the love of money.[87] It is convinced that avarice is always threatening the soul and is never far away. ''Souls are ever liable to avarice.''[88] So, it treats all of these as a personal matter, using the methods which we have seen; it stimulates the will, it warns, it exhorts, it depicts; in this way, its aims may be achieved, and thus, it can beseech this naturally niggardly disposition of man to attain a standard of nobility in dealing with that which he loved dearly and which has a powerful hold upon him. ''You will not attain charity until you expend in alms of that which you love.''[89]

In this way, man reaches the height of generosity, the limit of liberality, and the noblest form of beneficence which can possible arise from the human spirit. Thus, man is raised above his natural state, and thus the higher side of his nature overcomes the lower, his spiritual nature conquers his animal nature. By its very nature this is by itself a lofty and universal aim which must command all support. How much more so, then, seeing that it is also an objective for society. The purpose is to create a balance of wealth, to oppose destitution, to establish the responsibilities which exist between the rich and the poor, and thus to shape a society which has a sense of mutual relationship and mutual help, and which is therefore a healthy society.

Islam follows this method, with one example of which we have now dealt in detail. Islam is concerned with persuasion of the conscience in the case of every duty which it prescribes. It imposes no more duties than are demanded for the safety of society, and no more than can be accepted by the limited ability of the general mass of mankind.

Beyond that stage it appeals to the conscience, persuading it of its responsibility and seeking to raise it above its normal scope; thus it attempts to elevate human life, and to draw it ever onward and upward. It recognizes the wide gap which lies between the lower level of duty which is prescribed by the law and the higher level of conscience which is so desirable, and towards which individuals and nations have striven in every age and century.

Thus, as an example, Islam prescribes a principle of vengeance, awarding it as a legal right to the next kin, and permitting him to exact it in full; yet at the same time it exhorts as strongly as possible that men should forgive, forbear, and pardon. ''If any man is unjustly killed. We have given authority to his next of kin; but let him not be immoderate in killing; verily, he has been helped.''[90]

Again, it prescribes holy war in the way of Allah as a responsibility incumbent on everyone who is able for it. But over and above that it kindles a love for holy wars by inciting the conscience to accept it, by depicting it in glowing terms, and by emphasizing its justice and the glories which it brings to a society. "Allah has purchased from the Believers their persons and their wealth that the Prince of Paradise reserved for them; so they fight in they way of Allah, so they kill and are killed"[91] "And, if not Allah set some men against others, the cloisters had been destroyed, and the churches and synagogues and mosques in which the name of Allah is often repeated.[92] What is the matter with you that you do not fight in the way of Allah, and in defence of the oppressed, men, women and children."[93]

It forbids usury, and goes on to attack its evil character and the evil character of its results. It seeks to arouse the conscience to condemn usury and to reject it. Those who eat up the fruit of usury will not arise on the Day of Resurrection, except in the same way as he whom Satan has sent mad by a touch. That is because they have said: 'A bargain is just the same as usury.' But, Allah has allowed bargaining, though He has forbidden usury. If anyone receives a warning from his Lord and desists, he shall keep what he has already gained, and his destiny shall be in the hand of Allah. But if anyone continues to practice usury, then he is one of those destined to Hell, there to abide; Allah will blot our usury, but He will multiply money. Allah does not love any guilty unbeliever,"[94] " O! you who have believed, act piously towards Allah and abandon the usury which is still unpaid, if you are really Believers. And if you do not do this, then know that there will be war from Allah and from his Messenger."[95]

Islam forbids the drinking of wine and gambling, and it links up these things with the custom of divining the future by the casting of lost or sacred arrows; this occurs in one verse which places all these things together as being outside the bounds of commonsense and logic. Then it goes on to persuade the conscience of the reasons for this prohibition. "O! you, who have believed wine and gambling, scared lost and arrows are only an abomination, a work of Satan. Turn away from them, then, and it may be that you will prosper. Satan desires only to raise enmity and hatred among you by means of wine and gambling, to keep you from the remembrance of Allah, and from the prayers; so will you rafrain?"[93]

Islam, thus, continues through all its commands and prohibitions; the same course is followed. It is the wisest and the most profitable course for human nature, and its results have already been proved in the early history of Islam and throughout the long period of the past fourteen centuries. This method can be repeated for the present and the future, so long as its essential nature is understood, so long as this direction is followed, and so long as men will follow this straight path.

References

1. Ibn-Sina, known to the West as Avicenna, was born in Bokhara in 979 A.D. and died in 1039 AD. He is known as the outstanding Arab philosopher of the classical school, and, after the fashion of his time, as the outstanding physician. His philosophy was that of Aristotle, his medicine that of Galen and Hippocrates -- (Trans.)
2. Ibn-Rush or Averroes lived nearly a century and a half after Ibn Sina, and at the other end of the Muslim world. Born in Cordova, Spain, in 1126, he also was an Aristotlian in philosophy; and though he left comparatively little impress on Arab thought, he was exceedingly influential on the development of Mediaeval Europe an Philosophy. He died in 1198 A.D.
3. Sura 36:82.
4. Sura 13:2.
5. Sura 22:64.
6. Sura 36:40.
7. Sura 67:1.
8. Sura 67:3-4.
9. Sura 41:9.
10. Sura 67:2.
11. Sura 30:47.
12. Sura 16:15.
13. Sura 55:9.
14. Sura 67:15.
15. Sura 2:27.
16. Sura 67:5.
17. Sura 78:6-16.
18. Sura 11:8.
19. Sura 50:15.
20. Sura 40:62.
21. Sura 6:152.
22. Sura 49:13.

23. Sura 5:37.
24. Sura 49:9.
25. Sura 2:252.
26. See the chapter on 'History in the *Qur'an,*' "*Literary Artistry of the* Qur'an"
27. Sura 23:54.
28. Sura 100:8.
29. Sura 4:127.
30. Sura 17:102.
31. Sura 49:13.
32. Sura 58:12.
33. Sura 18:44.
34. Sura 50:37.
35. Traditions.
36. Sura 49:12.
37. Sura 24:27.
38. Sura 49:11.
39. Sura 17:39.
40. Sura 68:4.
41. Sura 24:4.
42. Sura 24:6-9.
43. Sura 2:282.
44. Sura 2:282.
45. Sura 2:283.
46. Sura 58:8.
47. Sura 50:15-17. (It is a Muslim belief that every man throughout the course of his life is attended by two angels: the one on his right side records the good that he does, and the other on his left records the evil. This is the reference whereto the two who meet and sit on either side of the man. This verse is also sometimes interpreted as being a reference to the meeting of the angel of life with the angel of death, but this seems less satisfactory.-- (Trans.)
48. Sura 20:6.
49. Sura 21:48.
50. Sura 99.
51. Sura 23:1-4.
52. Sura 27:1-3.
53. Sura 41:5-6.
54. Sura 24:5.
55. Sura 22:41-42.
56. Sura 19:55-56.
57. Sura 21:72-73.
58. Sura 60:8.
59. Sura 22:35-36.

60. Sura 32:15-17.
61. Sura 59:9. (The reference of this whole passage is to the *Hijra* or emigration of Muhammad from Mecca to Medina in the year 622 A.D. It is from this date, the Muslim era is reckoned, as it is with good reason held to be the turning point in Muhammad's career as a prophet. At the time of the emigration of Prophet there where already some converts at Medina, and it was these who received the emigrants with such grace, literally sharing with them all that they possessed.--Trans).
62. Ali was first cousin to the Prophet through his father AbuTalib who, though he never embraced Islam, extended his protection to Muhammad throughout a difficult period of the latter's mission in Mecca. Ali himself was an early convert to Islam, and through his marriage of Muhammad's daughter, Fatima, became the Prophet's son-in law. After the death of the Messenger, Ali was the fourth Caliph, though owing to the civil war he never was the sole ruler of the Muslim world. He met his death by assassination in 661 A.D. The connection of this Quranic passage with Ali and his family is given by Baidwi on the authority of Ibn-Abbas in the following story: "Hasan and Husain--the two sons of Ali fell ill, and the Messenger of Allah went to visit them with a company of people. They said to Ali, 'O *Abu-la-Hasan* if you had made a vow over your two sons, all would have been well; then Ali and Fatima and Fida, a slave-girl belonging to them, vowed that if the boys recovered and got well they could keep a fast for three days. So they had nothing in the house, and Ali borrowed three measures of barley from Simeon of Khaibar, and Fatima ground up one measure and baked five loaves which she put before them to break their fast. Just then a poor man arrived at their house, and they gave him what they had, and themselves spent the night without tasting anything save water. So, the next morning they were still fasting, and when again food was placed before them, an orphan arrived and they gave him what they had; then on the third day a prisoner arrived, and they did the same again. And Gabriel revealed this sura to Muhammad." --Baidawi on Sura 76.-- Trans.)
63. Sura 76:7-22.
64. Sura 57:11.
65. Sura 57:17
66. Sura 35:26-27.
67. Sura 2:237.
68. Sura 3:127-128.
69. Sura 9:103-105.
70. Sura 13:19-25.
71. Sura 2:191.

72. Sura 50:23-24.
73. Sura 68:10-12.
74. Sura 90: 12-16.
75. Sura 74:43-48.
76. Sura 3:175-176.
77. Sura 9:34-35.
78. They did not add the phrase "If Allah will."--Trans.
79. Sura 68:17-33.
80. Sura 14:36.
81. Sura 63:10-11.
82. Sura 64:15-16.
83. Sura 4:40-41.
84. Sura 2:211.
85. Sura 24:22. (The story of Mistah is connected with the well-known misadventure of A'isha. Having been lost in the desert during one of the Prophet's expeditions she was brought in to Medina under compromising circumstances. A tempest of scandal at once assailed her reputation, and one of the foremost in spreading the scandal was Mistah, a poor relation of A'isha's father, Abu-Bakr. The latter in his anger vowed that Mistah for this ingratitude would on longer enjoy his generosity to which he was accustomed. The forbearance which is indicated in the verse of the *Qur'an* here quoted is the most notable since Muhammad himself must have deeply resented the calumny of Mistah, A'isha being his favourite wife.--Trans.)
86. Sura 2:263-268.
87. Sura 2:273.
88. Sura 4:127.
89. Sura 3:86.
90. Sura 17:35.
91. Sura 9:112.
92. Sura 22:41.
93. Sura 4:77.
94. Sura 2:276-277.
95. Sura 2:278-279.
96. Sura 5: 92-93.

4

Evolution of Civil Society

The secular civilizations have been instrumental in eroding the noble feelings, righteous emotions and moral values of the human race, but even greater destruction has been wrought by the doctrine of social evolution. This doctrine took its birth from materialism. It was fostered by the utilitarian outlook and man's conquest of time and space which lent maturity to it. The doctrine was developed by Kant, Fischte, Hegel, Karl Marx and several other philosophers. With the rise of this theory, wrong took the shape of right and evil became good. Bloodshed, savagery and exploitation of the weak came to be regarded as the highest moral virtues of humanity.

The present chapter cannot admit of a detailed discussion on the subject. I shall, therefore, confine myself to a brief examination of the ideas which have gone into the making of this doctrine. We take up Hegel first, for although the doctrine of social evolution has been extant in the world for several centuries, it was Hegel who with profound conviction and full force of logic presented it to the world as a well-knit system of philosophy.

It is rather a marvel for the student of historiography that this astute German philosopher emphatically refutes Kantian system, yet strives with even greater force and energy to affirm the Kantian theory. He infuses logic into the dull philosophy of Kant and carries the philosophy started by the 'iconoclast' of reason to its final conclusion.[1]

Avoiding technical intricacies of philosophy, we may explain that in Hegel's view, the evolution of human civilization follows this process: the appearance of contradictions, their conflict and fusion. Each period of human history is a unit and a whole. In a given period, all phases of human life, economic, political, cultural, moral, intellectual and religious ideals are at a particular level. They are all closely interrelated, and they all reflect the age in which they exist. When at the behest of the "Absolute Spirit," the history of mankind advances some steps further, some antithetic ideas, tendencies and doctrines rise from within the body of politics of that age.

An intense conflict between the thesis and antithesis ensues which rages for some time. At last both come to terms. Weak elements on both sides are eliminated and thesis and antithesis merge to from a unity which consists of strong and pure elements of both side. Thus, a completely new system of thought and practice emerges, which in due course of time meets the same fate as its successor. Thus, human civilization continues to advance by this evolutionary process.

In his own terminology, Hegel calls it the Dialectical Process of History. According to this theory, a given period of history is a battleground in which a logical debate and conflict is constantly going on and it is the force of this conflict that propels mankind to further progress. First a thesis appears and then an antithesis arises to challenge the thesis. After a prolonged conflict between the two, the 'Absolute Spirit' brings about a reconciliation between them. Thus a new entity comes into being which in every respect is better and more comprehensive than its predecessors, for, it contains all the best elements of the preceding entities. Hence each step takes mankind to further advance. This is the Hegelian philosophy of social evolution.

Marx borrowed his philosophical framework from Hegel, but filled in details from his own intuition. He discarded the concept of soul and held that material causes or economic factors were the prime force in the process of historical evolution. Whereas Hegel regards ideas as the most effective power, in Marxian theory, the decisive factor is the material environment and even in this environment the real factors of importance are the means of production.

Hegel thinks that the conflict between thesis and antithesis occurs in the realm of ideas. Marx believes that the main battleground of life is the economic sphere and that it is in this sphere that the destiny of mankind is decided. Economics is the preeminent factor in human life and the superstructure of morality, religious doctrines, culture, arts and sciences is erected on the foundation of the economic system. The contours of intellectual and political life in a given period are determined by the various means of economic production in that period. According to Marx, the process of social evolution takes the following course:

> "To begin with a change in the means of economic production takes place, which directly affects the distribution of means of life and the modes of ownership of property. Consequently, all the values of life undergo a change, and a new system comes into existence."

At this stage, a conflict between the new and the old system in the sense of Hegelian dialectics takes place which ends eventually in conciliation and both systems merge to create an entirely new system which contains only the best elements of the preceding systems. Evidently, the emergent system is in every respect superior to former systems. This then is the Marxian view of the process of social evolution.

The third philosopher whose viewpoint lent force to the doctrine of social evolution was Darwin. According to him all living creatures have a natural tendency towards unlimited growth, development and changing their physical form. But the evolution of various creatures is not determined by any constructive process initiated by providence, but is the result of a destructive process.

The evolution of living creatures does not occur without mutual conflict, famine and death. Darwin reposed implicit faith in Malthusian theory of population and inferred from it that since the number of living creatures multiplies at a faster rate due to availability of food and other necessities for existence, hence each creature is constrained to fight constantly against other creatures in order to preserve his own existence.

In Darwin's view life is a battleground where at all moments and in every direction the strong are engaged in eliminating the weak in an overall struggle for existence. Only the fittest survive in this struggle and it is really they who deserve all that is best in life. Those who perish in this callous struggle receive a just punishment for their infirmity. In short, this earth, and the means of life on it sustain only those who are the strongest.

There is no room on earth for the weak and the sooner they liquidate their infirm existence from this universe the better. Thus under compulsion of circumstances the process of evolution is initiated and through a constant course of conflict produces higher forms of life. Man too, climbs the high rung of humanity through this complex struggle. Those who emerge victorious from the struggle of existence are pure and the universe belongs to them only.

The theory of social evolution which emerges from a combined view of the doctrines of these philosophers contains the following major principles:

i. The evolution of life takes place through conflict.
ii. Human progress is the consequence of this conflict.
iii. Only the strongest have the right to live and develop in this universe.
iv. Success by whatever means it may be achieved is the main object of existence.

For the moment, I do not intend to point out the intellectual flaws in this doctrine. What I wish to emphasize is that this philosophy instead of humanizing man has actually transformed him into a brute and rather than make this world a heaven of peace, it has changed into a veritable hell.

The Philosophy of Social Evolution

The first impact of the philosophy of social evolution is that man has come to regard material progress as the highest achievement of life, whereas upon a careful consideration it will be found that material development only aids the consciousness of man; it has no creative power of its own. Actually, spiritual power is the prime mover of human consciousness.

It is at this point that the exponents of doctrine of social evolution have committed the greatest blunder. When social evolution means only material development, it necessarily follows that different sections and classes of people should cast morality to the winds and launch a frenzied struggle against each other for expropriating the material means of life, for if they refrained from the struggle, they would perish. This philosophy has produced a permanent fear complex among the people. This savage competitive spirit has enveloped individuals as well as nations, and everyone is scared of the other. This permanent fear complex has developed the vilest qualities among human beings, such as, for instance, selfishness, callousness, avarice, bigotry, faithfulness, corruption and falsehood.

Modern psychologists have established the fact that human actions calculated to make a show of strength spring from a fear complex. Hence ostentations, display of military strength, assertion of superior authority and a craving of power without responsibility are various forms of the same fear complex.

Secondly, this philosophy has plunged the future of humanity into darkness. A philosophy which explains the creation of human ego in terms of time and place can provide man with the knowledge of laws and boundaries of this universe, but cannot liberate man from its cruel fetters. It is for this reason that modern man daily grows pessimistic about his future. The well-known Italian philosopher Croce comments on this problem as follows:

> "The shadow of pessimism covers from time to time the life of the individual and similarly the life of societies; and doubts, fears and despair over the future belongs to all eras of history. But in the years through which Europe is living, that shadow has become wider and darker, philosophers, or people who call themselves philosophers, have become prophets and describe to us, under the guise of philosophical and historical reality, the steep incline, we shall perforce descend...when, as frequently happens, we conceive it as a tangle of forces which act outside us and according to their own laws, we have, with the nightmare of these forces, the feelings of helplessness, since, if they are outside us, there is no way of getting among them and of dominating or regulating them. There is nothing left to do then but to speculate, seeking in the external world other forces which may oppose, defeat or check them, and to put our hope in these. But it is uncertain hope, always fearful, because it depends on others and not on us, and, whether fearful or hopeful, we feel ourselves in the clutches of others."[2]

Thirdly, because this doctrine is founded on the idea that the evolution of man takes place through conflict between hostile forces, hence instead of promoting cooperation among human beings, it has aroused in them a fierce sense of jealousy and competition. This doctrine inculcates in the minds of the people that prosperity and progress in life depend on total commitment to the struggle for worldly gains.

Consequently, it has transformed man into a callous and insensitive creature. This doctrine holds it perfectly natural for the strong to enrich himself at the expense of the weak, by doing so, he proves that only the fittest have the right to survive. Conversely, the weak deservedly suffer persecution and are rightly downtrodden by the strong. Not only has this doctrine turned human beings into savage tyrants, but it has also furnished a rational basis for capitalism and imperialism by endorsing that might is invariably right. Fighting has been a part of human history since long, but before now men considered fighting as evil, though at times a necessary one. This doctrine has baptized war as a definite blessing. In the past, people looked upon a tyrant as an evil-doer.

Today, they laud him as a just man. Max Eastman's comment on the materialistic interpretation of history is, in fact, truly applicable to the whole doctrine of social evolution. He remarks:

> ''Notwithstanding their high-sounding claims to humanism, the Marxists have become haughty and violent under the influence of this doctrine. The basic assumption of the doctrine is that man attains evolutionary progress through a process of severe and violent conflict. Good and evil in this doctrine are merely names for two material forces and man achieves glory only through a collision between these two forces.''[3]

A French author Boris Soyrarine comments:

> ''All respect for humanity has been erased from our hearts. Life has lost its real worth and use. At the present time, one has the spirit to eliminate the savagery of the tyrants. Actually, brutishness has reached its zenith.''

Referring to the Darwinian theory of evolution another writer Kenneth Walker in his book *Meaning and Purpose* states that the glories of war described by Trietsechke and Bernhardie is the fruit of the analysis of Darwin's theory of evolution.

In England, which according to the saying of Napoleon is more a land of shopkeepers than of armies, the theory of selection has provided a justification for the worst economic competition and a criminal inelegance on the part of the workers.

Again, this philosophy of life has imparted conviction to the people that movement and conflict of every sort, provided it is materially successful, ensures human evolution. This theory impelled man to worship power and force rather than truth and justice. Man devoted his intellect and skill to the exploration of those means by which he could augment his power and strength.

Aggressive colonialism and oppressive imperialism are mischiefs borne out of this theory. This doctrine represents the darkest period of human history as the most luminous. A famous critic of the Hegelian philosophy, Croce rightly declares that this theory provides instigation for everything, be it conservatism, revolution or restoration.

Similarly, another critic remarks that this doctrine has provided the Marxist writers with an opportunity to justify their stand in every matter. This notion is the major cause of tyranny and oppression in the modern age.

Finally, this theory taught men to repudiate the social significance of religion and morality. It preached that men should exclusively and relentlessly absorb themselves in the struggle for their survival, stability and the grasping of strength and power, wherefrom they may be obtained.

If religion and morality prove useful in achieving this purpose, they should be adopted. If, on the other hand, success is ensured by their repudiation, they should be instantly cast aside. The popularity achieved by the precepts of that high priest of deception Machiavelli, during the last four centuries has been largely owing to this false doctrine. The following words of Dr. Funk and Goebels represent a true definition of this theory.

> "The sole purpose of all power and strength is to secure the capitation of the enemy by all means, fair or foul. Our movement is perfectly free from moral restraints prescribed by religion. Every act performed for the purpose of dismantling the citadel of colonialism is a moral act."

This, then, is a brief analysis of the components of western civilization and their impact on human life. Modern man is immersed indeed by anxiety. He is at a loss to know why in spite of all the progress in art and sciences and abundance of material provisions, he is still unhappy. The earth yields millions of tons of grain every year, yet, its inhabitants suffer from hunger and privation. Innumerable fountains of knowledge are gushing forth, yet man is still wallowing in ignorance.

In point of fact, the groping for a millennium during the last three or four centuries has led men far astray from their goal. In a New Year message on Ist January, 1935, Iqbal referred to this failure of the secular civilization in the following words:

> "The modern age prides itself in its progress in knowledge and its matchless scientific developments. No doubt, the pride is justified. Today, space and time are being annihilated and man is achieving amazing successes in unveiling the secrets of Nature and harnessing its forces to his own service."[4]

In spite of all these developments, the tyranny of imperialism struts abroad, covering its face under the masks of democracy, nationalism, communism, fascism and heaven knows what else besides. Under these masks, in every corner of the earth, the spirit of freedom and the dignity of man are begin trampled underfoot in a way to which not even the darkest period of human history presents a parallel. He sums up the modern man, equipped with power but lacking in vision, in these striking and beautiful verses:

> Love is denied to him and intellect bites him like a serpent,
> He has failed to subordinate intellect to love!
> He has succeeded in tracing the course of the stars. But failed to make his way through the labyrinth of his own ideas!
> He has got so entangled in the maze of his knowledge,
> That to this day he does not know profit from loss.
> He ensnared the rays of the sun,
> But failed to illuminate the dark night of his life[5]

Having analysed the ingredients of secular civilization, we shall examine the contemporary social movements which have risen under the patronage of this civilization. Although, these movements bear diverse titles, the spirit which animates them is born of the same mother civilization.

State of Civil Society in Medina

Having seen the state of Nature and the social and governmental contracts in Medina, we now turn to the civil society. Here, we shall try to see how the individualism of the state of nature which was replaced by the acceptance of Islam by a community of Muslims soon gave way to an organic conception, that is, the individuals who had accepted Islam were yet individual Muslims of *Aus* and *Khazraj*, and they had not yet begun to think in terms of a common community and before the coming of the Prophet Muhammad (Peace be on him,) the community of Muslims was like the joint stock company of Locke.

It was like a bundle of sticks which is tied up by a common rope, but every stick keeps up its identity separate. The only common bond of the people of Medina was no doubt acceptance of Islam, but as yet they had not forgotten their individuality. The whole conception, yet, was arithmetical: it was in no sense organic.

It was, therefore, the first task of the Prophet to unite these scattered elements in an organic whole, and to this task he at once turned his attention. Says Wellhausen:

> "The first Arabic community with sovereign powers was established by Mohammed in the city of Medina, not upon the basis of blood which naturally leads to diversity, but upon that of religion which is equally binding on all."[6]

Margoliouth also affirms the same thing when he says:

> "In the new community all tribal differences were to be sunk, and the theory of the platonic republic, according to which the members of the community should share pains and pleasures to the same extent as the members of one body, is attributed to the Prophet."[7]

Thus, the first care of the Prophet in Medina was to build a mosque, for which he bought a plot of land, though every man offered his land and house free of any charge for the purpose, but the Prophet did not accept them.[8] In the construction of the mosque all worked with the greatest enthusiasm the more so because the Prophet himself was working with them,[9] and they chanted with loud and cheerful voices as they bore along their burdens:

> O Lord! There is no joy but the joy of futurity.
> O Lord! Have mercy upon the Citizens and the Refugees.[10]

In this way, the elected President of Medina gave practical proof of the fact that he was but the first citizen and the Prophet showed that he was only like an ordinary mortal, and because he was the representative of God, he has to prove and justify himself as the ''First Muslim' as the first servant of God. Thus, for the first time in the history of Medina (and even of all Arabia) the people began to meet on a footing of absolute equality in the mosque five times a day.

A new community had grown up out of heterogeneous and individualistic elements, and as the above couplet has shown, the tribal differentiation of Aus and Khazraj was done away with, for the Citizens of Median began to be called Ansar or helpers, and the people who had migrated and settled from Mecca with the Prophet were called *Muhajirin* or Refugees.

The Covenant of Brotherhood

But still, in the beginning, a greater attachment in the Muslim spirit of brotherhood was necessary between the *Ansar* and the *Muhajirin* for the latter were still no more than mere guests of the Ansar as they had forsaken everything of their own-house, wealth and other property at Mecca for the sake of God and their faith. They were, therefore, entirely ill-provided and ill-provisioned.

The Prophet at once created a new Tie of Brotherhood (*aqd-i-Muwakhat*) between the *Ansar* and the *Muhajirin*. 'Become brethren every two and two of you,' such ran the command of the Prophet; and he himself 'set the example by taking Ali', or as others say Uthman, for his brother. Accordingly, each of the refugees selected one of the citizens as his brother. The bond was of the closest description, and involved not only special devotion to each other's interests in the persons thus associated, but in the case of death, the 'brother' inherited the property of the deceased.[11]

This covenant or contract lasted only up to the Battle of Badr after which inheritance was allowed to be based on the law of consanguinity as laid down in the *Holy Qur'an*.[12] This contract of brotherhood makes it definitely clear that while the contract of Locke was meant for the preservation of property, the Islamic contract was based on the idea of the sacrifice of property and this sacrifice was done with the greatest sincerity.

Contract with the Jews

After, thus, providing for the two urgent needs of the hour, the Prophet turned his attention to the condition of Medina itself, where another elements could not be ignored. These were the Jews of the three tribes Banu Nadir, Banu Quraiza and Banu Qainua who were not prepared to accept Islam. They came to the Prophet and said:

> "We have come to make a treaty of peace with thee, to the effect that we shall be neither for nor against thee, that we shall aid no one against thee; nor injure any who aids thee; on condition that thou injures neither us nor our friends until we learn what becomes of thy affairs and of those of they people."[13]

The Prophet, 'complied with their request on condition that they would afford aid to no one against him; nor against any of his companions, neither by word, arms, or cattle, neither openly nor secretly.[14]

This must be pointed out that in spite of all efforts to win over the Jews, they could not be reconciled and from the very beginning were always bent on mischief. Even the*Holy Qur'an* refers to their adverse activities in a clear manner, for what they could not tolerate was the unification of Aus and Khazraj into one community under the leadership of the Prophet. One Shammas bin Qais (a Jew) set a mischief monger in a meeting of Aus and Khazraj with instructions that he should recall the events of the Battle of Bu'ath. As soon as couplets regarding that battle began to be recited the extinguished fire of hostility and ravage was rekindled and it took no time to move from verbal hot exchange of words to actual fight and hostility. When the Prophet, on hearing of what was going on, at once appeared on the scene and addressed them to fear God and not to go back to the state of ignorance out of which God had taken them out.

On hearing this, they threw away their implements of war and began to weep and embrace each other. Thus was the unity of the Islamic community maintained in the firm grip of the rope or Covenant of God. They took God to witness that, in case they should fail to keep this agreement and covenant His Lordship would be at liberty to shed their blood, to confiscate their property as well as to capture their wives and children.

A treaty was written for each tribe. Thus, the Prophet associated the Jews in a contract or 'Treaty of Mutual Obligation drawn up in writing between the Refugees and the Believers of Medina on the one hand and the Jews on the other, confirming the latter in the practice of their religion and in the secure possession of their property.'

Charter of Religious Toleration

This agreement was, therefore, the First Charter of Religious Toleration in the history of man's political development. It has been preserved in full by Ibn Hashan[15] and is a lengthy document. It begins thus: 'In the name of God,the Compassionate, the Merciful. It is a Covenant *(Ahad-Nama)* of Muhammad the Prophet of God, on behalf of the believers of Quraish and Yethreb (Medina) and those that are under them[16] and those that may join them and strive with them for the faith. Verily, they form a community apart from the rest of mankind.

Thus, the opening words definitely tell us that the Muslims were now a community and *the Holy Qur'an* refers to this unity in these words:

> 'Surely, this your community is one community and I am Your Lord, Therefore be careful (of your duty) to me." 23:52.

Wellhausen has expressed this aspect thus:

> "The Community, at the head of which God stands, and the Prophet as God's representative, has power to deliver the shedder of blood over to the avenger, and it is the duty of the community to see that this is done,[17] and in this covenant, as we shall see noted below, it is specifically stated that if a man kills a Muslim wrongfully, the Muslims shall joins as one man against him."

The other clauses of this covenant may now be given in brief, to make the above statements clear:

i. The Refugees and the Believers of Medina shall defray the price of bloodshed among themselves (respectively) and shall ransom honourably their prisoners.
ii. Whoever is rebellious or seeketh to spread enmity and sedition, thee hand of every man shall be against him, even if he be a son.
iii. No Muslim will kill a Muslim for an unbeliever and non-believer will be helped as against a Muslim. And verily, Allah's Protection is meant for one and all. The Believers

are pledged to protect each other against all others.

iv. Whosoever of the Jews followeth us, shall have aid and succour; they shall not be injured, not shall any enemy be aided against them.

v. No Unbeliever shall grant protection to thee people of Mecca, either in person or property, nor interpose between the Believers and them.

vi. Whosoever killeth a Muslim wrongfully the Muslim shall join as one man against him.

vii. The state of peace and war shall be common to all Muslims; no one among them shall have the right of concluding peace with, or declaring war, against the enemies of his co-religionists.

viii. The Jews who attach themselves to our commonwealth shall be protected from all insults and vexations; they shall have an equal right with our people to our assistance and good offices.

ix. The Jews shall contribute with the Muslims and join with them in defending Medina against a common enemy.

x. The Jews of the various branches of '*Awf, Najjar, Harith, jsham, tha'laba, Ans* and all others domiciled in Medina shall form with the Muslims one composite nation, *i.e.* one people with the Believers.

xi. The Jews will profess their religion as freely as theMuslim theirs.

xii. The interior of Medina shall be sacred and inviolable for all those who join this covenant.

xiii. All true Muslims shall hold in abhorrence every man guilty of crime, injustice or disorder.

xiv. Controversies and disputes shall be referred for the decision of Allah and His Prophet.

xv. None shall join the men of Mecca or their allies; for, verily, the engaging parties are bound together against every one that shall threaten Medina. War and peace shall be made in common. And verily! Allah is the protector of the righteous and the godly, and Muhammad is His Prophet.

A Free Church in a Free State

From this brief summary of the covenant, it is clear, that it does not merely assert the unity and oneness of the Muslim community, it even asserts the unity of the City State of Medina itself, for the

Jews and the Unbelievers also have been considered to form one nation with the Muslims, and they had equal obligations in the defence and the maintenance of peace in Medina.

Moreover, the fact Medina was made inviolable makes it clear that the Divine Laws of Peace had now been promulgated with full force in a land of war, turmoil and anarchy. Lastly, the tolerance that was granted to the Jews for the first time established a 'Free Church in the Free State of Medina', and it was the first charter of freedom of conscience and of religious worship in the history of the world.

The Prophet, thus reconciled the various parties in the city and introduced law, order and peace among its various elements. The covenant with the Jews was the crowning contract in the edifice of contracts which established the City State of Medina. Thus, in the words of Amir Ali, "the contract constituted the Prophet as 'the chief Magistrate of the nation, as much by his prophetic mission as by a virtual compact between himself and the people."[18] Dr. Hell regards this contract (ordinance) as a piece of fare statesmanship and of far-reaching importance"[19] of rare statesmanship because it was the only way of reconciling the tribe and the best means of Meccans with the united support of the whole of Medina; and of far-reaching importance because it made the Prophet the sole guiding power in a land which had known no common superior. Nicholson thus estimates the significance of this event:

> "Ostensibly a cautious and tactful reform, it was in reality a revolution. Mohammed dared not strike openly at the independence of the tribes, but he destroyed it, in effect, by shifting the center of power from the tribe to the community, and although the community included Jews and pagans as well as Muslims, he fully recognised what his opponents failed to foresee, that the Muslims were the active and must soon be the predominant partners in the newly founded State".[20]

The City State of Medina was founded on the basis of various contracts, and 'Islam thus became what, in theory at least, it has always remained-a political as well as a religious system.'[21] The First contract was the contract with God and this was the acceptance of Islam which every Muslim has to individually utter the 'Kalima' of faith: there is no god but God and Muhammad is His Prophet. Then the Second Contract was a contract for the Protection of the Prophet-not only as God's representative on Earth but also as their own elected ruler.

The Third Contract was the confirmation of the Second Contract by the whole of the Muslim population of Medina; and the Fourth Contract with the Jews was not merely à charter of toleration for freedom of belief and conscience, it was also a contract for the creation of a composite nation or community for common defence and protection. The Republic of Medina (of which the elected President was the Prophet) was thus recognised 'organic' even though the whole process of its creation was individualistic and therefore contractual.[22]

Islamic State: Contractual and Organic

It is a recognised principle of modern political philosophy that the theory of contract assumes a mechanical way of creating a state and it makes it a mere manufacture, but it is now universally held that the state is not contracted or made, it grows. And here, in the City State of Medina we have said that it is by contract that the state has been made 'organic' (and that too in a double sense); for it is primarily a Muslim state, the Muslim community was already one and every Muslim was an inseparable part of the whole, as it was the greatest sin to shed the blood of a brother Muslim; and if it was a common state of all the peoples of Medina, they were solemnly bound , 'under the protection of God which extends to one and all' to defend the common state against all foreign dangers, and internally too, its soil was made inviolable and free from all bloodshed. This was the Islamic City State of Medina made 'organic' by contracts and to this day both the ideas of contract and the unity of the community[23] continue to be the central features of Muslim religious life.

The idea of contract was, therefore, never a fiction in Islam. As has already been shown, the making of contract was a historical reality in Arabia. But in political philosophy, it is not only Kant who has called 'contract' an 'idea of reason', modern critics have tried to make it even unreal and unnecessary in those who are thee real classical writers of this theory. They have tried to show that these writers-Hobbes, Spinoza, Locke and Rousseau-have expressed their political ideas. Through the medium of the contract, not because it was essential for their political philosophy, but because it was the prevalent mode of expressing[24] political ideas in terms of contract. Thus, says Vaughan, "of the four philosophers in question, Locke comes nearest in principle of accepting the theory of contract."

But he rejects it in terms; and, even when in substance he seems nearest to it, he inserts so many limitations, he puts in so many hostile amendments, that, in the net result, he is much farther from it than, at first sight we might be tempted to imagine. Of the remaining three, one Spinoza accepts it in words but in fact, takes away with one hand what he professes to give with the other. The two that are adjudged as one in the interest of absolutism and the other in that of the sovereign people-reject it root and branch.[25]

According to Vaughan, Locke was only a half-hearted social contract writer. But Joad has absolved Locke also of this irrelevancy absolutely in these words: "But the social contract theory, in the form in which Locke maintained it requires us to suppose that the abolition of Government involves man's relapse into a personal condition would admittedly be a condition of peaceable and socially disposed persons, and it would not be the same as the condition introduced by society, since it is the establishment of government which puts an end to this condition and establishes the condition of society. Such, at least are the contentions of the social contract theory as Locke states it.

It is difficult in the light of these contentions to see how society could survive the abolition of government; yet that it does so, is precisely what Locke, in making his distinction between society and government, maintains. This social contract theory is however, no sense essentional to Locke's political philosophy. [26] Thus, critics have freed all the four political philosophers from being social contract writers, even though they have been the classical writers of this theory. This means that critics have made them what they had never thought about their own writings.

Contractual Organicity of Islamic State

In the Islamic conception of the State, as we have already seen, the 'contract' (social and governmental) is a reality just as much as the conception of the community is 'organic. "The Islamic State may, therefore, fittingly be called a 'contractual organism"[27] in the words of Fouillee, a modern French writer. The defect of the contract theory is that it makes the state a plaything of individual caprice even though it emphasises the 'consent' as the basis of the state; the defect of the organic theory is that though it emphasises the interdependence of the individual and the community, it entirely belittles individuality and the individual is made unreal. Both these defects are not to be found in the Islamic state.

A Muslim has to individually make a contract with God; but at the same time, he is an inspirable part of his community of which he is an equal member. Thus, the individual in the Islamic state is both individuality and his dependence upon the community. This explains the full significance of the conception of contractual organicity in Islam.

Abolition of Slavery: the Quranic Approach

Aristotle maintains that slavery is based on nature, and that certain races are intended to be subject. Whether this be true or not, it would be useless to hope for the abolition of slavery in Muhammadan countries under present conditions. Whether the Prophet of Islam could have abolished slavery altogether among his followers is very doubtful and his prescriptions regarding the just and humane treatment of this unfortunate class, taken all in all, are praiseworthy.

On the other hand, there is nothing whatsoever in Islam that tends to the abolition of this curse. As Muir has well said, "Rather, while lightening, he riveted the fetter. There is no obligation whatever on a Muslims to release his slaves."[28]

The Acquisition of Slaves

"The greatest of all divisions, that between a free man and slave, appears as soon as the barbaric warrior spares the life of his enemy when he has him down, and brings him home to drudge for him and till the soil."[29] The two main causes of slavery arewant and war, and of these two it may be said that the acquisition of slaves was chiefly connected with warfare. (In Sura 47 Muhammed commands his followers thus, i.e. verse 4.f.):

> "When ye encounter the Unbelievers, strike off their heads; until ye have made a great slaughter among them; then bind (the remainder) in fetters. And after this give (the later) either a free dismissal or exact a ransom, until the war shall have laid down its arms."

The usual expression for female slaves in the*Qur'an* as we have already seen is that which your right hands possess. Muhammed says nothing in *the Qur'an* regarding the purchase of slaves. According to Islamic law, a slave is:

i. a person taken captive in war, or carried off by force from a foreign hostile country, and being at the time of capture an Unbeliever
ii. the child of a female slave whose father is (a) a slave, or (b) is not the owner of the mother of the child, or (c) is the owner of the mother, but who does not acknowledge himself to be the father
iii. a person acquired by purchase.

War and slavery, as one would expect, is also closely bound together in the Old Testament. In Num, chap. 31, the Children of Israel are commanded to wage a war of vengeance against the Midianites. And in verse 7, ff, we read:

> " And they warred against Midinian, as the Lord commanded Moss, and they slew every male...(9) And the Children of Israel took captive the women of Midian and their little ones, etc."

As far as strangers were concerned, the Israelites were allowed to buy, sell, or transfer their male an female slaves. So, we read in Lev. 25, 44 ff.:

> "and as for thy bondmen, and thy bondmaids, which thou shalt have; of the nations that are round about your, of them shall ye buy bondmen and bondmaids. (45) Moreover the children of the strangers families that are with you, which they have begotten in your land; and they shall be your possession[30] (46) And ye shall make them an inheritance for your children after you.[31] to hold for a possession, of them shall ye take your bondmen for ever."

As among the Muhammadans slaves consist partly of children of female slaves, and partly also of those that are acquired, so in the Old Testament we have the two expressions:

> "he that is born in the house, and he that is bought with money."

This shows us that among the Israelites as among the Muhammadans, the number of slaves might be multiplied by birth. This, of course, is true of all peoples who trade in slaves; since the slaves are the "possession" of their masters, their children also belong to them.

A further agreement between the Muhammadan and Old Testament laws consists in the limitation of slaves to foreigners. In Lev. 25, 39. ff. we read:

> "And if thy brother be waxen poor with thee, and sell himself upto thee; thou shalt not make him to serve as a bond servant: (40) as a hired servant, and as a sojourner, he shall bee with thee; he shall serve with thee unto the year of jubilee: (41) then shall he go out from thee, he and his children with him. (42). They shall not be sold as a slave is sold."[32]

And so with the Muhammadans, who are strictly forbidden to take believers as slaves, thee Muhammadan like the Israelite is to regard his fellow-believer as a brother.[33]

Among the Babylonians, however, it was otherwise. Slaves were recruited both from within and without. If a son, whether natural or adopted, sinned against his parents, his father could see him as a slave. And likewise the husband had the right to dispose of a quarrelsome wife for money. Also the captured enemy naturally took the position of a slave, especially did the white (light complexioned) slaves from Gutium and Shubarti at that time appear to be much desired.[34]

The Treatment of Slaves

We have already seen how the Prophet in *the Qur'an* insists upon the just and humane treatment of the widow and orphan. And a like treatment is demanded by him also for slaves; and that in accordance with his teaching that all men belong to God, and are therefore in a certain sense alike. So, we read in Sura 16,73:

> "God hath caused some to excel others in worldly possession; Yet those thus excel do not give of their wealth unto those whom their right hands possess (their slaves) so that both may have an equal share thereof. Do they, therefore, deny the beneficence of God.?"

Also Sura 4, 40:

> "Honour God, and associate none with him and show kind-

> ness unto parents, relations, orphans, the poor, the neighbour who is of kin to you, and he who is not,[35] and to your trusted friends, and the traveller and to those whom your right hands possess for God loveth not the arrogant and the proud.''

In the year before his death, the Prophet, during a farewell pilgrimage at Mina, delivered an address to his followers, in which, among several other injunctions, we find the following:

> ''And your slaves! See that ye feed them with such food as ye eat yourselves, and clothe them with the like clothing as ye wear yourselves; and if they commit a fault which ye are included not to forgive, sell them; for they are the servants of the Lord, and are not to be tormented.'[36]

If Muhammed could not abolish slavery, he has certainly done what he could to secure for slaves a humane treatment. And if present-day Muhammadans disregard his injunctions, it is not fair to hold the Prophet himself responsible for it.[37] Also, as already observed, it must not be forgotten that the legislation of the *Qur'an* was enacted for a seventh-century people.

The position and treatment of slaves among the ancients in different lands naturally differed in accordance with the character of the various peoples, as well as the character of the slaves themselves, that is whether they be foreign or inland born, And there was also a difference of treatment by the same peoples at different times.[38]

But if the enactments of the Prophet were only faithfully observed by his followers, the treatment of slaves in Muhammadan countries would in all cases compare very favourably with what it was among the ancients. Also the treatment of slaves, as enacted in Muhammadan law, taken all in all, can only be regarded as just.

As we have already seen in the case of adultery, female slaves were held to be less guilty than free women, and consequently their punishment was to be less severe, And especially did the law enact that they should be sufficiently supported, and not made to suffer.

On the other hand, it must be remembered that slaves, like any other property, were transferable. A Muhammadan has the right to sell his concubine, as long as he has no child by her.[39] And even if he has a child by her, he can always deny the paternity (although this does not often happen). And in any cases, the slave would have to continue to serve him, and be his concubine, that is unless he, when she has borne a son to him, presents her with her freedom by way of compensation.

The Emancipation of Slaves

The founder of Islam not only insisted upon the humane treatment of slaves, but also that it should be made possible for them to secure their freedom, when they have shown themselves worthy of it by their conduct. Accordingly the emancipation of slaves among the Muhammadans must be regarded as a meritorious act[40]. Sura 24, 33 reads: "And those of your slaves who desire a deed of manumission, write it for them, if ye have a good opinion of them, and give them of the wealth of God, which he has given you."

The manner in which this emancipation is brought about in Muhammadan countries varies. Sometimes complete and immediate emancipation is granted to a slave gratuitously, or for a monetary compensation to be paid later. This is done by means of a written document, or by a verbal declaration in the presence of two witnesses; or again by the master presenting the slave with the certificate of sale obtained from the former master. Also, in conformity with the Prophet's demand in Sura 24. 33.

Future emancipation is sometimes agreed upon to be granted on the fulfillment of certain conditions; or more frequently, upon the death of the owner. In the latter case the owner cannot sell the slave with whom the agreement has been made.[41] Also, as the owner cannot alienate by will more than one-third of the whole property that he leaves, the law ordains that, if the value of the said slave exceeds that portion, the slave must obtain, and pay to the owner's heirs the additional sum. We shall see further on that for certain offence, such as manslaughter, etc., the freeing of a captive is reckoned in part-punishment.[42]

It is not impossible that Muhammad to some extent, at any rate, was acquainted with the Old Testament enactments concerning the emancipation of slaves. While, however, the Old Testament deals only with the emancipation of Israelite slaves, who has become bondmen through debt, Muhammad speaks of the emancipation of all slaves.

References

1. Bertrand Russel, *History of the Western Philosophy*.
2. Benedotto Croce, *Politics and Morals,* George Allen and Unwin, London, 1946, p. 136.
3. *Ibid*.
4. Iqbal, New Year's Message broadcast from the Lahore Radio Station on Ist January, 1938; see Vahid, *Thoughts and Reflections of Iqbal,* Ashraf, Lahore 1946, p. 373.
5. K. G. Saiyidain,*Iqbal's Educational Philosophy,* Ashraf, Lahore, 1960, 5th edition, pp. 142-43.
6. Wellhausen,*Historians, History of the World*-Article, ND, p. 291.
7. Margoliouth, *Muhammadanism*, p. 75.
8. *Al Baladhuri,* (Hitti's Translation), p. 19.
9. *Ibn Khaldun, p. 53; Raudatus Safa, p. 251.*
10. Muri, *Life of Mahomet,* 1894, p. 168;*Ibn Hisham*, p. 176.
11. Muri (1894 edition) p. 1671; Ibn Khaldun, p. 62; Abul Fida, p. 301. Raudatus Safa notes that this brotherhood was created between Mahajirin and 45 Ansar (p. 261):*The Translation of Zaidan* (named as *Tamaddun-i-Islam),*Part-I, by Shaikh Ghulam Muhammad that I possess gives one more Contract which I do not find in otherbooks. Before the creation of this Fraternal Contract, the Prophet hadbrought about a written Contract between the Ansar and the Muhajirin in which they had declared themselves to be one nation (Qaum) (p. 47). It was after this Contract of one nationhoodthat brotherhood between two and two was made. Zaidan says that this Contract occurs in *Iban Hisham* in full but this translation has omitted all that part of it. But such a Contract seems to be feasible because in the Contract with Jews Muslims are treated as one community or nation (*Qaum*).
12. *Raudatus Safa*, p. 261.
13. *Ibid*., pp. 255-56.
14. For further dctails, sce*thc Holy Qur'an* translated by the late M. Mahumudul Hasan and M. Shabbir Ahmad 'Uthmani', pp. 80-81.
15. *Ibn Hisham*, pp. 179-80;*Ibn Khaldun,* pp. 53-61, see also Muir, pp. 177-78, and Amir Alri's *Spirit of Islam,* pp. 54-55.
16. 'Those under them, means those unbelievers in Medina who had not yet accepted Islam but were a hopeless minority.
17. *Historians: History of the World,* p. 291.
18. *The Spirit of Islam,* p. 55.
19. Hell, *Arabian Civilisation*, p. 23.
20. Nicholson, *A Literary History of the Arabs,* p. 173.
21. Arnold, *Preaching of Islam,* p. 32.
22. Vaughan, 'It is manifest that the idea of Contract naturally lends itself to an individualist theory of the State,' p. LVI;*Du Contract*

Social-Modern Language Texts, Longmans, 1918.

23. The Prophet said: 'None of you shall be a Momin (faithful) until wish the same thing for a brother Muslim what you wish for your own self.'(Bukhari); Abu Susa reports that the Prophet said: 'A Momin is like a building for another Momin for one of its parts is a source of strength to the other, and then he crossed the fingers of both his hands (to suggest that union is strength). (Bukhari).
24. *The Contract of Rousseau* by Cole (Everyman's Library), p. IX.
25. Vaughan, Du, *Contract Social,* p. LXV.
26. Joad, *Guide to the Philosophy of Morals and Politics*, p. 492.
27. Coker, *Recent Political Thought*, p. 412.
28. Sir W. Muri, ''*The Qur'an*, its Composition and Teaching,'' p. 58.
29. Tylor. *Anthropology*, p. 434 ff; also Hastings, D. B., Vol. 4, p. 461.
30. ''Possession'' esp. of land and landed property (Gen. 17, 8, etc): then also, as here, of persons.
31. So also with the Babylonians, Die Sclaven drafting one Erlaubnis ihers herrn nicht die Schoole varlassen and gingen bei dem Tode des Besitzers one writers in die hande seience Erben Uber.''-Meissner. ''Beitrage zum altba by to nischen Provatrcht: p. 5; See also Meissner, ''Aus d. Altabably. Recht'' (''Alter Orient'', VII, I), p. 8f.
32. This law, however, can only be regarded as an ideal. That Israelites could be taken as slaves and in fact, were often so taken, usually on account of debt, we find from such passages as 2 Kings, 4, I; Ex. 21.
33. See Syed Ameer Ali, *The Personal Law of the Mahommedans,* p. 37f.
34. Meissner, ''*Beitrage zum altbaylonischen Privatrecht,*'' p. 6.
35. ''The person who is one's neighbour, but who belongs to another people,'' Lana, Lex.
36. Muri, *Life of Mahomet*, Vol. I, London, p. 486.
37. Prof. Fischer says, ''Dass man sich die Lage der Sklaven in Heutigen Muslimischen Landern im allgemeinen nicht zu schlimm vorstellen darf, hat, abgeschen von andern (S.Z.B. Lane, ''Moder Egyptians,: p. 168), besonders Snouck Hurgronje gezeigt (''Mekka,'' 2. p. 18ff). Bei meinem zweimaligen Aufenthalte in Marokko have ich gleichfalls den Eindruck jewonnen dass die lage der Muslimichen Sklaven nur formell von der christlicher Dienerverschieden its.'' Cf. also Doughty, ''*Arabia Deserta,*'' I. p. 554; ''The condition of the slave is always tolerable and is often happy in Arabia; bred up as poor brothers of the sons of the household, they are a manner of God's wards of the pious Mohammedan householder who is army [properly 'my uncle'] of their servitude and buy ['my father']...It is not many years 'if their houselord fears Allah; before he will given them their liberty; and then he sends them away not empty; but in pland Arabia (where only substantial persons are slave holders) he good man will marry out his free servants, male and female, endowing them with somewhat of his own substance, whether camels or palm

stems.

38. As regards the Babylonians cf, Meissner, "Beitr. Z. Altba, Privatrecht," p. 6f.," Der Sclave war each altably lonischem Reechte kein Mensch, sondern eine Sache, welche man stickwise berechnete; deshalb ward von hm immerals I, SAG *ardu*-I Stuck (eightlich Kopf-caput geredet, und aus eben dem Grunde wird auch nie der Name seienees Vaters Genannt. Von den Freien Waren sie Schon ausserlich druch ein eingle branntes Mal unterschienden, haubing, usd besonders whol, wenn sie als Ausereisser bekannt waren, trugen sie sogar Ketten.. ....Auch die Todesstraf knnote naturlich one witeres gegen sie ange wandt werden..Trotzdeem die Sclaven ihern Herrn absolute rechtlos regenuberstanden, wird das Verhaltnis zqischen Herrn und Diener gewohnilich ein recht freundliches gewesen sein. Die Sclavin war gewohnlich die Nebenfran ihres Gebieters..der ihre kinder zu erziehdn verpfichete war...Ingleicher Weise wird auch der Sclave gut behandelt worden sein; je es kam sogar vor, dass Sclaven adoptlert wurden..Ein anderer Weg, die Freiheit zu erlangen, war der Loskauf durch Geld (imptiru)." Also as regards the Israelites, cf. Guthe: Bibelworter bunch,' art. "Sklaven." Der altests Haussklave..hatte eine sehr angesehence Stellung and unter Urnstanden Erbrecht (gen 15, 2f.). Even Sklvin knnote duch den Herrn Zur Gattin and Gebieterin des Hauses rehoben werden. Man gab den Sklaven Weiber aus den eigenen Tochterni, Chron. 2m35 und den Sklandlung von Sklaven, aur die Luc. 12, 46 ff, an spielt, ist romisch order herodeisch, nicht isrealeitisch."
39. Cf, Hammurabi & 119.-"If a debt has seized a man, and he has handed over for the money a maidservant who has borne him children, for the money the merchant paid to him, the owner of the maid shall pay (back) and he shall ransom his maid.
40. Sachau, "*Muh,Recht,*" p. 131.
41. See Lane, "*Modern Egyptians,*" p. 155f.; also Sachau, "Muh. Recht," p. 131ff.
42. Margoliouth, *Mohammed*, p. 461f.

5

Social Foundation of Justice

Social foundation of Islamic justice does not treat the matter as a question of pure theory, nor as a counsel of perfection. For by its own nature Islam is a faith of achievement, of work in the sphere of practical life; it is not a religion of mere words, or idle theory existing only in a world of shadows.

As we have already seen, Islam has a basic theory of the universe, of life, and of man. We have seen also that the thought of 'social justice' has its roots in that basic theory, and enters into its general scheme. We have discovered that the nature of Islamic belief about human life makes social justice essentially an all-embracing justice which does not take account merely of material and economic factors.

Islam does not divide the individual into body and soul, into differing intellectual and spiritual sides. It holds that the values of this life are material and spiritual at one and the same time, and that no division is possible in such a unity. It holds also that mankind is essentially one body, its members mutually responsible and interdependent, a body in which there are no isolated and outcast societies.

Many times, it has seemed that the reality of history falsifies this fundamental Islamic theory. So first we must discover what is this reality of history. The reality which Islam regards as ultimately true is not the state of affairs of any one individual, or in any one group or nation; rather it is that limited, definite, and fixed reality on which the faculties of frail human individuals are set, when they turn away from the pursuit of immense and fix their thoughts on the larger and more comprehensive things in human life, the things which endure from eternity to eternity. For Islam scans all standards, and reckons with all kinds of interests; its aim is the achievement of a purpose which includes all humanity from beginning to end.

It may appear to be an inconsistency when we take the comprehensive view, which embraces all men, rather than merely one individual, one group, or one nation. The comprehensive view of social justice with its far reaching aims will serve later on to explain the regulations which Islam lays down. These cannot be correctly understood when they are taken individually; nor when they are understood only of the individual in relation to society, of society only in relation to the group; nor when they are understood only of the group in relation to the nation, or of the nation only in relation to other nations.

This comprehensive view will serve to explain the regulations on individual possession, on the poor-tax, on the law of inheritance, on the rules for estates, on politics, in commercial transaction, in a word, it will explain all the regulations prescribed by Islam for Individuals, societies, nations, and races. At this point, we have no intention of dealing with all this; we shall, then content ourselves to deal with the general foundations on which Islam established its regulations for social justice, within the limits of its universal theory. And from the nature of these we will see that Islam believes in the unity of body and soul in the individual, and in the unity of the spiritual and the material in life.

Similarly, it believes in an identity of aim in the individual and in society, in the identity of interests of the various societies within a race, and in an identity of purpose among all the races of mankind. And this despite the apparent divergence of their more immediate and limited interests. The following are the foundations on which Islam establishes justice:

1. Absolute freedom of conscience.
2. The complete equality of all men.
3. The permanent mutual responsibility of society.

With each of these foundations we shall deal in turn, explaining its nature and its objective.

Freedom of Conscience

Complete social justice cannot be assured, nor can its efficiency and permanence be guaranteed, unless it arises from an inner conviction of the spirit. It must be claimed by the individual, it must be needed by society. There must be a belief that it will serve the highest purposes of mankind. It must arise also from some material circumstances which prompts the individual to demand justice, as being required by the situation, yet unobtainable. No man can claim justice by law unless he first claimed it by instinct and by the practical methods which accompany instinct. Similarly, society will not proceed with such legislation, even when it is started, unless there is a belief which demands it from within, and practical threats which demand it from without. It is these facts which Islam has in mind in all its ordinances and laws.

It is the Christian view that freedom of conscience is one of the luxuries of life; and that to turn towards the Lord's Kingdom of Heaven and to spurn the life of this world is true way of guaranteeing to man his freedom and to the soul its happiness. Now this is true; but it is not the whole truth. The needs of life are not paramount under all circumstances, nor do material necessities always outweigh man's final destiny; but at most times man must submit to their demands.

So to ignore the material needs of life, or to refuse them, is not always the better way. It was Allah who created life, and He did not create it for man, to neglect it and to check its growth. Certainly it is desirable that man should rise superior to material needs and above his bodily appetites. But it is not desirable that because of these aims he should neglect life altogether.

That is one way to achieve the realization of the powers latent in human nature together with the elevation of that nature above submission to the demands of material necessity; it is even the soundest and the safest way. But what Islam aims to do is this-to integrate the needs of the body and the desires of the spirit in one unity, and to satisfy by a freedom of conscience the inner instinct which is borne of practical reality. So, it is not unmindful of either side of the question.

On the other hand, the communist view is that economic freedom alone satisfies the need for freedom of conscience, and that it is purely economic pressure on the individual which prompts him to overstep his legal rights of justice and equality. This too is true; but it is not the whole truth. For economic freedom of itself has no guarantee of permanence in society, unless there is also freedom of conscience within the mind. For alone it produces only another from of tyranny-the repression of individual gifts and abilities and inclinations; and these are things which cannot be satisfactorily dealt with by legal methods alone.

It produces also a repression of the individual, inasmuch as his natural abilities are unable to find an outlet and have no opportunity of growing in competition with others. Thus, inevitably the individual is cheated in his desire for that equity which the law has promised him, because he has the inner conviction that he is getting less than he deserves, And similarly on the other hand, laziness and pride are encouraged.

The man who has the greatest abilities and who can produce the most will always overcome the law of absolute equality. If he cannot do that, he will hate and resent it; in which case, either he will rebel, or the divine spark will be extinguished, his abilities will atrophy, and his power of production will be lessened.

But where equality has its roots in a profound freedom of the conscience as well as in civil and religious law, and if the instinct for it is powerful among the strong and the weak alike, then it will be accepted as a rise in status for the weak, and for the strong, a fall. It will answer the need of the soul for a belief in Allah, and in the unity and mutual responsibility of the community.

It will inculcate a belief in the unity of human nature and its attributes. Such is the aim of Islam when it grants complete and absolute freedom to the human conscience; but at the same time it stipulates that first the needs of the body and the material necessities of life must be guaranteed alike by the authority of the law and by the authority of the conscience.

Islam began by freeing the human conscience from servitude to any one except Allah and from submission to any save Him. There is no supreme authority anywhere except in Allah, nor can any other have power for evil or good. None save He can supply provision of anything on Earth or Heaven, nor can there by any mediator or intermediary between man and Him. Allah is the only possessor of power, and all others are but underlings, without control either over themselves or over others.

> "Say; He is Allah the One, Allah the Undivided. He brought not forth, nor was He brought forth, there has never been any equal to Him."[1]

Since, Allah is One, His worship is also one, and to Him alone must all men turn. There is no object of worship except Allah, nor can men take one another as Lords apart from Him. No man among them can excel any other except by Allah's doing and through His grace.

> "Say, O people of the Book, come to a word which is fair between us and you; namely that we worship none but Allah, that we associate nothing with Him, and that we do not take one another as Lords apart from Allah."[2]

Islam has an intense interest in this belief, and *the Qur'an* emphasizes it in various passages. The Prophets in their day imagined that their people would turn to them with some sort of worship, or with a reverence of some kind or another; but Islam strove to free he human conscience completely from this belief. So, Allah says of His Messenger, Muhammad:

> "And Muhammad is only a messenger; messengers have passed away before him. So, if he dies or if he is killed, will you then turn back upon your heels?"[3]

And He addresses the Prophet himself with a great sincerity, saying:

> "Thou hast nothing to do with this matter, either He may relent towards them, or He may punish them."[4]

In the same way, he addresses to Muhammad in another place something like a threat:

> "If we had not made thee stand firm, thou hast almost leaned towards them a little. In that case We would have made thee, taste the double of life and the double of death; then thou couldst not have found a helper against Us."[5]

So too He commands him to proclaim openly his true position:

> "Say, I call only upon my Lord, and with Him I associate nothing, Say: Verily I wield no power over you, either to harm you or to set you right. Say: No one can protect me from Allah, nor can I find a shelter from Him."[6]

And He speaks of those who deify Jesus, the son of Mary, charging them with unbelief and folly:

> "They are unbelievers who say that Allah is the Messiah, the son of Mary. Say: Who, then, will control Allah in the least if He wishes to destroy the Messiah, the son of Mary, together with his mother and all those who are on the Earth."[7]

Or in another passage He says of the Messiah:

> "He is only a servant whom we have favoured, and whom We have made a parable for the Children of Israel."[8]

He takes him as one of the witnesses of the Resurrection, and in *the Qur'an,* Jesus the son of Mary, himself answers the assertion which some people make about his divine nature; he establishes his own innocence of this assertion in which he had no part, answering it in a strong, forceful, and impressive manner. When Allah said:

> "O Jesus! Son of Mary, was it thou who didst say to the people, Take me and my mother as Gods apart from Allah."

He replied:

> "Glory be to Thee, it is for me to say what to me is not the truth. If I did say it, then You knowest it. Thou knowest what is within me, but I know not what is within Thee. Verily, Thou art He who knoweth secret things. I said nothing to them save what Thou didst command me; Serve Allah, my Lord and your Lord.' I was a witness to them as long as I was among them; but when Thou didst take me away, then Thou Thyself was a watcher over them. Thou art a witness over all things. If thou dost punish them-they are The servants; if Thou dost forgive them-Thou art the Glorious, the Wise."[9]

And other passages are similar. *The Qur'an* places insistent emphasis on this belief, on its proof and on its clarity, in order to ensure freedom of the human conscience from any form of association with Allah as regards His divinity and His holiness. For such association would oppress the conscience, and would make it worship some created thing among the servants of Allah.

If Jesus was a prophet or a messenger, he was still only one of His servants. And if it is held that he was not a servant in His, then all mediation between Allah and His servants is denied; there can be no priesthood and no mediator. So, every individual can make his own practical relationship with his creator and can strengthen his own weak and frail nature with the power which is from eternity to eternity. So he can draw from that power, strength, glory and courage, can know His mercy and care and sympathy, can strengthen his faith and empower his spirit.

Islam insists most strongly upon the reality of this experience, and upon the individual realizing that he has the ability to call upon that great Power day and night.

> ''Allah is gentle with His servants.''[10]
>
> ''And when My servants ask thee about Me, verily, I am near to answer the prayer of him who prays, when he prays to Me. So, let them ask an answer from Me, let them believe in Me, and perhaps they may be guided all right.''[11]
>
> ''And despair not of the comfort of Allah; verily, none despair of the comfort of Allah except the unbelieving people.''[12]
>
> ''Say: O My servants who have squandered your own resources, do not despair of the mercy of Allah; verily Allah forgives all faults.''[13]

Islam has prescribed five times of prayer, in which every day the worshipper stands before this Lord, in which the creature draws near to his Creator. These are at stated times, and not merely when it occurs to anyone to stand before his God, and to draw near in adoration and prayer. The purpose of these prayers is not only words or movements; rather their aim is to direct the whole man, heart, mind, and body at the same time, towards Allah. This is in line with general theory of Islam on the unity of human nature in its creatureliness, and of the unity of the Creator in His divinity.

> ''So woe to those who pray, and of their prayers are careless.''[14]

When the conscience is freed from the instinct of servitude to and worship of any of the servants of Allah; when it is filled with the knowledge that it can of itself gain complete access to Allah; then it cannot be disturbed by any feeling of fear of its livelihood or fear for its station. This fear is an ignoble instinct which lowers the individual's estimation of himself, which often makes him accept submission, or abdicate much of his natural honour of many of his rights.

But Islam insists strongly that glory and honour are the rights of man, and that to be proud of his rights and to persevere in the search for justice is deep-seated in the human soul. By reason of all this-over and above its religious law-it insists on the guarantee of an absolute social justice, under which man shall not suffer from neglect.

Therefore, it is particularly anxious to oppose the instinct of fear, whether of life or of livelihood, or of station. For life is in the hand of Allah, and no creature has the power to shorten that life by one hour or by one minute. No creature has the right to cut off from life one single soul, nor has any creature the right to inflict the slightest mark or the least injury on any single living being.

> "But it is not given to any soul to die, except by the permission of Allah, a permission written and dated."[15]
> "Say: Nothing will come upon us save what Allah has prescribed for us; He is our Master."[16]
> "Each community has its appointed time, and when their time comes they will not be an hour behind, nor will they go before their time."[17]

In which case there can be no cowardice and no cowards; for life and destiny, good and evil are in the hand of Allah, and of no other.

> "Say: Shall I choose as a patron any other than Allah, the Maker of Heaven and Earth? He, it is who giveth food, and who needeth not to be fed."[18]
> "Allah maketh wide provisions for whom He will, or He is sparing."[19]
> "And how may beasts do not carry their own provision. Allah maketh provision for them and for you."[20]
> "Say : Who giveth you your provision from Heaven and Earth? Or who hath power over hearing and sight? Who bringeth forth the living from the dead, and bringeth forth the dead from the living? And who settleth the affair in order? They will say, Allah."[21]
> "O ye people, remember the favour of Allah towards you. Is there any Creator save Allah, who giveth you from Heaven and Earth your provision? There is no god save He How, then, are ye kept from him?"[22]
> "And do not kill your children because of poverty; We shall provide for you and for them."[23]
> "And if you fear poverty; Allah will enrich you from His bounty if He wills."[24]

The Qur'an lays it down that the fear of poverty is inspired only by the Evil One, in order to weaken and impede the soul in its trust in Allah and in its own nature.

> "The Evil One promises you only poverty, and bids you to indecency; but Allah promises you pardon from Himself, and bounty; Allah is bountiful, wise."[25]

In that case, there is no reason for any man to be oppressed by anxiety about his livelihood, for his provision is in the hand of Allah, and in His hand alone; and not one of His created servants has the power to cut off any man's provision, or to withhold from him any part of that provision. This belief certainly does not rule out trade and commerce, but it does strengthen the human heart and empower the human conscience. It sets the poor man who is anxious over his livelihood on a level with the man who thinks that his provision is in his own hand, to be won with all his own strength and resource.

The instinct of fear does not then keep the poor man from seeking what is his due, or from taking pride in himself, it means that does not have to give up any of his rights or compromise his honour in order to ensure his provision. This is the meaning of the Qur'anic teaching, as it is the objective of Islam; this is the true application of the general Islamic philosophy in hortatory and legal form.

Fear for one's position or station in life often runs back to the fear of death or injury, or to the fear of poverty or destitution; and Islam is insistent that the individual be freed from this fear also, for no creature can have any power over another creature in this matter,

> "Say: O Allah, wielder of the kingly power, thou givest that power to whom Thou willest. Thou wilt; in Thy hand is the good. Verily, Thou over all things art powerful."[26]
>
> "Allah hath not chosen any son, nor is there any Gog along with Him; else would each God have assuredly championed that which is created, some of them would assuredly have overcome others. Glorified be Allah above that they allege."[27]
>
> "Say: In whose hand the rule over all things? Who giveth protection and seeketh none? If you have any knowledge, you will say: when Allah help you, then none can defeat you; but if He abandon you, then who will help you after Him."[28]

"Whosoever there be who desires honour, to Allah belongs all honour."[29]

"To Allah belongs all honour, and to His Messenger, and to the Believers."[30]

So here again there can be no fear, for all power belongs to Allah alone, and all honour, is Allah's:

"And He is supreme above His servants; He is the Wise, the Informed."[31]

But sometimes the human spirit is freed from servitude to priestly things, and from subservience to a fear for its life or its livelihood or its station, only to fall a prey to social values. Even though it derives from them neither profit nor loss, it still may be under the influence of such values as money, power, rank or lineage. When the conscience recognizes its practical allegiance to any of these values, its very observance of them renders it incapable of true freedom, so that it cannot feel any real equality with its fellows.

So here Islam applies itself to all these values, and puts them in their proper place; it pays them neither too little attention nor too much, and thus it restores the true values to their proper and essential status, the true values which are either latent in a man's spirit or given expression in his acts. Thus it minimizes the effect of the material values, and checks their impact on the human spirit. So it makes this matter also-so far as Islam can undertake to give practical and legal guarantees-a means towards the complete freedom of the conscience.

"Verily, the noblest of you in Allah's eyes is the most pious of you."[32]

And thc nobel man in Allah's eyes is he who is really and truly noble.

"The Arab has no eminence over the foreigner except his piety."[33] "

And then said:

"We are the greater in wealth and in children, so we shall not be punished. Say: Verily my Lord maketh wideth provision for whom He will, or He is sparing. But the majority of people will not understand. Neither your wealth nor your children are things which bring you near to Us; but only he who believes and who acts righteously will be near to Us. For such men there is a double recompense for what they have done, and they shall be safe in Upper Chambers.''[34]

So let them have their greatness in wealth and children, this is no value which will bring them any discrimination or any fame, but only he who believes and acts righteously. For faith is the permanent value apparent in life; these are the two real values which can command respect. At the same time Islam does not depreciate the value of wealth or of family:

> ''wealth and sons are an ornament for life in this world.'' An ornament. But it does emphasize that such things are not such as to elevate or lower a man's true status. ''the things which endure, the works of righteousness, are better in the Lord's sight-better for reward, and better for hope.''[35]

The Qur'an deals with material values and spiritual values by coining a parable about them in the souls of two men; it lays down no formal preference for one of them over the other, but at the same time it paints a clear and appealing picture of the believing soul, and of the reality of its values. Coin for them a parable. There were two men, to one of whom we gave two gardens of vines which We surrounded with palm trees. And between them, we set a patch of arable land. Each of the gardens produced its fruit without failing in any way, and between the two of them, we caused a stream of flow. So this man had his fruit, and in dispute with his neighbour he said to him:

> 'I have more wealth than you, and my family is mightier.'

So he went into his garden, sinning against his own soul, and saying:

> ''I do not think that this will ever pass away, nor do I believe that The Hour will come. But even if I am taken back to my Lord, I will surely find something better than this in exchange.''

But his neighbour said to him in dispute:

> 'Have you no belief than Him who created you out of dust, then out of semen, and then formed you as a man? Nay, Allah is my Lord, and I will not associate any other than my Lord.

Why did you not say when you entered you garden:

> ''As Allah will; there is no power save in Allah.''[36]

If you thought me inferior to yourself in wealth and children, it may be that my Lord will give me something better than your garden; and that He will send down on this a thunderbolt from Heaven, so that next morning it will be only smooth, bare soil. Or the next morning the water may have sunk so deep in the ground that you cannot find it.

> "Then his fruit was encompassed, and the next morning he was turning down the palms of his hands in dismay at what he had spent on it, for it had fallen down upon the trellisses; and he was saying. Would that I had not associated another with my Lord. He had no party to help him except Allah, and so he was helpless."[37]

In this there is apparent, both the pride of the believer in his faith, and his contempt for those values of which his neighbour boasted, when he disputed with him. What confuses the issue is that his neighbour, who is so proud of his garden, does not appear to associate any other with Allah. But *the Qur'an* accounts him as one who does so, and makes him finally admit such an act of association. That is to say, he associated with Allah a purely material value, and gave to it a high mental regard; while by contrast the true believer would not associate anything with Allah.

So too in the story of Korah *the Qur'an* portrays two characters in face of the temptation of wealth and property. There is a portrait of the character which is made conceited by such values, the character which is weakened and made mean, and which is seen to be small in contrast with the great. And on the other hand there is the portrait of believing souls which are mighty and strong, and which never stoop to smallness or weakness.

> "Now Korah was one of the people of Moses, and had authority over them. We gave him so much of the treasures that the keys of it weighed down a band, strong though they were."[38]

Then his people said to him:

> 'Do not exult; for Allah loveth not those who exult. But rather, through what Allah has given you, seek the future above, without foregetting your part in this world. Do good, as Allah has done good for you, and do not seek to cause corruption on the Earth; for Allah loveth not those who cause corruption.'

He said:

> "This has been given to me solely on account of the knowledge which I possess."

Did he not, then, know that before his time Allah had already destroyed generations which were stronger than him in power, and which had gathered more wealth? The sinners will not be asked about their crimes.

> ''So Korah went out among his people in his pomp, and those who were eager for the life of this world said: 'Would that we had something the same as has been given to Korah. Indeed he is a very fortunate man.''

But those who had been given knowledge said:

> 'Woe to you. The reward of Allah is better for him who believes and acts righteously; but only those attain it who have had endurance.'

Then we craft the Earth for him and for his house, and he had no party to help him except Allah, nor was he one of those who could help themselves. So in the morning those who the previous day had envied his station were saying:

> ''Ah, How wide a provision does Allah make for His servants as He wills, or how sparing He is. If Allah had not been gracious to us, He would have cleft the Earth for us. Ah, how the unbelievers fail to prosper.''[39]

Islam is organized around its view of these teachings; and so Allah forbids His Prophet, Muhammad, to attach any value to those things in which some men find a deceitful enjoyment.

> ''Do not cast your eyes longingly at those things which We have given for the enjoyment of some classes of men, things which are the follower of the life of the world. For We gave them in order to test these men; the provision of your Lord is better and more enduring.''[40]

Some authorities interpret this verse and its implications as meaning merely that the rich should be left to enjoy their riches, while the poor should be content with their poverty. But this is a false exegesis which is inconsistent with the general spirit of Islam. This explanation is typical of those crafty Churchmen of despotic ages who use it to quieter the public conscience and to divert it from the quest for social justice. Such men must bear the responsibility themselves, for Islam cannot countenance such an exegesis.

In point of fact, this verse and others similar to it refer rather to the rehabilitation of the true human values, and to the necessity of rescuing the poor from their state of weakness and helplessness under the purely material values of wealth and possessions.

Corroboration of this exegesis is to be found in the fact that Allah commands his Prophet not to attach importance to these values, and not to encourage the people to respect them.

> "Content yourself with those who pray to their Lord in the morning and in the evening, as they seek His presence. Do not let yourself wander from them, seeking the adornment of the life of this world. Do not obey anyone whose heart We have made careless of Our remembrance, who follows his own desires, and who lives in excess."[41]
>
> "Do not let their wealth astonish you, nor their children; Allah intends only to punish them in the life of this world, intends that they may themselves perish while they are yet unbelievers."[42]

In this connection we must also remember the story of Muhammad with the blind beggar, Ibn-Umm Maktum, and with Al-Walid ibn al-Kughira, the chief of the people. It is a story in which Allah delivers a sharp rebuke to His Prophet.

> "He came forward and turned away because the blind man came to him. That will teach you whether perhaps he will purify himself?"[43]
>
> "Or whether he might let himself be reminded, and the reminder profit him? The man who is rich-to him you have given your attention caring nothing that he has not purified himself. But the man who comes to you earnestly inquiring and in fear-him you neglect."[44]

A moment of human weakness had assailed Muhammad in his desire that Allah might bring Al-Walid over to Islam, and he was intent upon this matter when Ibn-Umm Maktum came to him, seeking some knowledge of the *Qur'an*, calling to him again and again while he was still occupied with Al-Walid. The Prophet was annoyed with the beggar, and forward upon him; but his Lord rebuked him sharply for it in these words which are almost the strongest possible rebuke. Therein He endorses the values for which Islam stands, he points out what must be its true path and its constant endeavour-namely, to free the conscience.

So finally the human soul is freed from its bondage to holy things, is freed from its fear of death and injury, of death and humiliation-save for what Allah ordains, it is freed from all regard for outward appearances, and for the values of society; yet after all this it still remains in subjugation to its own nature, swayed by its pleasures and its appetites, by its desires and its longings. Thus an inner tyranny replaces the outer which the soul has escaped, and the complete freedom of conscience which Islam desires is nor achieved; nor can there be any realization of that supreme human aim, social justice.

Islam is not unaware of this hidden weakness in the freedom of the conscience, and it bestows upon it a profound attention. This is evidenced by its care for the innermost depths of the soul, and again by its preoccupation with all the abilities and endowments of the individual. And here Islam comes to the same point as Christianity makes its supreme objective:

> ''Say, there are you fathers and your sons, your brothers and your wives; there are your tribes, and the money you have earned, the commerce which you fear may suffer, and the dwellings in which you take pleasure. If these things are dearer to you than Allah and his Messenger, if they are dearer than a holy war in His cause, then wait in idleness till Allah starts on His work. Verily Allah does not guide people who are impious.''[45]

Here, in one verse are gathered up all the attractions, the longings, and the desires-all the weak points of the Human soul; and they are placed on one side of the balance.

On the other side are placed the love of Allah and of His messenger, and the love for holy war in his cause. It is a striking contrast, and it provides a complete escape from strangling desires. The soul which it thus completely freed is the soul which Islam seeks, and which it summons to its true destiny. Thus man can rise superior to humiliating necessities, can control the direction of his own course, and can seek after things which are greater and farther reaching than his own little ephemeral pleasures. Again he says:

> ''The love of desires is made to appeal to men in their wives and their children, in hoarded hoards of gold and silver, in excellent horses, and cattle, and land; these things are the treasures of the life of this world. But of a better thing than these? For those who are pious there are gardens in the presence of their Lord, through which rivers flow; and long

> shall they dwell there. There are pure wives for them, and there is favour from Allah; Allah is observant of His servants."[46]

This is not an attempt to drug the mind, nor yet is it a summon to austerity or to a neglect of the good things of life, although in this way some have seen fit to interpret *the Qur'an,* and in this way others have understood Islam. This is simply a summon to freedom, and to an independence of the weakness of desires and passions.

Accordingly, there can be no harm in the enjoyment of the good things of life, so long as man can control them, rather than they him.

> "Say who has forgotten the adornments of life which Allah has made for his servants; or who has forbidden the good things of his provision?"[47]
>
> "And do not forget your part in this world."[48]

To this same line of thought belongs the ordinance of fasting; for its purpose is to raise the soul for a space of time above the necessities of all-powerful human nature. By fasting; the will is strengthened and elevated, making man superior to his nature, because he has risen above his necessities.

To this end *the Qur'an* recommends various methods, among them being the inspired warning about the temptation of wealth and children, which occurs in the phrase:

> "Your wealth and your children are only a temptation."[49]

In this there is a stern warning which is sorely needed by human weakness in the face of wealth and children.

This is particularly shown in the covetousness which assails a man where his possessions or his family are concerned; he accepts what he would not otherwise accept, submits to what he would otherwise not submit to, and commits sins that he would not otherwise commit. So that "a child is an inducement to avarice, a cause of cowardice," as said by the Messenger of Allah.

Yet even after this, when a man is freed from all things which would deprive him of his full spiritual status, he may still be in need. He is in need of food, and so he is humiliated; for there is no need which is more humiliating. The empty belly cannot appreciate high-sounding phrases. Or else he is compelled to ask for charity, and all his self-esteem leaves him, lost forever. This is met in Islam by the religious law which aims at preventing the causes of such need, and at putting an end to them where they can be found.

Accordingly it makes the claim of the individual to a competence, a responsibility of the state, and of the rich member of the community; it is a responsibility whose neglect will be punished in the world to come, as it is punishable by death in the present world. A full discussion of this will follow when we come to elaborate the economic theory in Islam. For this reason Islam forbids begging, and envisages a community of Muslims who have suffered loss by fighting in the cause of Allah, and who cannot travel the Earth for wealth; it describes their nobility on the grounds that:

> "they do not beg importunately from the people."[50]

So too, the Prophet gives a coin to a beggar, and then says:

> "Verily the better that one of you should get a rope and collect a bundle of firewood on his back and sell it, even if Allah does not give prosperity; better this than that you should beg from the people that they may give to you or refuse you."

And again he says:

> "A generous hand is better than a stingy hand."

And he exhorts men to avoid all shameful means of getting money other than begging; for begging is regarded by Islam as a necessary evil. As for the proceeds of the poor-tax,[51] this is the law. It is to be taken as a right, and is not to be given as a charity.

> "And of their wealth there was a settled share for the beggar and the outcast."[52]

Thus share is taken by the state, and is spent on the welfare of Muslims, to supply their bodily needs, to preserve their self-esteem, and to retain to them their power of conscience. If this is not sufficient, provision is made to take sufficient from wages and salaries from the wealth of men of means and the richer classes to meet the needs of the poor and the humble.

Thus Islam approaches the question of freedom from every angle and from all points of view; it undertakes a complete emancipation of the conscience. It does not deal only with spiritual values, or only with economic values, but with both together. It recognizes the practical reality of life, and equally the spiritual power of the soul; it attempts to awaken in human nature the highest desires, and to evoke the loftiest abilities, thus bringing that nature to complete freedom of conscience.

Without such complete freedom human nature cannot prevail against the force of humiliation and submissiveness and servility, nor can it lay claim to its rightful share in social justice; nor can it state the responsibilities of such a justice when it has attained it .

This freedom is therefore one of the corner stones for the building of social justice in Islam. More so it is principal corner stone on which all the others must rest.

Human Equality

Suppose, then, that the human mind has come to know all this freedom of conscience; it is free from the least shadow of servility, be it to death or injury, to poverty or weakness, unless what comes by Allah's permission. It is released from the tyranny of the values of social standing and wealth; it is saved from the humiliation of need and beggary, and it can rise superior to its desires and its bodily appetites.

It can turn towards its one sole Creator, to whom all things must turn without exception and without fail; and so it can find a complete independence of the material necessities of life. When the human conscience has come to know all this, it will have no need of anyone to preach equality to it in words, for it will already have experienced the full meaning of equality. It will also not endure the distinctions which arise from worldly values at all. It will seek equality as its right, and will strive to ensure that right; it will guard it carefully when it is gained and it will accept no substitute for it. It will bear the responsibility of guarding and defending its equality, whatever it may cost in effort and labour.

When the establishment of equality is rooted in the conscience, when it is safeguarded by religious law, and when it is guaranteed by its own adequacy, the poor and the humble will not be the only persons to desire it. Even the rich and the powerful will support it, because their conscience acknowledges those values which Islam is intent on establishing and confirming, as we have already outlined them. This is what actually happened in Islamic society fourteen centuries ago, as will be shown in the course of this book.

But despite this, Islam is not content with the acknowledgement, assured and profitable results of freedom of conscience; rather it emphasizes the principle of equality in word and precept, so that everything may be clear and firm and definite. There was an age when some men asserted their claim to be of the progeny of the Gods, while others asserted that the blood which flowed in their veins was not of the nature of common blood, but was blue blood-royal or noble blood. It was an age when there were faiths and religions which divided the nations into classes; some were created by the head of a God, and hence they were holy, while others, having been created by the feet of a God, were despised.

A dispute centered around woman; had woman a soul, or had she not? It was age in which a master was permitted to kill his slave, or to punish him in any way, because slaves belonged to a different class of humanity from that of their masters. In this age Islam was born; it taught the unity of the human race in origin and in history, in life and in death, in privileges and in responsibilities, before the law and no nobility except in piety. That formed a revolution in human thinking, and it has continued to this day; it was an achievement to which humanity had not till then aspired. That is to say, what was theoretically established by human laws during and after the French Revolution was established as a matter of practice by Islam more than fourteen centuries ago. No God can possibly have progeny:

> "Say, He is Allah the One, Allah the Undivided. He brought not forth, nor was He brought forth; there has never been any equal to Him."[53]
>
> "And they said, 'The Merciful has taken a son.' You have committed a terrible thing, at which the very heavens almost are torn apart, and the earth cleft asunder, and the mountains fallen down in pieces. For they attribute a son to the Merciful, But the Merciful has no need to take a son. There is nothing in Heaven or in Earth which does not approach the Merciful as a servant; He has counted them and given to them an exact number, and all of them must come before Him singly on the Day of Resurrection."[54]

Or again, there can be no such thing as blue or noble blood; and as for one being created by the head and another by the foot of a God:

> "Did We not create you out of mere water which We stored

in a secure place until a decreed time? We set the time, and good was Our setting.''[55]

So let man consider from what was he created? He was created from the dropping water, from water issuing from between the lions and the ribs.[56]

''It was Allahwho created you from dust, the from the seed and who then set you in pairs. Nor female conceives or gives birth without His knowing it; none is given long life and none is given short life, unless it be in a Book. Verily that is easy for Allah.''[57]

''We have created man out of an extract of clay; when We made him a seed lodged in a secure place; We made the seed a clot of blood, and We created the clot into a morsel. We created the morsel bones, and We clothed the bones with flesh. We made him grow as a new creation; blessed be Allah, the best of Creators.''[58]

The *Qur'an* goes on to repeat this teaching in many passages, to impress on the mind of man the oneness of his origin and his growth. The human race as a whole is made from dust, and the individual-every individual-from mere water. And the Prophet repeats this truth in the Traditions:

''Each of you is man; and man is of dust.''

Thus he increases man's reliance in his sense and his intelligence.

When it is thus denied that one individual can be intrinsically superior to another, it follows that there can be no race and no class which is superior by reason of its origin or its nature. Yet there are some races which to the present day insist that there does exist such a superiority. There cannot be:

''O, ye people, revere your Lord who created you from one soul, creating from it his mate; and He spread abroad from these two many men and women.''[59]

There was originally only one soul; from it came its mate; and from the two of them there spread abroad both men and women, So all are of one origin, all are brothers in descent, all are equal in origin and nature. The noble Prophet of Islam said:

''O ye people, We created you male and female, and We made you race and tribe. That you might know one another. Verily the noblest among you is the most pious.''[60]

These races and tribes were not made for the purpose of rivalry or enmity, but for mutual knowledge and friendliness; all of them in the eyes of Allah are equal, and there can be no superiority except in piety. But this is another question, unconnected with origin and nature; in these respects,

> ''People are all equal as the teeth of a comb''

as said by the noble Prophet of Islam.

This equality extends its compass over all mankind, and transcends both patriotism and religion; for since the Messenger said, ''All Muslims are of one blood,'' Islam grants to men of other faiths rights of blood equivalent to those enjoyed by Believers-so long as there is a compact between them and the Muslims.

> ''Whoever kills a Believer by mistake, the penalty is to set free one Believing slave, and to deliver the blood-money to the dead man's family-unless they give it as alms. If the killer is of a people who are at enmity with you, but is himself a Believer, then he must set free a Believing slave. If he is of a people with whom you have a compact, then he must deliver the blood-money, and set free a Believing slave.''[61]

Thus, the atonement to be made by a non-Muslim killer whose people have a compact with the Muslims is exactly the same as that to be made by a Muslim killer. The same tendency to equality is shown by the fact that Islam fixes the atonement for an accidental killing as the liberation of a slave; this indicates that it regards freeing a slave as a means of giving life to a soul. Thus, this new life is given in exchange for the life which has been taken by the accidental killing; for in the eyes of Islam slavery is akin to death, while freedom is akin to life.

As for deliberate murder, in vengeance or in hatred, the principle in ''A life for a life;'' and there is no difference between a prince and pauper, a seigneur and a slave. the Messenger said:

> ''Him who killed his slave We have killed; him who mutilated his slave We have mutilated; him who gelded his slave We have gelded.''

Thus Islam has freedom from the conflict of tribal and racial and religious loyalties, and thus it achieved an equality which civilization in the West has not gained to this day. It is a civilization which permits the American conscience to acquiesce in the disappearance of the Red Indian race, a disappearance which is being organized in the sight and hearing of the government. It permits also Field-Marshal Smuts in South Africa to introduce racial laws which discriminate against coloured Indians.

Islam follows up any suspicion of discrimination between men, or of superiority of one over another; no matter what its form or guise, nor matter what its cause, Islam condemns it. Even in the cause of the Prophet Muhammad, the *Qur'an* constantly reminds his people that he is human like the remainder of mankind; and Muhammad himself reiterates the same fact that he was a Prophet, loved and respected by his people, yet always afraid that the love and respect might lead to make him pre-eminent or superior to others. So here he is, telling his people:

> "Do not venerate me, as the Christians venerate Jesus, son of Mary; I am only a servant of Allah, and His Messenger,"

Or again, when he comes into a meeting in which all present rise to their feet out of respect for him, he says:

> "Whoever wishes that men may stand to greet him, let him take his seat in hell-fire."

And when Muhammad's family thought that as a Messenger he would raise their status or their rank, and would confer on them a form of aristocracy above the ordinary, Muhammad refused them everything of that kind, save the nobility of good works and he said to them plainly:

> "If my people cannot approach me through their good works, shall you, then, approach me through your genealogies? Verily the noblest of you in the sight of Allah is the most pious."

If Muhammad's family enjoyed no superiority except that of good works to raise them above the level of the people, no one ever can enjoy such a superiority. And again, when Muhammad was accosted by the blind man, when he turned away from the poor man, Ibn Umm Maktum, to pay attention to Al-Walid ibn al-Mughira, who was the chief of his people, there came swiftly upon him a stern reproof which was almost a condemnation; thus he was brought back to recognize the absolute equality and complete parity of all men, or when some of the rich nobles looked with contempt on marriage for themselves or for their families with poor men or women, there came the command of Allah:

"Settle the unwed among you in marriage, and those who are upright among your male and female slaves. If they are poor, Allah will enrich them of His bounty; Allah is generous and wise."[62]

Relation between the Sexes under Islam

As for the relation between the sexes, Islam has guaranteed to women complete equality with men with regard to their sex; it has permitted no discrimination except in incidental matters connected with physical nature, with customary procedure, or with responsibility, in all of which are customary procedures, or with responsibility, in all of which the privileges of the two sexes are not in question. Wherever the physical endowments, the customs, and the responsibilities are identical, the sexes are equal; and wherever there is some difference in these respects, the discrimination follow that difference. In the spiritual and religious sphere, men and women are equal.

"Whoever does goods works, man or woman, and is a Believer-such shall enter into Paradise and shall not be wronged one jot."[63]

"Whoever does good works, man or woman, and is a Believer-We shall make their life a good life, and We shall give them their reward for the best that they have done."[64]

Then their Lord answered them:

"I shall not waste the work of any one of you who works, male or female; you belong to one another."[65]

Or again in the sphere of possessing and administering money they are equal.

"Men shall have a portion of what their parents and their near relatives leave; and women shall have a portion of what their parents and their near relatives leave."[66]

"Men shall have a portion of what they have gained; and women shall have a portion of what they have gained."[67]

In the law about a man getting double the share of a woman in an inheritance, the reason is to be found in the responsibility which a man carries in life. He marries a woman, and he undertakes to maintain her and their children; he has to bear the responsibility of the whole structure of the family. So it is no more than his right that for this reason, if for no other, he should have the share of two women.

The women, on the other hand, if she is married, has the responsibility of providing for herself from what her husband gives her; if she remains unmarried or if she is widowed, she must provide for herself out of what she inherits. So the question here is one of difference in responsibility, which involves a similar difference in the law of inheritance. Or there is the case of men being overseers over women.

> "Men are overseers over women because of what Allah has bestowed of His bounty on one more than another, and because of what they have contributed in the way of wealth."[68]

The reason for this discrimination lies in physical endowment, and in use and not in the matter of oversight. Because a man is free from the cares of the family, he can attend to the affairs of society over considerable periods, and can apply to these affairs all his intellectual powers. On the other hand a women is restricted most of her life to these family cares. The result is that these responsibilities promote in women in the direction of reflection and thought. So when man is made to oversee woman, it is by reason of physical nature and custom that this ordinance stands.

Besides which, the man has the financial responsibility, and the economic sphere is closely linked with that of oversight, which is essentially the acceptance of responsibility. Ultimately the fundamental point here is one of the balance of privileges and responsibilities in the sphere of the sexes, and in that of life as a whole.

> "The same is due to women as is due from them; but men have a precedence over them.[69]

This Precedence is the oversight, the reason which we have demonstrated. Again there appears to be an instance of discrimination in the question of the giving of evidence.

> "Call two of your men as witnesses; or if there are not women, then call one man and two women from those on whom you agree among the people who are present. So if one of the women goes astray, the other may remind her.[70]

In this verse itself the explanation is made clear; by the nature of her family duties the growth of the woman's spirit is towards emotions and passions, just as wellas in man it is towards contemplation and thought, as we have already said. So when she is forgetful, or when she is carried away by her feelings, the other will be there to remind her. Thus the question in this case is one of the practical considerations of life rather than one of the inherent superiority of one sex to the other, or of a lack of equality.

But the strongest point in Islam is the equality which it guarantees to women in religion, as in their possessions and their gains. It also gives them the assurance of marriage only with their own consent and at their own pleasure; they need not marry either through compulsion or through stipulated price.[71] They must also have the remainder of their married rights, whether they be married or divorced:

> "Retain them honourably, or send them away honourably. Do not retain them by compulsion in order to transgress."[72]
> "Associate honourably with them."[73]

We must notice that Islam guarantees these rights to women, and gives them full enjoyment of these privileges, in a sincerely humane spirit which is not influenced by the pressures of economic or material interests. Islam opposed the idea that a girl child was a disaster, and that she was better put away while she was still an infant. It was implacably opposed to the custom of burying daughters alive, which was current in the life of some of the Arabian tribes. It looks at mankind, and it stringently prohibited such murder altogether and without exception.

> "Do not kill the person whom Allah has forbidden, except with justification."[74]

It specifically forbids the killing of children, though the only children who were killed were the girls:

> "Do not kill your children out of fear of poverty; We will provide for them and for you."[75]

In this verse providing for the children is mentioned first because they are the cause of the fear of poverty; thus it fills the heart of the fathers with trust in the provision of Allah, and in His care for the children even more than for the father. Then as the instincts of justice and mercy gain force He says concerning the Day of Resurrection:

> "And when the girl child buried alive shall be asked for what fault she was killed."[76]

So He poses in this passage a clear and decisive question for that terrible Day.

Thus Islam, in granting to women their full spiritual and material privileges, had regard to their human nature, and was acting in conformity with its own belief in the unity of mankind.

> "He created you from one soul, and He created from it its mate to dwell with it."[77]

Islam's aim was to raise women in status to the point where they would be of necessity the half of the one single Soul. For this reason it grants to women, besides the right of spiritual faith and that of material independence, the right of intellectual achievement; also it makes it obligatory for them.

> "The search for knowledge is incumbent upon all Muslims, men and women."[78]

Similarly it grants to women the right to pay the poor-tax; and it lays it down as their duty; for payment of the tax is obligatory for them as it is for men. In the giving of alms also they have the same part as men:

> "Verily men and women who have given alms, and who have lent to Allah a fair loan-they will be recompensed double."[79]

We must also remember this about Islam-and in its favour-that the freedom which the material West grants to women does not flow from this noble and humane source; nor are its objectives the innocent objectives of Islam. It is well not to forget history, and not to be led astray by the misleading appearances of this present age.

It is well to remember that the West brought women out of the home to work, only because their menfolk shrank from the responsibility of keeping them and caring for them; and that too although the price was the chastity and honour of women. Thus and only thus were women compelled to work.

It is to be remembered also that when women did emerge to work, the material West seized upon the opportunity offered by this event, and paid them lower wages; thus employers were able to dispense with men who were beginning to raise their heads and demand their true value. So when women in the West came to demand equality with men, it was first and most essentially an equality of wages that they wanted, so that they might be able to eat and to support life. When they could not gain this form of equality they demanded the right of the franchise, so that they might have a voice to speak for them. And finally they demanded access to Parliament, so that they might have the necessary representation when their equality was being established.

It is well to bear in mind also that to this day France does not grant to women the right of administering their property-a right which Islam does allow, except by the consent of a guardian. Yet at the same time France grants to women the right of every kind of unchastity, public or private. This Privilege is the only one which Islam denies to its womenfolk, just as it also denies it to men; thus it guards the honour and the instincts of man, and makes the relationship between the sexes a mutual affair, in the belief that there is a physical bond over and above the ties of home and family.

And while today we watch the material West preferring women to men in some professions, particularly in commerce, in embassies, in consulates, and in information services such as newspapers and the like, we must not forget the regrettable and unsavoury significance of this advancement. It is a form of slavery and servitude in an atmosphere of the smoke of incense and opium. It is the employment of the sexual instinct by the tycoons and potentates of the merchant world; and similarly the government sends women into embassies and consulates, and newspaper editors send women to glean news and information. All of them are merely attempting to make use of women; and they know what success a woman can have in these fields. They know, too, what she must give to achieve her success. And even if she gives nothing-which is an absurd supposition-they know that hungry passions and eager eyes are on the watch about her body and about her reputation. But they take advantage of women's hunger for material gain, and for some slight success; for humane and noble feelings are far from them.

As for Communism, it has a wide claim to uphold the equality of women with men; its equality is that of work and that of pay. But when there is equality of work and pay, women become free, and they gain also the right of license, just the same as men. Because in Communism generally the question does not go beyond the sphere of money; whereas in reality all the desires of man and all the instincts of human nature are involved in this one aspect of life.

The essential fact is that men refused to support women, and hence women were compelled to work like men and in masculine circles, in order to live. Thus, it is that Communism is the natural and logical outcome of the spirit of the material West-at least in this respect; for the spirit of the West lacks the generous and humane aspects of true human life.

All these things must be borne in mind before the false flame blinds our eyes. Islam has for fourteen centuries granted to women privileges which France does not yet grant them. It has always granted them the right to work and the right to earn which Communism now grants them. But, it retains for them the primary duty of upholding the family circle; and that for several reasons in the Islamic view life is more than merely economic or physical, and in itself can offer higher objectives than food and drink.

Again Islam looks at life from many sides, and envisages for individuals duties which differ one from the other, but which are all mutually connected and ordered; within this scheme is envisaged the respective duties of men and women, and it lays on each of them the charge of fulfilling a duty primarily towards the growth and the advancement of life as a whole; and it ordains for each of them his guaranteed privileges, in order to ensure this universal and humane aim. Finally the whole race has a nobility which cannot allowably be lessened.

> "And We have ennobled the sons of Adam; We have carried them by land and sea, and having given them their provision of good things. We have given them preference over much of that which We have created.[80]

We have ennobled them, that is, by their nature, and not by thei persons or their races or their tribes. And that nobility attaches to all men, producing absolute equality, for all alike are men. It was man who came of dust; it was man who was ennobled, therefore all the sons of man are equal in every respect.

Thus, all alike have a nobility which must not be degraded, and at which none may scoff.

> "O ye who have believed, let not one people mock another who are possibly better than themselves. And let not women mock other women, who are possibly better than themselves. Do not scoff at one another, or pour shame on

> another with nicknames; it is bad to get the name of evil conduct when you are a Believer; and those who do not repent are evil doers."[81]

The complete and far-reaching point of the verse is:

> "Do not scoff at one another." For when a man scoffs at his neighbour, scoffs at himself, for all men came of one soul.

So there are some things which are prohibited for all men:

> "O ye who have believed, do not go into houses other than your own, until you are received as friends and have greeted the inmates. That is better for you; perhaps you will remember. If you find no one at home, do not go in until you receive permission; and if you are told to go away, then go away; that is more innocent for you, and Allah knows what you do."[82]
>
> "Do not spy into one another's affairs, and do not indulge in backbiting against one another."[83]

The value of these regulations is to make every individual aware that he has a certain sanctity which must not be violated by others; the sanctity of one man is no less than that of another. In this respect also they are equal, and are trusted. Thus, Islam deals with every aspect of human life, spiritual and social alike, in order firmly to establish the concept of equality. There was, in fact, no need for it to do so; for it, treats equality verbally and legally only after it has established in fact and in spirit, through the complete freedom of the conscience from all material necessities. It has an intense passion for equality; it demands that it be universal and complete,not limited to one race or one nation, to one house or one city. Similarly it demands that equality embrace a wider sphere than merely the economic, to which the teaching of the material West have confined it.

Mutual Responsibility in Family and Society

No form of life can be satisfactory in which every individual is bent on the enjoyment of his absolute freedom, without bounds or limits, he might be led to expect such freedom by his belief in the absolute equality which exists between himself and all other individuals, in respect of all privileges; but such speculation is responsible for the destruction not only of society, but also of the individual himself. For there is the important matter of the welfare of society, short of which the freedom of the individual must stop;

there is also the private welfare of the individual himself, which entails his giving up his freedom at certain specific limits.

Thus, on the one hand, he may not allow himself to be carried to extremes by his passions and appetites and pleasures; and on the other hand his freedom may not conflict with that of others. For when this latter takes place, it produces unending disputes, and makes liberty an unendurable burden; through it the growth and improvement of community life are checked by the claims of individual welfare, which is a much narrower interest.

Islam grants individual freedom in the most perfect form and human equality in the most exacting sense, but it does not leave these two things uncontrolled; society has its interests, human nature has its claims, but a value attaches also to the lofty aims of religion. So Islam sets the principle of individual responsibility over against that of individual freedom; and beside them both it sets the principle of social responsibility, which makes demands alike on the individual and on society. This is what we call mutual responsibility in society.

Islam lays down the principle of mutual responsibility in all its various shapes and so that forms in it we find the responsibilities which exist between one community and other communities, and between one nation and various other nations.

We have the responsibilities which a man has to himself. He must restrain from being carried away by his appetites, and he must cleanse and purify these appetites; he must make them follow the path of righteousness and salvation, and must not let them go down in degradation.

> "As for him who has been presumptuous and has sought the life of the world verily Hell will be his place. But as for him who has feared the greatness of his Lord and has restrained himself from desire, verily Paradise will be his place"[84]
>
> "By a soul and what formed it, implanted in its wickedness and its piety, he who purifies it prospers, while he who corrupts it fails."[85]
>
> "Do not hand yourselves over to destruction."[86]

But at the same time man is charged to enjoy himself within those boundaries which will not admit the corruption of his natural self, instead he must give himself his due, both of work and of rest, and he may not exhaust or weaken himself.

> "Through what Allah has given you seek the future abode, without forgetting your part in this world."[87]
> "O ye sons of Adam, take your adornment in every mosque; eat and drink, but be not immoderate; verily He does not love those who are immoderate."[88]
> "Verily you have a duty to your body."[89]

Thus individual responsibility is complete; every man has his own works, every man is responsible for what he does to his soul, good or evil, benefit or harm; and in his place no other can ever stand, either in this world or in the next.

> "Each soul is held in pledge by what it has gained,"[90]
> "Or has-he not been told of what is in the pages of Moses, and of Abraham, who fulfilled his task? That no burden bearer can bear the burden of another; that man gets no more than he has striven for; that the result of his striving will be seen; and that he will be fully recompensed."[91]
> "What it (i.e., the soul) has gained stands to its credit, and what it has piled up stands against it."[92]
> "Whoever is rightly guided, that is of profit to himself; and whoever goes astray, he does so to his own loss; you are not in charge of them."[93]
> "And he who acquires guilt acquires it only against himself."[94]

According to all this, man is ever a watcher over his own soul, to guide it if it goes astray, and to ensure for it, its legal rights, to call it to account if it sins, and to bear the responsibility of neglecting it. In all this Islam postulates two personalities in each individual, keeping watch on one another and observing one another, responsible, the one to the other, for the good or the evil which is shared. This fact lies over against the other fact that Islam gives complete freedom of conscience to the individual, and complete equality with others; but freedom and responsibility are mutually compatible and mutually necessary.

We have also a mutual responsibility between the individual and his immediate family.

> "And use kindness with parents; whether one or both of them attain old age with you, do not say to them, Baj'. Do

> not rebuke them, but speak to them fair, lower the wing of humility to them in mercy, and say; 'O my Lord, have mercy upon them, as they brought me up when I was little.''[95]
>
> ''And We have laid a charge on man concerning his parents; mother bore him in weakness upon weakness, and he was weaned in two years, Show gratitude to Me and to your parents.''[96]
>
> ''But blood relations are nearer to each other in the Blood of Allah.''[97]
>
> ''Mothers shall suckle their children two full years, where it is desired that the period of suckling be complete; and the man to whom the child was born must feed and clothe them both suitably.''[98]

The value of this responsibility within the family circle is that it is the basis on which the family stands; and the family is the basic unit on which society is built; hence there must be a regard for its value. It rests on the permanent characteristics of human nature, on the emotions of pity and love, and on the necessity of material needs and welfare. Thus it is the nest in which and around which are produced all the morals and the manners which are peculiar to the human race; these are essentially the morals of society, which is raised by them above the license of the animals, and above the anarchy of a rabble.

Communism has sought to condemn the family, on the plea that it fosters ideas which are essentially selfish and produces the love of private possession; whereas communism itself forbids wealth, instead there the control of private individuals by the state. But so far as may be seen, communism has failed completely in this matter; for the Russian people are a domestically inclined people, in whose life and in whose history the family has a large place.

Further, the family is a biological and a spiritual institution, as well as a social institution; and the idea that a woman should belong exclusively to one man is biologically sound, and is conducive to the reproduction of healthy children. It has been noted that a woman who is shared by a number of men soon becomes barren or produces unhealthy children. From the personal point of view the feeling of love and compassion grow better in the atmosphere of the family than under any other form of institution; and the growth of personality is more complete in the family circle than under any other form of institution.

Tests carried out during the last war among children in nurseries proved that the child whose upbringing is in the hands of a succession of nurses lacks personality, and has no self-control; nor his the normal growth or the feelings of life and action. So too, the child who has no father has to struggle against a feeling of inferiority; from this hard reality he escapes by inventing a father who does not exist, a father to whom he can go in imagination, and whom he invents in various shapes and forms.[99]

But biological and personal factors are not the only ones; we have here also the question of material needs and welfare which bind a man and a woman together to set up a home and to rear children. There are also the ties which unite the individuals of one family and make them a social unit: this unit relies upon its own members in good or in ill, and its members are mutually responsible in work and in reward, for one generation after another.

Another of the aspects of family responsibility in Islam is the law of material inheritance of property which is analyzed in the following two verses:

> "With regard to your children Allah commands you the males shall have the portion of two females; if the children are all female, and more than two in number, than they shall have two thirds of what their father has left; if there is only one, then she shall fare a half."

Each of a man's parents shall have one sixth of what he has left, if he had any children; but if he had no children and his parents are heirs, then his mother shall have a third. If he had brothers, then his mother shall have a sixth-after any bequests have been made and any debts paid. Whether your fathers or your sons bring you more advantage you do not know.

This is an ordinance from Allah. Verily Allah is understanding and wise. You shall have half of what your wives leave, if they had no children; but if they had children, then a quarter of what they left shall be yours, after bequests have been made and any debts paid. Your wives shall have a quarter of what you leave, if you have no children; if you have children, your wives shall have an eighth of what you leave, after any bequests have been made and any debts paid.[100] They ask you for a decision. Say:

> "Allah gives you a decision about distant relations. If a man dies, leaving no children, and if he has a sister, then she shall have half of what he leaves; and he shall bear her if she has no children. If there are two sisters, then they shall have two thirds of what he leaves. If there is a family, both male and female, then the male shall have the portion of two females. Allah makes it clear to you, lest you fall into error; Allah has knowledge of all things,"[101]

Concerning the bequest which is the subject of the first passage, He has explained it by saying:

> "A command is prescribed for you when one of you is near to death and has property to leave; he must make a declaration, leaving a suitable amount to his parents and his near kin. This is a duty upon all who are pious."[102]

This bequest cannot exceed one third of the estate after the payment of debts, and it does not apply to the principal heir:

> "there can be bequest for the heir."[103]

This legislation is aimed only at obviating conditions under which the proper person may not inherit the kinship gift which the testator wished to give and bequeath to him.

It is aimed also at making available from the legacy some money for spending for good and proper purposes. Thus this ordinance enacted by Islam is one of aspects of the mutual responsibility which connects the individual members of the same family. It is also one of the means of distributing property, so that it may not become too great and prove injurious to society. A discussion on this will follow in the chapter on economic theory. As far as we are concerned here, we need only say that the Islamic law of inheritance is and equitable balance between effort and reward, between credits and debits, within the family circle. The parent who works knows that the fruits of his labour will not be realized in the short and limited span of his own life, but will stretch forward to be enjoyed by his sons and his grandsons, who are his natural successors in life.

Such a parent must give of his very best, and must produce as much as he can; by which the welfare of the state and of the human race as a whole is served. And besides, there is here an equal balance between the effort which he puts as a part of himself. He knows that in them his life is perpetuated.

On the children's side it is but right that they should profit from the efforts of their fathers and their mothers; for the connection between parents and children would not be broken even if the connection in property inheritance were broken. Parents bequeath to their children traits and endowments in their physical and mental composition; and these qualities remain with them all their lives, and to a great extent determine the course of their future, either for good or for evil. And children have no power either to refuse or to nullify this legacy.

Sometimes the state or society steps in and refuses a fair chance to a child to whom his parents have bequeathed an evil legacy; he cannot be given physical health or strength of constitution, because his parents may have given him only weakness and trouble; he cannot be given long life or ample health, because his parents have bequeathed to him only a tendency to swift decay or chronic illness. Therefore, if he must necessarily inherit all this evil, then it is only his right in society to inherit even the material possessions of his parents; thus there may be some fair balance between credits and debits in his case.

The *Qur'an* coins a parable of the mutual responsibility of fathers and children, when it tells the story of Moses:

> "one of Our servants upon whom We had bestowed mercy from Us, and whom We had taught knowledge from Us...And the two of them set out and travelled until they came to the people of a town. From these people they asked food, but they refused to entertain them. In the town they found a wall which was ready to fall down, and Moses' companion set it up."

Moses said to him,

> "If you had wished, you could have claimed a wage for that."

But the people of the town still would not give them food...Then his companion explained to Moses his secret reason for setting up the wall, saying:

> "As for the wall it belonged to two orphan youths in the town, and under it was a treasure belonging to them. Their

> father was a worthy man, and your Lord wished that they might reach full age before finding out their treasure as a mercy from your Lord."[104]

Thus the two sons profited from the virtue of their father, and inherited what he left to them, both in the way of property and in the way of virtue. That this is just there can be no doubt.

When there is a fear that property may by kept in a narrow circle, then remedy is at hand for the state to set things right. This rectification Islam provides for in its own particular way, as we shall see in the chapter on economic theory.

We must think also of the responsibility which the individual has to society, and of that which society has to the individual. On each of these two Islam lays responsibilities, and for each of them it defines the limits to which he may go. In dealing with these responsibilities Islam tries as far as possible to harmonize their interests, and to remedy or to punish any loss which either of them may suffer in undertaking the duties which attach to the various fields of life, spiritual and material.

Every individual is charged in the first place conscientiously to perform his own work; for the results of individuals work are in the long run advantageous and beneficial to the community.

> "Verily Allah is glad when one of you does work which He can be sure of."[105]
>
> "Say work and Allah will see your work, as will His Messenger and the Believers."[106]

Again every individual is charged with the care of society, as if he were a watchman over it, responsible for its safety.

> "Yours is the care of one of the frontiers of Islam, so let none overcome you."[107]

Life is like a ship at sea whose crew are all concerned for her safety; none of them may make a hole even in his own part of the ship in the name of his individual freedom.

> "Verily some people travelled in a ship, and they were partners, of whom each one had his own place. One man among them struck his place with an axe, and the remainder said to him 'What are you doing?' He said, 'This is my place, and I can do what I wish in it'. Then if they restrain him, he and they are saved, but if they let him be, he and they all

perish."[108]

This is a striking picture of the way in which the various interests are inextricably bound up together; over against it stands the selfish outlook which takes account of the outwards appearance of actions, without reckoning their results in practical terms. So here we have an exact indication of what the individual must do and what the community must do in cases such as this.

No individual, then, can be exempt from this care for the general interest, but everyone must have a constant care for the community.

> "Everyone of you is a watchman, and everyone of you will held responsible for his ward."[109]

Similarly, the welfare of the community must be promoted by mutual help between individuals-away within the limits of honesty and uprightness.

> "Help one another in innocence and piety, but do not help one another in crime and hostility."[110]
>
> "Let there be a community of you exhorting to good, urging to virtue, and restraining from evil-doing."[111]

Each individual will be held personally responsible for having urged to virtue; and if he has not done so, then he is a criminal and will be punished for his crime.

> "Take him and chain him; then roast him in Hell; then thrust him into a chain of seventy cubits' length. Verily he would not believe in Allah the Great; he would not urge the feeding of the poor. So he has no friend here today, nor any food save corruption which only sinners eat."[112]

Not having urged to feed the poor will be accounted as one of the signs of unbelief and of repudiation of the faith.

> "Have you seen him who repudiates the faith: He it is who repulses the orphan and does not urge the feeding of the poor."[113]

Every individual, again, is charged with the duty of putting an end to any evil-doing which he sees.

> "Whoever among you sees any evil-doing, let him change it with his hand; if he cannot do that, let him change it with his tongue; and if he cannot do that, let him change it with his heart; and that shows the weakest faith."

Thus every individual will be held responsible for every evil-doing in the community, even if he has had no part in it. For society is a unity which is harmed by any evil-doing, and the duty of every individual is to guard and to protect it.

The whole community is to blame and merits injury and punishment in this world and in the world to come if it passively accepts evil-doing in its midst by some of its members. Thus it is charged with the duty of watching over every one of its members.

> "When we wish to destroy a town We command its luxury-loving citizens, and they deal corruptly in it; thus the sentence upon it is justified, and We destroy it utterly."[114]

Even if the majority of the people in it were not corrupt, but merely accepted the corruption passively, He would still have counted their destruction justifiable.

> "And fear a trial which will not fall only upon those of you who have done wrong."[115]

There is no injustice in this, for the community in which there is an immoral element, and in which evil-doing flourishes unchecked is a community which is exhausted and decayed, on the way to its end. The ruin which will overtake it is a natural fate, brought on by its own condition.

So the Hebrew people merited the curse which their prophets laid upon them; the nature of their kingdom changed, and their spirit left them because they would not change the wrongdoing in their midst, nor did they restrain one another from it.

> "Those of the Children of Israel who became unbelievers were cursed by the tongue of David and of Jesus, son of Mary. That was because they rebelled and transgressed; they did not restrain one another from evil-doing, but practised it. Bad indeed is what they were doing."[116]

Or again in the Traditions:

> "When the Children of Israel fell into rebellion, their wise men rebuked them, but they would not desist. they sat in company with the evil-doers in their assemblies, and they ate and drank with them. So Allah struck the hearts of some of them with others. He cursed them in the words of David and of Jesus, son of Mary, Because they rebelled and were hostile."

As for the Believers on the other hand, they are of the number of those of whom the *Qur'an* says:

> "And the believing men and women are friends one of the other; they urge to virtue, and they restrain from evil-doing."[117]

Now concerning the verse: "O you who believe, look after yourselves; he who goes astray will not harm you, so long as you let yourselves be guided."[118] Some have argued that this verse justifies an abstention from combatting wrongdoing and from changing it. But Abu Bakr[119] (Allah be pleased with him) reminds them that this is a mistaken interpretation. He said:

> "O people, you read this verse, and you put a wrong construction on it. I myself have heard the Messenger of Allah say: 'verily people who see wrong-doing and do not change it-Allah will speedily inflict punishment upon all of them."

This is the true interpretation, which is in conformity with the aims of Islam. For what this verse actually contains is a statement of individual responsibility. Wickedness is negative, which has no compulsive force on others is a matter which concerns only him who indulges in it; the duty of others is to seek guidance; if the sinner does not seek guidance, the responsibility is on himself and his own possessions.

The community is also responsible for the care of its weak members; it must watch their welfare and guard them. It has also the duty of fighting in defence of those whom it guards.

> "It is not for you to refuse to fight in the cause of Allah and in defence of the weak, men, women, and children."[120]

It must also exercise discretion.

> "Make trial of the orphans until they reach the age of marriage; them if you perceive discretion in them, hand over their property to them. Do not eat it up it in extravagance before they grow up. Let him who is rich restrain himself from touching any of it, and let him who is poor use a reasonable amount of it. When you hand over their property to them have witnesses present for them. Allah is sufficient as a reckoner."[121]

Or in the Traditions:

> "He who strives on behalf of the destitute or the poor is like

> one who wages holy war in the cause of Allah, or like one who rises to pray by night and fasts by day.''[122]

The community is responsible for the provision of a substance for its poor and destitute members; it has the care of the money from the poor-tax and of its expenditure on various objects. If this is not enough, the rich are obliged to contribute as much as will meet the wants of the needy; there is no restriction and no condition, except that there shall be sufficient. If any individual pass the night hungry, the blame attaches to the community because it did not bestir itself to feed him. Nay, but you do not honour the orphan, nor do you urge the feeding of the poor; you eat up the inheritance altogether, and you love wealth with an excessive love. Nay, but when the Earth is ground down, Hell is brought forth-then indeed man would let himself be reminded; but whence shall he find the Reminder? He will say:

> ''Would that I had sent forward good works during my life.' On that day no one will punish as He punishes, and none will bind as He binds.''[123]

Or again in the Traditions:

> ''Whatever people suffer knowingly that a man remain hungry among them, the protection of Allah is taken from them-Blessed and Great is He.''
>
> ''He has an abundance of profit, let him use it on behalf of him who has none.''
>
> ''He who has food for two, let him take a third man with him; and he who has food for three, let him take a fourth.''
>
> ''He has no faith in Me, who sleeps replete, while his neighbour beside him is hungry, and he is aware of the fact.''

Where neighbourliness is concerned, prosperity obliges a man even to give away one garment out of two. So the story goes that a man came to the Prophet, and said to him,

> ''Give me clothing, O Messenger of Allah.''

He turned away from him, not having the means to comply, and the man said again:

> ''Give me clothing, O Messenger of Allah,''

Muhammad replied:

> ''Have you no neighbour who has more garments than he

needs? Certainly I have. More than one."

Then Muhammad said:

"Then let Allah not put both you and him in Paradise."

The whole Islamic community is one body, and it feels all things in common; whatever happens to one of its members, the remainder of the members are also affected. This is the perfect, descriptive simile which the noble Messenger uses when he says:

"The loneliness of the Believers in their mutual love and mercy and relationship is that of the body; when one member is afflicted, all the rest of the body joins with it to suffer feverish sleeplessness."

In the same way he portrays the mutual help and responsibility between one Believer and another in a second finely expressed description:

"One Believer strengthens another as one building strengthens another."

And this is the best possible description that strengthens power of mutual help and responsibility in life. On this foundation the laws against social crimes are built up; they are very severe, because mutual help cannot exist except on the basis of the safety of a man's life, property, and rights.

Every Muslim is sacrosanct to a fellow-Muslim-his blood, his honour, and his property. Thus the penalty for killing or wounding is laid down as an exact equivalent:

"free man for free man, slave for slave, female for female."[124]

The crime of murder is reckoned as equal in punishment to that of unbelief:

"Whoever kills a Believer intentionally, his punishment is Hell, and there shall he continue."[125]

"Do not kill the person whom Allah has made inviolate, except for some justifiable cause; if anyone is unjustly killed, We have given authority to his kinsman."[126]

"We have prescribed a law for them in this matter; a life for a life, an eye for an eye, a nose for a nose, an ear for an ear, an eye for an eye, a tooth for a tooth, and for wounds the equivalent."[127]

He emphasizes the retaliation, seeing in it the life of the community:

> ''In this retaliation there is life for you, O ye have understanding; perhaps you may be pious.''[128]

And in fact it does mean life: for it safeguards life by discouraging murder, and because it preserves the vitality and the power of the life of society.

The punishment for immorality, again, is severe, because it involves an attack on honour and a contempt for sanctity and an encouragement of profligacy in society. From it by a gradual process there come license, the obscurity of family ties, and the loosening of those essential feelings of fatherhood and sonship. The penalty for this must be severe; for married men and women it is stoning to death; for unmarried men and women it is flogging, a hundred lashes, which in most cases is fatal.

> ''The man or woman guilty of fornication shall be flogged with a hundred lashes; and let no pity for them affect you in the faith of Allah.''[129]

A punishment of eighty lashes is fixed for those who stone chaste women, Believers, who have been innocently careless; such men cowardly and falsely impugn the women's honour. In this case the crime of falsehood is closely akin to that of immorality, for it is an attack on reputation and honour, an incitement to hatred and bitterness, and an evidence of corruption of thought.

> ''As for those who cast imputation on chaste women and then cannot bring four witnesses, flog them with eighty lashes, and never again accept evidence from them.''[130]

The punishment for theft is likewise severe, because it is an offence against property; it is fixed at the cutting off of a hand; for a second offense the other hand is cut off.

> ''For the thief, man or woman, cut off their hands and recompense for what they have piled up-a chastisement from Allah.''[131]

There are some today who profess to find this a shocking punishment for the theft of property from an individual; but Islam looks at the matter only from the point of view of the safety, the security; and the stability of society. So too it has regard to the nature of the circumstances of a crime. This is a crime which is committed secretly; such secret crimes have need of stern punishments, firstly to recompense the criminal adequately, and secondly to make him an example through his suffering and his fear of the punishment. And in addition, this stern penalty is not exacted in full if the theft was committed under compulsion, such as the need to ward off the evil of hunger from oneself or from one's children.

The general rule is that no guilt attaches to things done under compulsion.

> "He who is under compulsion, who acts against his will and not of malice, has committed no crime."

Thus Umar enacted during his Caliphate. As for those who threaten the general security of society, their punishment is to be death or to be crucified, or to have their hands and feet cut off, or to be banished from the country.

> "The punishment of those who wage war on Allah and His Messenger and who strive to cause revolt in the land is to be put to death, to be crucified, to have their hands and feet cut off on opposite sides, or to be banished from the land."[132]

For the consensus of public opinion holds that revolt and civil war are a greater crime than individual crimes, and that they justly merit being followed by a rigorous punishment.

Islam, thus, legislates for mutual responsibility in society in all shapes and forms; these forms take their rise from the basic principle that there is an all-embracing identity of purpose between the individual and society, and that life in its fullness is all interrelated. So Islam lays down a complete liberty for the individual, within limits which will not injure him and will not favour society, at his expense. It safeguards the rights of society, and at the same time specifies its responsibilities on the other side of the balance. Thus it enables life to progress on a level and even path, and to attain to the highest ends which can be served by the individual and by society alike.

On these three foundations, then-an absolute freedom of conscience, a complete equality of all mankind, and a permanent mutual responsibility in society-social justice is built up, and human justice is ensured.

References

1. *The Holy Qur'an*, Sura 112.
2. Sura 3:57 (''People of the Book : or ''Scriptures,'' as Lammen translates the phrase, is the Muslim expression in *Qur'an* for religions which possess a body of Scripture, and particularly for Jews and Christians. The verb sharaka renders ''associate'' characterizes the darkest crime in Muslim theology, that of placing other objects of worship alongside Allah, and thereby compromising His unity and His uniqueness. This verse dates from a period of Muhammad's life soon after the Hegira when he still believed it possible to make some accommodation with the Jews and Christians--Trans.)
3. Sura 3:138.
4. Sura 3:123.
5. Sura 17:76-77.
6. Sura 72:20-23.
7. Sura 5:19.
8. Sura 43:59.
9. Sura 116:118.
10. Sura 42:18.
11. Sura 2:182.
12. Sura 12:87.
13. Sura 39:54.
14. Sura 107:4-5.
15. Sura 3:139.
16. Sura 9:51.
17. Sura 10:50.
18. Sura 6:14.
19. Sura 13:26.
20. Sura 29:60.
21. Sura 10:32.
22. Sura 35:3.
23. Sura 6:152.
24. Sura 9:28.
25. Sura 2:271.
26. Sura 3:25.
27. Sura 23:90-91.
28. Sura 3:154.
29. Sura 35:11.
30. Sura 63:8.
31. Sura 6:18.
32. Sura 49:13.
33. The Noble Traditions.
34. Sura 34:35-36.
35. Sura 18:44.

36. The usual Muslim formula to express winder-Trans.
37. Sura 18:44.
38. The legend here referred to runs that Joseph concealed three treasures in Egypt, one of which fell to Korah. The keys of the treasure chambers are said to have been a sufficient load for 300 white mules. the Biblical account of Korah is in Num. 16.-Trans.)
39. Sura 28:76-82.
40. Sura 20:131.
41. Sura 18:27.
42. Sura 9:55.
43. (i.e., by giving alms,-Trans.)
44. Sura 80:1-10. (The story here in question is best introduced to the English reader in the form in which it is given by Baidawi in his commentary on this passage "It is related that Iban-Umm Maktum came to the Messenger of Allah while he was in company with some ofthe prominent men of Quraish, Whom he was seeking to convert to Islam. Ibn-Ummaktum said to him, 'O Messenger of Allah, teach me something of what Allah has taught you', This he repeated, not knowing that the Prophet was busy with wither People: so Allah's Messenger, unwilling to rebuke him, frowned and turned away from him, then this passage was revealed to him, and ever after Allah's Messenger, unwilling to rebuke him, frowned and turned away from him, Then this passage was revealed to him, and ever after Allah's Messenger honoured the blind man, saying to him whenever he saw him, 'Welcome to one on whose account my Lord remonstrated with me and he made him his regent in Medina on two occasions-Trans.)
45. Sura 9: 24.
46. Sura 3:12-13.
47. Sura 7:30.
48. Sura 28:77.
49. Sura 64:15.
50. Sura 2:274.
51. The "poor-tax" is the zakat, one of the practical obligations of Islam. By the end of Muhammad's life it appears that this tax was a fixed contribution made by all Muslims to a common fund which was used for the relief of certain classes of the community, specified in Sura 9:60. These include the poor, slaves, debtors, travel lers, and those who suffer loss in the 'way of Allah." to the true Muslim the *zakat* is not so much a tax as it is a loan made to Allah, which He will repay manifold. In the later books of jurisprudence the amount is fixed , generally at one-fortieth of a man's posses sions. A full account of the institution will be found in L. Bevan Nones:" *The People of the Mosque,"* p. 115.-Trans.)
52. Sura 51:19.
53. Sura 112.

53. Sura 112.
54. Sura 19:91-95.
55. Sura 77:20-23.
56. Sura 86:5-7.
57. Sura 35: 12.
58. Sura 23:12-14.
59. Sura 4:1.
60. Sura 49:94.
61. Sura 4:94.
62. Sura 24:32.
63. Sura 4:123.
64. Sura 16:99.
65. Sura 3:193.
66. Sura 4:8. To this day French law grants to women fitness to possess property, but not to administer it.
67. Sura 4:36.
68. Sura 4:38.
69. Sura 2;228.
70. Sura 2:282.
71. Sura 4:28.
72. Sura 2:231.
73. Sura 4:23.
74. Sura 6:152.
75. Sura 17:33.
76. Sura 81:8-9.
77. Sura 7: 189.
78. Traditions.
79. Sura 57:17. (The alms-giving of this quotation is the Sadaqa or free-will offering, and is independent of the*zakat*, or poor-tax mentioned above. *Sadaqa*, which in the *Qur'an* is sometimes used as the equivalent of *zakat*, later came to refer to alms-giving or charity in general-Trans.)
80. Sura 17:72.
81. Sura 49:1.
82. Sura 24:27-28. (It was the custom of par-Islamic Arabia to enter any house announced-with regrettable moral results. Hence the *Qur'anic* prohibition of the practice.-Trans.)
83. Sura 49:12.
84. Sura 79:37-41.
85. Sura 91:7-10.
86. Sura 2:191.
87. Sura 28:77.
88. Sura 7:29.
89. The Noble Traditions.
90. Sura 74:41.

92. Sura 2:286.
93. Sura 39:42.
94. Sura 4:111.
95. Sura 17:24-25.
96. Sura 31:13.
97. Sura 33:6.
98. Sura 2:233.
99. From "Children Without Families" by Anna Freud and Dorothy Burmingham. (Published in London by George Allen and Unwin in 1942, under the title, "Small Children in Wartime,"-Trans.)
100. Sura 4:12-14.
101. Sura 4:175.
102. Sura 2:176.
103. Traditions of the Prophet.
104. The story here quoted in abridged from will be found in the *Qur'an*, Sura 18:59-81, where this incident is linked with two others of a similar encidence. The unnamed servant of Allah is generally taken to be Al-khadr, the Green One, so called wither by reason of his eternal youth, or, more probably, because of the green garments which he is said to wear when he appears to Muslims in distress. He is variously identified with Elias (i.e., Elijah), St. George the patron saint of England, and the prime minister of Alexander the Great. (The origin of the legend is unknown.-Trans.)
105. Traditions of the Prophet.
106. Sura 9:106.
107. Traditions of the Prophet.
108. Traditions of the Prophet.
109. Traditions of the Prophet.
110. Sura 5:3.
111. Sura 3:100.
112. Sura 69:30-37.
113. Sura 107:1-3.
114. Sura 17:17.
115. Sura 8:25.
116. Sura 5:82.
117. Sura 9:72.
118. Sura 5:104.
119. Abu-Bakr was one of Muhammad's most intimate friends, an early convert to Islam, and the first Caliph or successor of the Prophet. He was renowned alike for his mildness, in sharp contrast to Umar, and for his uprightness and mental integrity. From this comes the appellative, "The True".-Trans.)
120. Traditions of the Prophet.
121. Traditions of the Prophet.
122. Traditions of the Prophet.

123. Sura 89:18-26.
124. Sura 2:173.
125. Sura 4:49.
126. Sura 17:35.
127. Sura 5:49.
128. Sura 2:175.
129. Sura 24:2.
130. Sura 24:4.
131. Sura 5:42.
132. Sura 5:37.

6

Islamic Theory of Social Contract

We have now seen the state of Nature as it prevailed before the advent of Prophet Muhammad (Peace be on him!) and we already briefly touched upon the excellence of the laws of peace that transformed that country of war, anarchy and moral degradation into one of unity, harmony and moral excellence. Now we will try to see how that contract was made which brought about the civil society in which the laws of the sword were replaced by the articles of peace.

We will begin with a brief sketch of the life of the Prophet for he was the moving spirit which restored the laws of reason from oblivion and brought light in a country of darkness and sin.The Prophet was born at Mecca as a posthumous child in 570 A.D. and was bred and brought up by his grandfather who entrusted him to the care of Halima, a nurse of the clan of the Banu Sa'd. From his fourth year, he began to accompany the sons of Halima when they went out to graze their cattle.

When he was only six years old, his mother died and he was left without any protection. His uncle Abu Talib then became his guardian. In his thirteenth year, he went to Syria for trade (with his uncle) and in his 20th year occurred the notorious Sacrilegious War (*Harb-al-Fijar*), so-called because it was waged during the sacred month of *Dzulqu'd*. It was fought out between the Quraish (the Prophet also belonged to this clan) and the Banu Kinana on the one side, and the Banu Qais bin Ghailan on the other[1].

In this war, the Prophet did not take any part save that of gathering up the arrows discharged by the enemy and handing them over to his uncles.[2]

The Hilfal-Fudul and the beginning of Social Contracts

After four years of fighting, peace was restored and as there was no government worth the name at Mecca, the descendants of Hashim and the families of Zuhra and Taim formed an association known as the *'Hilfal-Fudul'* and agreed to stand by the oppressed and get justice done for them. Ibn Sa'd thus notes the character of this contract:

> "This contract was better and superior to all such previous pledges."[3]

It was initiated by Zubair bin 'Abdul-Muttalib and he called upon others to pledge. The Banu Hashim, the Banu Zuhra and the Banu Taim gathered in the house of 'Abdullah bin Jad'an for purposes of agreement. They first met on a common dinner and then they organized the meeting. In the presence of God, they made a contract among themselves that they would fight on behalf of the oppressed against the aggressors up to the time the latter agreed to pay compensation to the former. Ibn Hisham puts this affair in this way:

> "All unanimously agreed on oath in the city of Mecca whether the oppressed be a traveller or be one of the residents, they would force the oppressor to pay compensation."[4]

The Prophet was also present at the time of this contract and he said:

> "if further such contracts be made for the cause of the oppressed and 'I be called, I would certainly respond."[5]

But other clans did not join this contract and they remained in the state of hostility in which they were passing their lives.

The Prophet as *Amin*

However, the Prophet's gentle-sweet disposition, his austerity of conduct, the severe purity of his life, his scrupulous refinement, his ever-ready helpfulness towards the poor and the weak, his noble sense of honour, his unflinching fidelity, his stern sense of duty had won him among his compatriots the high and enviable designation of *Al-Amin* the trustworthy.[6]

In his twenty-fifth year, he married Hadrat Khadija who was much influenced by his honesty, virtue and the nobility of the soul.

In his thirty-fifth year, the Quraish decided to build the Ka'ba which was now in a shattered condition, but they began to quarrel on the fixing of the 'Black Stone.' The Prophet at once took a sheet of cloth and asked four men of the four divisions of the Quraish to hold each corner and the Black Stone was placed in the middle of the cloth. When it had been raised to the proper height, it was affixed by the Prophet himself.[7] This settled a quarrel which might have again brought in a state of war as Hobbes pictured it. Says Tabari:

> "When the time came of affixing the Black Stone, every one desired to place it at the Spot. On this basis, all of them began to get out of the limits of patience and, one oath, became ready for war and bloodshed. The Banu 'Abdud-Dar went to the extent, according to the Arab custom of swearing on such hard occasions that they filled a cup with pure fresh blood and following the practice of the Arabia of ignorance they dipped their hands and of those of the clans of the Banu' Adi bin Ka'b into this cup of blood thus signifying with steadfastness their readiness for bloodshed and war."[8]

Because of his God-fearing nature, the Prophet used to retire to the Cave of Hira and there offered prayers to the Almighty--the only 'Light of Nature.' It was here in his fortieth year, that the mantle of Prophethood fell upon him and he received the "Light". His wife--Hadrat Khadija-at once accepted the Light of Islam and she was followed by Abu Bakr, 'Ali Zaid and a number of other followers such as 'Uthman bin' Affan so that the number of his followers in no time reached forty.[9] This began to perturb the heathen Quraish and there was no meeting in which the growing power of Islam was not discussed.[10]

The Muslims dared not offer prayers openly for fear of growing opposition. However, for three years the Prophet preached his religion of peace secretly. But when he began to do it publicly, the Quraish at once felt infuriated and they approached his uncle Abu Talib to refrain the Prophet from reviling their Gods and condemning idolatry. When Abu Talib advised the Prophet to refrain from such activities, he received the prompt reply:

> "if these people would place the sun on my right hand and the moon on the left, even then I would not give up my work until God fulfils it or I die in its pursuit."[11]

The First Hijrat to Abyssinia

When, however, the Quraish found that the activities of the Muslims could not be abated, they decided on their heartless persecution[12] and the Prophet was forced to advise them to leave for Abyssinia. Eighty-one Muslims thus said good-bye to their hearth and home simply because they had got the 'Light' which they could not forsake for an exchange of worldly life.

However, in spite of growing opposition, Islam went on gaining converts after converts and even Hamza and Umar became Muslims. Muir writes:

'These conversions were a real triumph of Mahomet.' Hamza and Umar both passed, with great bodily strength, and indomitable courage which added to social position, secured an important influence at Mecca. Muslims now began to offer public prayers at the Ka'ba.[13]

This open challenge alarmed the Quraish beyond imagination and all of them gathered together and all of them unanimously made a written contract under which they decided for a social boycott of the Hashimites agreeing that they would not marry their women nor give their own in marriage to them, nor buy aught from them; and that dealings with them of every kind should cease.[14]

The written document was then hung in the Ka'ba duly sealed. This contract or agreement has been called the 'Covenant of Tyranny' as distinguished from the earlier contract of the*Hilfal Fudul*. The former was a contract for the oppressed and the latter was made to oppress: the one was an instrument of human sympathy, the other an instrument of intolerance and cruelty.

For three years, the Hashimites were put to the greatest trouble because of this boycott, but when, on the suggestion of the Prophet, that document of tyranny was examined, it was found out that it had been devoured by the insects (only in the name, of Allah! remained).[15] Thus, the whole opposition was set at nought and the obligation of boycott was lost. The Covenant of Tyranny was annulled.

Contract between the Quraish and the Prophet

Soon after, however, the Prophet not only lost his wife--Hadrat Khadija-but also his uncle Abu Talib who had suffered so much because of his affection for his nephew (the Prophet).

Immediately before his death, another attempt was made by the Quraish to come to some agreement with the Prophet. Some of the well-known leaders went to Abu Talib and said that after his death quarrels and contentions would arise between the Quraish and Muhammad (peace be on him!) and therefore it was desirable that the Prophet should enter into a contract (a treaty of peace) with them for 'ceasing injuring their religion,' and on their part they would also 'let alone his'. Abu Talib at once sent for the Prophet and when he came he said:

> "My son, the nobles and chiefs of the Quraish have gathered here to make a contract (Muahada) with you and they agree to promote thy interests, and act according to thy behests, if thou will comply therewith".

The Prophet at once said:

> "My uncle! It is excellent. I request them to utter only one expression and the result of pronouncing this will be that they will reign over the whole of Arabia and the whole of Persia will accept their religion."

That expression is 'there is no god but God and Muhammad is His Prophet.' On hearing this, they clapped their hands and said:

> "O! Muhammad wishest thou to reduce our gods from one thousand to one." After this they arose and dispersed.[16]

The passing away of Abu Talib emboldened the Quraish for further persecution and they even threw dust and dirt and even the intestines of goats and camels[17] when the Prophet was busy in prayers, but he bore all this patiently. He then went to preach to the people of Taif but was not only hooted and treated in an unbecoming manner, he was also pelted with stones and pursued by a relentless rabble.[18] In this way, he was forced to go back to Mecca.

Then the Prophet adopted the practise of preaching to the peoples of the suburbs of Mecca when they gathered for the performance of the *Haj* but here too he was relentlessly opposed by the Quraish and made the target of calumny and ridicule. But the Prophet undaunted by adversity carried on his mission, and it is to this sublime attitude that Muir refers to in these words:

> "Mahomet thus holding his people at bay, waiting in the still expectation of victory; to outward appearance defenceless and with his little band as it were in the lion's

> mouth; yet trusting in His Almighty power Whose messenger he believed himself to be, resolute and unmoved, presents a spectacle of sublimity paralleled only by such scenes in the sacred records as that of the Prophet of Israel when he complained to his Master, 'I even I only am left.''[19]

However, it now became quite clear that the blind Arabs of the age of ignorance were not prepared to accept the Light of Allah and they were determined to live a life of darkness and error. They were wedded to their ancient customs and traditions and did not want to follow the laws of Nature as they were disclosed by the religion of peace--Islam. Hence, the first institution of civil society was not be on the land of Mecca: it was to be in a far, distant city--the city of Medina.

This contract of Aqaba practice of preaching to the people of the suburbs who came for the *Haj*, after all, was crowned with success. The Prophet met six people of the Banu Khazraj from Yethrib (Medina) and they accepted Islam (that is, made a contract with God)[20] and unanimously agreed to forsake the ways of their tribe; and when they went back 'there remained hardly a family in Medina in which mention was not made of the Prophet,'[21] for they had already declared that on their return they would call their people to the principles of Islam.

Next year, during the same pilgrimage, twelve people came from Medina (of these seven were newcomers and five from those who had accepted Islam last year). They belonged to the two tribes that inhabited Medina--ten belonged to the Banu Khazraj and two to the Banú Aus. They met the Prophet near Aqaba and those who had not yct accepted Islam now accepted it and all of them pledged their faith to the Prophet in these words:

> ''We will not worship any but God, we will not steal neither will we commit adultery, nor kill our children; we will not slander in any way, nor will we disobey the Prophet in anything that is right.[22]

The Prophet then said:

> ''If you keep this covenant, Paradise will be your lot. But if you commit any sins excepting idolatry and infidelity your pardon or chastisement will depend on the will of God.

This first contract or pledge is known as the 'Pledge of Women' as not embracing any stipulation to defend the Prophet, it was the only oath required of women. However the twelve men went back to Medina as missionaries of Islam and with them the Prophet sent Mus'ab to teach the *Qur'an,* that is, to call them to the religion of peace-Islam, and to the divine laws of Nature.

Thus, it is clear that the spread of Islam or of the religion of peace was now to occur in a far distant city of Medina. It would, therefore, be advisable to know the condition of Medina before Islam, for though we have already read of the state of Nature as it prevailed in the whole of Arabia, we have not yet specifically stated the condition of Medina before the Light of Allah dispelled the all-pervading darkness.

From the first pledge of Aqaba and its provisions, it is evident that the worship of idols, stealing, adultery, infanticide and slandering were prevalent in the people Yathrib (Medina) also and hence they made a Covenant with the Prophet of God that henceforth, they would abstain from those practices. Thus socially and morally, this part of Arabia was as low in the scale of civilisation as any other part of that country.

The Political Conditions Existing in the Prophet's Time in Medina

Politically, however, besides the Arab tribes, the Jews had settlements round about Medina and the Banu Nadir, the Banu Quraiza and the Banu Qainuqa were their chief tribal settlements. They had even taken possession of the old city of Yathrib (Medina) and 'had built for themselves strong castellated houses capable of resisting armed attack'.

In the 4th century, several Arab tribes had migrated from Yemen[23] towards the north, and they had gained a footing in Medina, thus supplanting the Jewish control in that city. They were divided into two clans--the Aus and the Khazraj, and both of them had developed strong enmity against the Jews. But, according to the general condition of Arabia, they themselves could not live at peace and were in the beginning of the 6th century in a state of 'chronic'[24] enmity, if not actual warfare with one another. Only four or five years earlier, hostilities had reached a crisis between them. Each was reinforced by allies from other Arab tribes; the Jews were divided, the Quraiza and the Nadir siding with the Banu Aus, the Qainuqa with the Khazraj.

In the year 616 A.D., there was fought the great battle of Bu'ath. This battle, like the so-called hundred years' war of Europe was a culmination of hostilities which had been going on for the past hundred and twenty years. At first, the Aus were worsted, but later on 'they dispersed the Khazraj with great slaughter. The Banu Khazraj were humbled but not reconciled. No open engagement after this took place, but numerous assassinations gave token from time to time of hardly suppressed ill-blood. No one yet appeared bold enough to seize the reins of government; the citizens, both Arab and Jewish, lived in uncertainty and suspense'.[25]

The State of Nature in Islam and Christianity

Thus, in Medina also there had been prevailing the State of Nature as Hobbes pictured it and in the words of Wellhausen[26] it was a state of 'hideous anarchy' conjured up by bloody feuds, which prevailed in Medina before the coming of Mohammed...Life was then indeed impossible. But at the time of the first pledge of Aquaba as has just been said, there was, what Muir terms, grave 'uncertainty and suspense.' This means that there was a sort of armed peace and 'enjoyment of life or property' was 'very uncertain and constantly exposed to the invasion of others.' Thus, everything was 'very unsafe, very insecure.'

Apparently, therefore, it seemed that there was peace, goodwill, mutual assistance and preservation because it was a state of equality--and of liberty of each individual; in fact, however, men had become tired of that suspense and uncertainty and they were ready to quit that condition, 'which, however free, was full of fears and continual dangers'. This meant that self-love and passion and heart of controversy easily turned that life of apparent peace into one of enmity, malice, violence and mutual destruction and revenge carried everybody too far. Thus confusion or disorder was the rule, and men living together in this State of Nature lacked:

1. A settled known law;
2. A known and indifferent judge with authority to determine all differences according to established laws; and
3. The supreme power to maintain order[27] again, in the words of Wellhausen, 'There are neither officers nor officials,

> neither jailors nor executioners. There is no magisterial authority, no sovereign power with a revenue of its own drawn from taxation and an independent administration by official organisation'.[28]

The Laws of Nature prevailing in Medina

Hence, the necessity of an orderly government was keenly felt by the individuals of Medina. But how could unity be brought about for they could not accept the sovereignty of any individual from either tribe--the Aus or the Khazraj? Nor had they accepted the Jewish faith, though they had heard from them that a Prophet was soon to rise to establish the Kingdom of God again

> "to make a permanent peace."[29]

Thus, when six of them went to the annual pilgrimage to Mecca, they met the much heard of Prophet himself and accepted Islam, that is, they made a contract with him in the acceptance of the formula that 'there is no God but God and Muhammad is His Prophet.'

These people, as we have already seen, then went back to Medina and next year, twelve people made a similar contract with God and His Prophet by accepting Islam--the religion of peace. Thus, on their return Islam began to be accepted by the different individuals of the state of Nature in Medina. This means that they also renounced the law of the sword that had always existed in that city and they at once accepted the divine laws of Nature as they were given out by Prophet Muhammad (Peace be on him!).

Thus, the state of Nature in Medina had no natural laws in Locke's sense which was understood and apprehended by every one's reason, though there were news that such laws were going to be promulgated soon by a new Prophet. From this comparison of Locke's State of Nature and of the condition of pre-Islamic Medina, it is evident that by recognising the laws of Nature in the state of Nature, Locke had given a moral tone, and therefore he had no justification left for the people to quit the state of Nature (as it was one of peace) and create a civil society which was in no sense an improvement upon it. It was without doubt a fall. In the words of Vaughan:

> "Neither materially, nor morally is there any marked barrier between his natural and his civil state. Neither materially

> nor morally, therefore, is there any sufficient motive for the individual to go to the cost and trouble of removing such slight fences as divide them. He already possesses, already owes allegiance to the 'law of Nature,' a law which, on Locke's showing is at least a very tolerable substitute not only for the law of the land, but also ever for the Gospel.''[30]

However, about the coming of the Prophet, the individuals of Medina had already heard and hence when he came, they individually agreed (contract of acceptance of Islam is always made by every individual) to accept the divine laws of Nature and quit that condition of insecurity and uncertainty.

According to Locke, when the people decide to quit the state of Nature each individual from amongst them unites with others for the preservation of life, liberty, and property, and thus by this social contract they create a community for peace, safety and the public good of one and all. Similarly, after the first contract of the *Qur'an*, we shall see now, the majority of the various tribesmen had already accepted Islam.

Thus, out of the scattered individuals of two hostile tribes of Aus and Khazraj, they were now becoming compacted as individuals of one community of Muslims. But still they were individuals as they had also remained in Locke even after the contract, for in spite of their commonality in Islam they could not yet tolerate the idea that they should be led in prayers by either an Ausite or a Khazrajite. Hence, Mus'ab not only taught them the *Qur'an*:

> ''he led the prayers and thus kept in abeyance the rivalry of the state of ignorance.''[31]

We have already said that after the first contract at Aqaba, the twelve Muslims with Mus'ab went back to Medina as missionaries of Islam and when they began calling people to the religion of peace, so zealous was their propagation that 'the new faith spread rapidly from house to house and from tribe to tribe.'[32] 'In spite of the jealousy of the tribe of Aus towards Khazraj, by the energy of the learned Mus'ab, whom Muhammad sent to Medina as his forerunner and as reader of the *Holy Qur'an,* Islam soon obtained a firm foothold in the city, so that two years later his adherents could venture to invite the Prophet to visit them.'[33] Thus says Muir:

> ''the Jews looked on in amazement. The people whom for

> generations they had vainly endeavoured to convince of the errors of heathenism were now of their own accord casting their idols to the moles and to the bats, and professing belief in the one true God--the only Light of the Heaven and the Earth, or of all creation.''[34]

However, in the month of *Haj* next year, Mus'ab along with certain Muslims and the unbelievers of Medina again went to Mecca. Among the Muslims[35] there were 73 men and two women (62 of the Banu Khazraj, 11 of the Banu Aus). The meeting with the Prophet was again arranged secretly [36] at 'Aqaba' and there he reached at the appointed time with his uncle Abbas (who had not accepted Islam by that time). When all were seated, Abbas thus began addressing them:

> ''You men of Banu Khazraj! You know it full well that Mohammed lives amongst us in honour and safety, and we are his protectors against his opponents. But he prefers to leave this city and seek protection with you. If you see the consequences of what you are going to do and feel that you will be able to defend him against his enemies, then give the pledge; but if you doubt your ability, you must at once give up the idea, for up to this time Mohammed is under our protection and in that case, I fear, you may hand him over to his enemies.''

On this Bara' one of their leaders replied:

> ''We have listened to your words. Our resolution is unshaken: our lives are at the Prophet's service. It is now for him to speak, and take whatever promise he takes from us.''

The Prophet then began by reciting the *Holy Qur'an,* and inviting all present to the service of God said:

> ''I want to take such a pledge from you that you protect me in the way you protect your wives and children''.

On this Bara got up and taking the Prophet by the hand pledged to defend him in the way they defended their wives and children, and then followed the noise from those present for individual 'bai'at' (pledge) even at the cost of life and property.[37]

The second contract[38] made at 'aqwaba (the women pledging only in the words used in the first contract and the men in addition pledging for defence and protection of the Prophet) and their treaty (contract) was ratified by the people (of Medina), who unanimously embraced the religion of Islam.[39] The Prophet appointed twelve leaders from amongst them (9 from Khazraj and 3 from Aus) and addressing them said:

> "I appoint you as the sureties (*Kafil*) of your people just as the Apostles (*Hawari)* of Jesus were, and I am the Surety of you all."[40]

Another Version of Contract

Besides this, another version of this second contract also had been given by the Raudatus-Safa[41] and that too is interesting from the point of view of the study of the contract theory. According to this version, Abbas had said to the assembly:

> "O ye tribe of Khazraj and of Aus, Mohammed is my nephew, and I love him most of all creatures. If you believe him, place faith in him, and if you desire to take him with you. I want to establish a covenant between you, so as to specify my mind and to preserve him from injury and harm during his exile, especially as the Jews, who are your neighbours, harbour, enmity towards him, and I fear their cunning devices against him."

On this Sa'd bin Zararah stood up and among many other things addressing the Prophet said:

> "We are a people aware of our dignity, and no one could rule or govern us except one of our number. How much less could a man do so who has been abandoned by his own tribe and from whom his own relatives have withdrawn their hand of protection? We have, nevertheless, in good faith, of our own free will, concluded to submit to thee...We assent to follow thee, we promise to, and make a Covenant with God, Who is thy and our Creator, and Whose power is above all powers, that we shall sacrifice our lives for thine and shall protect thy body in the same manner as we guard the bodies of our children and wives. We know that if we keep this Covenant we keep our faith towards Allah the Most High, and we will become partakers of eternal felicity, and that if we break this promise, we break our faith towards Allah the Most High, and will be of the number of the damned. O Apostle of Allah, these words of ours are true, so help us God."

Then turning to Abbas, he said that they were ready to make any agreement or covenant he liked. On this the Prophet said:

> "The conditions of our Covenant with reference to the Creator are: that you worship Him alone and attribute to Him no companion; and with reference to myself, they are that you protect me in the same manner as your own lives, those of your children and women."

The assembly then said:

> "O Apostle of Allah, we assent to what thou hast said."

When the Covenant was established the Prophet then selected the twelve leaders already noted above.

The news of this pledge soon spread to Mecca and it made the Quraish furious. They made up their mind to vehemently persecute the Muslims. On this the prophet advised his followers in Mecca to emigrate to Medina, and within two months, they settled in their new abode, with their families. The Quraish were thus paralysed by a movement which though unnoticed and suddenly planned, made their several quarters deserted. They at once met in the *Darul-Nandwa* (Council Hall) and began to plan the imprisonment, the assassination or the expulsion of the Prophet. They ultimately agreed (made a contract among themselves) that a young man of each clan be selected and all of them should at once attack and kill the Prophet. It this way, no blood feud would be raised by the Hashimites as they would dare not oppose all the clans put together.[42]

But before they could act on their decision, the Prophet had already left his place and had sought refuge with his bosom friend Abu Bakr in the Cave of Thaur. There, they lived for three days and then made off to Medina. This is known in Islam as Hijrat or flight and it is from this that the Muslim year begins.

After eight days of tiresome journey, the Prophet and his companion reached Quba safely where the people (of the Aus tribe) had been expecting him morning and night. As soon as he was sighted, a thrill of joy spread all over the city. The converts from all quarters flocked to Mahomet and made obeisance to him. He received them courteously and said:

"Ye people! Show your joy by giving to your neighbours the salutation of peace, send portions to the poor, bind close the ties of kinsmanship, offer up prayer whilst others sleep. Thus shall Ye enter paradise in peace."[43]

After four days, the Prophet started for Medina and when he entered the city, he found tribes and families ready to honour him.

> "As the people of Medina received Mohammed with joyous enthusiasm, his entrance into the town resembled that of a triumphant prince rather than a poor fugitive."[44]

Muir also thus draws the picture of the Prophet's reception:

> "The tribes and families of Medina came streaming forth, and view with one another is showing honour to their noble visitor. It was indeed a triumphal precession. Around the camels of Mahomet and his immediate followers, rode the chief men of the city clad in their best raiment in glittering armour."

The cavalcade pursued its way through the gardens and palm groves of the southern suburbs; and as it now threaded the streets of the city, the heart of Mahomet was gladdened by the incessant call from one another as they flocked around:

> "Alight here, O Prophet! We have abundance with us, means of defence and weapons and room. Abide with us."

So urgent was the appeal that sometimes they seized hold of Al Caswa's halter. Mahomet answered them courteously and kindly:

> "The decision, he said, rests with the camel; make way for her; let her go free."

It was a master stroke of policy. His residence would be hallowed in the eyes of the people as selected supernaturally, while the jealousy which otherwise might arise from the quarter of one tribe being preferred to that of another would thus receive decisive check.[45] However, the camel halted at an open yard and the Prophet stayed with Abu Ayyub whose house was the nearest. There, he stayed in the lower story for the convenience of those who used to visit him, and

> "dishes of choice viands, bread and meat, butter and milk, presently arrived from various houses and this hospitality was kept up daily so long as the Prophet resided in the house."[46]

Consolidation of Medina as Political Capital of Islam

Thus was Medina conquered by the Prophet? As he himself said in a Tradition:

> "All cities or districts were conquered by force, but All

Medina was conquered by the Qur'an''[47]

And certainly, it was the Qur'an that conquered it. It was a conquest of heart rather than of territory, and the means was the willing consent of the people rather than the sword of the conqueròr. And the contract, which gave this consent, had taken three steps in its fulfillment.

In the first, the laws of Islam which were the divine laws of Nature were explained and promulgated; in the second the representatives of the two chief tribes entered into a definite covenant of protecting the Prophet; and in the third, each citizen, nay every child of Medina welcomed the Prophet as their saviour.

Religiously considered, therefore, the Kingdom of God was thus established in a land of darkness and terror, and heathenism or idolatry vanished with the onslaught of the Light of Islam.

Socially and politically considered, the state of Nature with its state of war or, at least, of uncertainty and inconvenience was done away by the acceptance of the laws of Nature, and the contract with the Prophet at once transformed that state into one of civil society. Gibbon says:

> ''In the state of Nature every man has a right to defend, by force of arms, his person and his possession: to repel, or even to prevent, the violence of his enemies, and to extend his hostilities to a reasonable measure of satisfaction and retaliation. In the free society of the Arabs, the duties of subject and citizen imposed a feeble restraint; and Mahomet, in the exercise of a peaceful and benevolent mission had been despoiled and banished by the injustice of his countrymen. The choice of an independent people had exalted the fugitive of Mecca to the rank of a sovereign; and he was invested with the just prerogative of forming alliances and of waging offensive or defensive war.''[48]

Thus, if the city state of Medina was the Kingdom of God in one sense and the Prophet was the Vice regent of God in that divine kingdom, it was also in another sense a true state of the people created by the people themselves, and the Prophet was an elected sovereign of a sovereign people. To summarize the whole of our survey, we may now say that:

1. The state of Nature in Medina also was a state of war but

immediately at the time of the first contract, there was apparent peace, and therefore, it most truly resembled Locke's picture of the state of Nature.

2. The laws of Nature-of Islam-brought the individuals together into a contract (with God); that is, they accepted Islam and hence a community of Muslims was created, though that community was not yet organic in nature.
3. The absence of a well-known authority or judge wasthen provided for by the second contract with the Prophet, and this contract was then ratified by the whole community. This was a government contract. The Prophet thus became an elected chief of a people and he appointed their own leaders to look after them.

The Western Interpretation of Contract Theory of Islam

After this, we may now compare the character of this second contract from the point of view of political philosophy. From what we see of the addresses of Abbas, Bara and the Prophet, it becomes quite clear,that while Bara' pledged to protect the Prophet with life and property, the Prophet himself (in the worldly sense) promised nothing. That is, the Prophet in the literal sense of the contract of give-and-take, was not a party to the contract and the contract was only one-sided. This means that after the contract, and after its ratification by the people of Medina they got pledged to protect their elected 'Sovereign' and they had agreed to obey him in everything.

From this point of view, it becomes clear that this second contract resembled the contract of Hobbes in which the sovereign had promised nothing and yet he was to be obeyed absolutely. There was to be no rebellion because it would again result in the state of Nature from which they had run out for the law and the religion of peace.

Would it then be too fantastic on my part, to again ask, if Hobbes (as well as other social-contract writers) had this condition of Arabia in view, and that they were only interpreting things and events which were already past history?

Besides this interpretation, there can be another interpretation of this second contract in the view of Locke, if we take into account another 'report' regarding the proceedings of that contract. When that contract was going to be made Abul Hashim (one of those present) said to the Prophet:

> "O Apostle of Allah, between us and the Jews there are treaties and alliances, but if we break them, and Allah the Most High grants the victory, thou wilt possibly rejoin thy tribe, and abandon us to our foes."

His Lordship smiled and said:

> "Blood is blood, and destruction is destruction, You are mine and I am yours. I shall fight those who fight you, and make peace with those with whom you make peace."[49]

It is clear, that if after the first contract at Aqaba, the Muslim community was created in Medina (this resembles the social contract of Locke), by the second contract a governmental contract was made by which the Prophet became the chief authority of the city-state of Medina. In one point more, the resemblance of the events in the second pledge can be made with those on which Locke's contract was based. It is argued that Locke wanted to justify the Glorious Revolution of England in which William and Mary had been called from Holland (by seven notables of London). The Prophet was also a non-party man in Medina and he was called by 73 men to their land and then their contract or pledge was kept up by the people.

This governmental contract in Medina resembles, no doubt, the second (governmental contract) in Locke, but critics do not agree as to the making of a second contract. Thus, Vaughan emphatically asserts (and I think he is right) that there is only one contract in Locke-the social contract which creates the community. He observes;

> "it has often been said that Locke represents the relation between the community and the executive as one of contract: the original contract between King and people of the famous convention resolution of 1689."

This may not be very far removed from the spirit of his doctrine, but it is doubly wrong as to the letter. For, on the one hand, the appointment of the Executive is apparently conceived by him as belonging normally not to the community, but to the Legislature. And, on the other hand, what is far more important, he never once uses the term contract to describe the instrument from which the

Executive derives its authority. It is always a trust, or a fiduciary trust.[50]

Hence, if according to this argument there is only one contract in Locke, the two contracts in Medina bear resemblance to the two contracts in Milton and Althusius and other anti-monarchist writers, though the purpose of their contracts was not the same. But the social contract of Medina does not fully accord with the first or social contract of Althusius or of Milton for in them even the king was a party to the original contract (which is of course not true of Medina, for the Prophet was still in Mecca when the social contract was made in Medina). Hence, the two contracts of Medina wholly and fully accord with the framework (and not the spirit or purpose) of the contract theory as it was stated in Vindicia Contra Tyrannos which was formerly ascribed to Brutus or to Languet, but is now understood to be the work of Mornay (1579). Mornay in his book has two contracts:

1. The first contract is between God on the one side and the people and their ruler on the other side for maintenance of true religion. It was upheld by the state in return for the protection and favour of Almighty God.
2. The second contract is between ruler and subjects to preserve and protect the natural rights of subjects in return for their loyal support of the Prince.

The first of these contracts is true of the social contract of Medina also for the people whose representatives had already accepted Islam at the hands of the Prophet himself had now accepted Islam at the hands of Mus'ab who was the representative of the Prophet at Medina. This was certainly a contract of the ruler and the people with God to maintain the right religion which was Islam.

The second contract was made by the Prophet with the peoples' representatives and when he reached Medina the whole Muslim community ratified the *bai'at'* (pledge or contract) that had already been made and the Prophet declared, as has been already noted above, that he was heart and soul with the people of Medina for they had declared to support him in thick and thin and he was also prepared to fight with their enemies as his own enemy.

Thus, from the above account of the contracts at Medina, it is clear that the social contract theory is not a mere fiction: it is a historical reality and ancient Arabia was the scene of such contracts even in the making and the construction of the state itself. The contracts in Medina do explain not only the origin of civil society in contract but also of its government. Contract in Islam, therefore, is a reality and not a mere fiction or only a mere idea of reason.

References

1. Ibn Hisham, *Sirat* (Urdu Translation), Lahore, 1915, p. 56; Also *Tarikh-i-Abul-Fida* (Urdu Translation), p. 270. *Matba-i-Ulum Madrasa*, Delhi, 1847. The cause of this war, as usual in the Arabia of those days, was murder. *The Tabqat of Iban Sa'd quoted* in original Arabic by Khan Bahadur Syed Aulad Haider in his *Uswatual Rasul,* Vol. II, p. 69.
2. Ibn Hisham, p. 56. The *Usdul Ghabah* adds that the Prophet was also guarding or looking after their goods.
3. Ibn Sa'd, *Tabqat* reproduced in the *Uswatul Rasul*, pp. 71-72. As regards 'previous pledges' Margoliouth says, "It seems there was an arrangement between the tribes whereby warfare should cease for four months in each year in order to permit safe pilgrimage to the sanctuary." *Mohammedanism*, p. 43.
4. Ibn Hisham, p. 41.
5. *Tabqat Ibn Sa'd* as reproduced in the *Uswatual Rasul.*
6. Amir Ali, *The Spirit of Islam*, p. 13. The same sketch of character occurs in Iban Sa'd, Ibn Hisham and in Tabari.
7. *Tarikh-i-Abul Fida,* p. 272.
8. *Tarikh i-Tabari,* Vol. I, Part III, translated into or from Urdu by S. Ibrahim M. A. Hyderabad, p. 52.
9. Ibn Hisham gives the full list, pp. 83-85.
10. Ibn Khaldun, p. 24.
11. Ibn Hisham, p. 86.
12. For details of the horrible persecution See Usdul Ghabah under Khabbab, *Bilal, Khalid bin Sa'id Naufal* also Ibn Hisham. p. 88.
13. Nicholson, *A Literary History of Arabia,* p. 157; Ibn Hisham, *op. cit.*, p. 115.
14. Muir, p. 99; Ibn Khaldun, op. cit., p. 32; Ibn Hisham, p. 49; Abul-Fida, p. 282; *Raudatus-Safa* (Oriental Translation Fund), Part- II, Vol. I, p. 185.
15. *Raudatus-Safa,* p. 190.
16. *Raudatus Safa*, pp. 196-197; also Ibn Hisham, p. 146.
17. Ibn Hisham, pp. 145-46.
18. Ibn Khaldun, p. 35.
19. Muir, p. 122 (1894 edition).

20. Hobbes thus expresses himself on making a covenant with God: ''to make covenant with God, is impossible but by mediation of such as God speaketh to, either by supernatural Revelation or by his Lieutenants that govern under Him and in His name; for otherwise we know not whether our covenants be accepted or not.''-Levia than, (E.L.), p. 71.
21. Ibn Hisham, p. 150; Abul-Fida, p., 237; Tabari, (Hyderabad Edition), p. 113.
22. Ibn Hisham, p. 151; Abul-Fida, p. 289.
23. Abul-Fida, p. 187.
24. Muir, *Life of Mohamet,* p. 111 (1894 Edition).
25. *Ibid*, pp. 112-13.
26. *The Historian's History of the World,* Vol. VII, p. 291.
27. This picture of Medina which I have presented in Locke's language, is a more faithful picture of the State of Nature of Locke for it saves him from the inconsistencies and contradictions that he has made in his account. See Locke, *Civil Government* (E.L.) Ch. III, pp. 126-27.
28. *The Historian's History of the World,* p. 286.
29. *Margoliouth Mohammedanism*, p. 54.
30. Vaughan, *Studies in the History of Political Philosophy,* Vol. I, p. 136.
31. Ibn Hisham, pp. 151-52; also Muir, p. 116.
32. Ibn Khaldun, p. 43; Muir, p. 115: Raudatus Safa, p. 225.
33. *The Historians' History of the World,* p. 47. For Mus'ab's detailed activities *Raudatus-Safa,* pp. 223-25; Abul-Fida, p. 289, Ibn Khaldun, pp. 41-42; Ibn Hisham, pp. 152-53.
34. Muir, p. 115.
35. Abul-Fida, p. 29. According to Tabari, there were only 70 men including 2 women (p. 115) but according to Ibn-Khaldun there were 72 men and 2 women (p. 44). We have adopted the version of Ibn-Hisham, p. 154. See also Muir, p. 125.
36. The details of this secrecy have been will given by Tabari.
37. Muir gives all these proceedings on pp. 125-26 (1894); also Ibn Hisham, p. 155; Abul-Fida, p. 292; Ibn Khaldun, p. 43.
38. With this object seventy-three believers journeyed to Mecca, and in an assembly held at night on the same hill of homage they made a covenant with Mohammed The *Historians History of the World*, p. 117.
39. *Cambridge Modern History,* p. 357; Also See Tafsir Muwahibur Rahman, *Sura-i-Baqr*, p. 62. Even women made a contract (bai'at) with the Prophet on Islam. Thus Um-'Ata' herself declares that she made a contract with the Prophet on Islam (*Bukhari Kitabus Salat.* Also Um 'Atiyya says 'At the time of contract the Prophet had taken our word that we won't weep and wail over the dead and this contract was not fulfilled except by five women-Um-Slim, Um At'a

wife of Mu'adh, and two others. (*Bukhari-Kitabus Salat).*

40. Ibn-Hisham, p. 155; Ibn-Khaldun, p. 44.
41. *Raudatus Safa, pp. 227-32.*
42. Ibn Khaldun, pp. 47-48: Ibn Hisham, pp. 169-70.
43. Muir, p. 162 (1894 Edition)
44. *The Historians' History of the World*, p. 118.
45. Muir; p. 164 (1894 Edition). For further interesting details, Ibn Hisham, pp. 175-76: Ibn Khaldun, p. 52; Abul Fida, p. 300; Raudatus-Safa, pp. 250-51.
46. Muir, p. 165; *Raudatus-Safa*,p. 251. The Prophet lived in this house for seven months.
47. Al-Baladhuri, *Futuhul; Buldan* (Hitti's Translation), p. 21.
48. Gibbon, *Decline and Fall of Roman Empire, Bury'a Edition,* pp. 358-59.
49. *Raudatus-Safa* pp. 229-30. Also Tabari (Hyderabad Edition), p. 117.
50. Vaughan, Vol I. p. 145. Also see Lord, *Principles of Politics,* pp. 53-54; 'He appears to think, though he does not say so quite explicitly, that it rests upon two contracts. The first puts an end to State of Nature.

41. Kamalu's Safa, pp. 227-32

47. [illegible] (India's Translation), p. 71

7

The Social Justice in Modern Perspectives

We have already examined the theoretical bases of society as they are outlined in the *Qur'an* and the Traditions, and we have looked briefly at Muslim society as it evolved in the course of history. It now remains for us to ask: Is it possible today to renew something similar to that form of Islamic life for the present and for the future? It is not sufficient that Islam should have been a living force in the past; it is not enough that it has produced a sound and well-constructed society in the time of the Prophet and in the age of the Caliphate.

Since that distant time, there have been immense changes in life--mental, economic, political, and social. There have even been material changes on the Earth, and in its powers relative to man. All these things must be carefully considered before an answer can be given to our question. There is also the further consideration which cannot be overlook in any discussion which is directed to a practical and particular end, rather than to a theoretical and general; we must discover why it was that the spread of the Islamic spirit came to a halt in matters of political and economic theory only a short time after the era of the Prophet. Was this the longest possible span of life which the inner spirit and resources of Islam could command?Before dealing with these two considerations, we must emphasize the following truths:

> "that Islamic society today is not Islamic in any true sense."

We have already quoted a verse from the*Qur'an* which can not in any way be honestly applied today:

> "Whoever does not judge by what Allah has revealed is an unbeliever."[1]

In our modern society, we do not judge by what Allah has revealed; the basis of our economic life is usury; our laws permit rather than punish oppression; the poor-tax is not obligatory, and is not spent in the requisite ways. We permit the extravagance and the luxury which Islam prohibits; we allow the starvation and the destitution of which the Messenger once said:

> "Whatever people anywhere allow a man to go hungry, they are outside the protection of Allah, the Blessed and the Exalted."

The Imam Obn-Hazm also delivered a *fatwa*[2] on the same subject, to the effect that if a man dies in starvation in any town, the people of that town are regarded as having killed him, and the blood-money may be demanded of them. We permit this and similar things which have long been the subject of vain protest. Yet, the Qur'anic text is undeniably applicable to such things.

It refers to the existence in our modern society of such laws as those which permit usury, adultery, and refusal to pay the poor-tax, which thereby prove themselves to be in opposition to the divine laws laid down in the *Qur'an*. So long as Muslim society adhered to Islam, it manifested no weakness and no tendency to abdicate its control of life. It was when it fell away from Islam that these things took place. Emphasis on this fact will compensate for the idle aspersions which Western scholars have cast on our faith, and which they have evidenced from history.

These aspersions have been taken up by some in the East who were either gullible or mercenary, and have been the cause of the sullying of hundreds of pages by such men, under the claim of being liberal thinkers and accurate scholars. This is nonsense, and can only serve as a pretext for the false, the gullible, or the mercenary mind. We may now return to treat the two considerations whose discussion we deferred until we had noted the above points. We may start by answering the second question, why did the spread of the Islamic spirit come to a halt a short space after the time of the Prophet? Here again, we must emphasize two historical facts:

> "This halt was only partial, never complete. It took place only in a limited sphere, that of politics."

The tolerant Caliphate became a tyrannical monarchy:

> "the public funds were made accessible to the monarch, his relatives, his courtiers, and his flatterers, while they became inaccessible to those who had a true claim on them by the laws of Allah and His Messenger. But the remainder of the teachings of Islam remained in force; the charity and benevolence, the mutual help and responsibility tolerance and freedom of conscience and human equality, the payment of the poor-tax and the alms, and all the other positive and negative ordinances of Islam--all these continued in force to a greater or a lesser extent in many Muslim communities."

The Shari'a even continued in force as the system of civil law until the nineteenth century, when we introduced French law, thus giving the *coup de grace* to another tie which bound us to the beliefs of Islam.

The change which overtook the system and the development of politics--a partial change, as we have just said--was the product of an unfortunate mischance, as we have already contended. The mischance was that the control should fall into the hands of the Umayyads, first in an indirect way in the reign of Uthman, and later quite openly in the reign of Mu'awiya. If we are to be fair to Islam we cannot hold it responsible for the Umayyads; for it was injured far more by this clan of the Quraish than by the fiercest of its enemies.

It is certain that, if the life of Umar had lasted several years longer, or if Ali had been the third Caliph, or even if Uthman had become Caliph when he was twenty years younger, then the course of Islamic history would have been very considerably changed. For the policy which Umar enunciated was:

(a) to take excessive wealth from the rich and give it to the poor;
(b) to equalize the stipends assigned to the people, as had been the practice under Abu-Bakr.

If Umar had done this, there could have been no opposition to a policy so consistent with Islam. Umar's conscience was above all question, as was his zeal for the faith; the reverence in which he was held for his fidelity to the faith was similarly above the attacks of jealousy and doubt.

If this programme had been carried out by Umar, it would have restored economic and social equity to the Islamic world, and the civil war would have been averted at its very beginning, or, at the least, would have been postponed for a long time. Or if Ali had succeeded Umar, he would have guided the people in Umar's policy, whatever might have been the position of the Quraiship, who had more self-confidence in dealing with Ali than they had in dealing with Umar.

In this case, the matter would not then have come to the stage of rebellion or civil war. The Umayyads would not have later aspired to power; for their nobles had no high standing in Islam because of their early conversion or their renown in the early wars; they were only among the "forced" converts who embraced Islam at the conquest of Mecca, when the success of the new faith was already assured. Under such circumstances they could have held office in the army or in provinces, but with no special reason for holding or being kept out of office, such as they gained in thirteen years under the reign of Uthman.

But it will be asked: How were the Umayyads able to effect such a speedy revolution during a period of turmoil in Islam? Does this not indicate that the Islamic system is unsteady by nature, or at least unsuited to permanancy? Does it not indicate that by nature Islam provides no adequate safeguards against such revolution? We must here take account of the conditions of the Islamic state in that age, and we must reckon not only with factors of external power, but also with those of internal agitation.

The truth is that, at that stage Islam was in a ferment, and the really strange thing is that the Umayyads did with it only as much as they could. For the fact is that the astonishing speed of the conquests, to which history can produce no parallel, added to Islamic society a huge territory, teeming with various races and skills, intellects and languages, systems, traditions, and heritages.

However strong the spirit of Islam may have been, and however powerful in suppressing all these heritages, an element of time was essential before all this new material could be homogenized, before a change could be wrought in the old moral ideas, the rooted traditions, the cherished social systems and customs. Thus, the Umayyad attack on the spirit of Islam just at this juncture took place at a unique point of time; if it had been stayed for a space, it could never have accomplished all that it did.

We have seen that the bulk of Mu'awiya's support lay in Syria, a conquered country, rather than in Arabia itself. Those of his supporters who did hail from the Peninsula, such as Amar ibn al-As, were of a nature akin to Mu'awiya himself, men who trampled down the moral element in their reckonings, who justified the means by the end, and who justified the end simply on the grounds that they desired it.

As for the suggestion that the Islamic system does not provide by nature adequate safeguards against revolution, for one thing we must bear in mind that this system was assailed by revolution before it had properly struck roots; and for another thing we must remember that in practice no system has any real such safeguards. Where, for example, are the safeguards of democracy in Europe? This is a strongly entrenched system, which has achieved a definite form, and which has had time to establish itself and to spread its influence over a long period into every quarter of life.

Yet, where were its safeguards at the time of the Nazi revolution, or the Fascist, or the Spanish? Or again take the institution of free speech in the United States, whose people fled from Europe to form a free society--where are its safeguards? Today a few newspaper and radio companies can hold a monopoly of both information and opinion, and can forbid any contrary opinions to find their way to the eyes, the ears, or the thoughts of the people.

The truth is that any suspicion that the Islamic system does not afford safeguards against revolution is due to ignorance of what is practically feasible in any system. It betrays also an ignorance of the true facts of Islamic history; we have the evidence of the minor rebellion in the Hejaz, and of the great rebellion against Uthman; we have the evidence of the Qarmatian rebellion[3], and of many others, all of which were directed against exploitation, arbitrary power, and class distinctions. The spirit of Islam has continually and successfully resisted all such things, in spite of the grievous injuries which it has suffered at their hands throughout thirteen hundred years.

The spread of the spirit of Islam, then, was not halted because that spirit was unable to establish itself, nor because it was found inadequate to cope with the demands of the life. As we shall shortly see, this spirit has been continuously operative in many of the aspects of life and society. The halt in its spread was the product of an unfortunate mischance at a unique point of time. And it was when that mischance brought to Islam a Caliph who retained something of the true spirit of the caliphate in the person of Umar II, that the spread of Islam became again apparent, and the government again truly Islamic. But then the times were not propitious for such a truly Muslim Caliph to restore what had been destroyed, or to establish the roots of Islamic traditions in the political system.

But, nonetheless the attempt of Umar II does give us a clear indication that the inner power of Islam was really strong and capable of application in very different times. For his attempt followed the oppressive and evil age of the Umayyads, and it indicated clearly that a renaissance of Islamic government was possible, and not out of question.

We must repeat our contention that even when the spread of the Islamic spirit came to a halt in the realm of politics-though even here it was only a partial halt-it still continued to operate in other aspects of both social and individual life. It continued to realize many of its ideals, and to achieve many of its aims; indeed even to the present day it is still effective in such spheres as are not strongly under the influence of politics. As the Frenchman, Gouilly, says in *Islam and the Great Powers*:

> " The number of Muslims in Madagascar is not less than three quarters of a million. Most European authorities explain the spread of Islam in the native villages by the fact that it is a unifying religion which ensures for the negro an equality and justice for which he longs; it emancipates him finally from the bondage of priesthood and superstition, and even from the nightmare of evil spirits."[4]

H.A.R., Gibb writes in *Whither Islam*?:

> "Islam still has it in its power to render a conspicuous service to mankind. There is no other society which can show such a record of having united various races in one unity based on equality. The great Islamic community in China, and the still smaller community in Japan, all show that Islam has still the power completely to reconcile such divergent elements as those of race and class. If ever the

opposition of the great states of the East and West is to be replaced by understanding, this can only be done through the medium of Islam."[5]

The Muslim's Conduct during the Crusades

The conduct of the Muslims during the Crusades showed the full inspiration of the strong spirit of Islam, as it rose superior to worldly considerations, treachery and ruthlessness. It showed a belief in the unity of mankind and the relationship of humanity beyond all differences of faith, and above all temporal and ephemeral enmities. Saladdin was not the only one whom the history of the Crusades has recorded as being of the true and lofty Islamic spirit; rather would this description apply to all the Muslim armies which took part in these long and bitter wars. And this remained true despite the foul deeds of the Crusaders. These may be exemplified in the fall of Jerusalem on the fifteenth of July, 1099 A.D. (492 A. H.), during the first Crusade.

The Muslims sought refuge and sanctuary in the Aqsa Mosque, but the Crusaders followed them inside and dispatched them with their swords, so that blood flowed through the sacred precincts in a flood. In this act, the Crusaders violated a solemn treaty which their leader had made with some of the Arabs.[6] This was only one example of the barbarity of the Crusaders, involving as it did a violation of their honour, punishment of the living, and retaliation on the infirm and the children.

Even after that, when fate turned against the barbarians, their treatment at the hands of the Muslims was imbued with the Islamic spirit, which was strong enough to check the desire for vengeance in Muslim hearts, and to keep them within the bounds of humanity and religion.

Again, within our own times, the recent war against the Jewish settlers in Palestine had revealed the penetration of the Islamic spirit. Even after the long interval during which Muslims have been divorced from the spirit and traditions of their faith, these have proved effective in keeping the Arab forces from taking vengeance for the most horrible and inhuman crimes committed by the Zionists in the Holy Land. They have been effective in keeping Muslim armies true to the lofty tradition which their religion has maintained for fourteen centuries, and that in the midst of a constant record of inhumanity.

While we are discussing the inner vitality of Islam, we must not overlook the succession of disasters and calamities, both internal and external, to which Islam has been subjected throughout its long history. Yet, it is still a powerful element in human history, and commands the attention even of some occidentals as a means of saving humanity from it present dilemma, as we have already seen in the quotations from Gouilly and Gibb.

Despite the fact that such men are unable fully, to comprehend the Islamic spirit, but confine themselves rather to a review of its practical profit as it now exists, than to an appreciation of its profound spiritual content. For it is difficult for occidentals who have been brought up in the shadow of a deeply rooted materialistic civilization--and such we shall later see that it is-to appreciate this subtle spiritual element.

We have already indicated that the first internal disaster which overtook Islam, namely its subjugation by the Umayyads. This was an interlude which neither permanently affected the practical traditions of Islam nor altered its spiritual exhortations and laws. It did not produce any permanent social principles, any accepted practical traditions, or any rooted practices.

We must now examine quickly the more important developments which befell Islam, and mark their influence through the following centuries. The first of these is to be found in the rise of the Abbasid state, with its reliance on racial elements newly converted to Islam. The attitude of these people to their new religion was never whole-hearted, because of the national loyalties whose roots remained strong within them.

But as time passed on, the Abbasid state deserted these elements on which it had been founded, and which were now beginning to acquire a tincture of Islam, for others whose nucleus was a body of Turks, Circassians, Dailamites and such like. So, this dynasty continued to find its support in elements which were opposed to the spirit of Islam, and to which it gave a favoured position because it relied on them. There was nothing to withstand these racial elements--and hence to withstand the power of the dynasty--except the spirit of Islam, with all the inner force and vitality which it could muster.

Then followed the destructive raids of the Tartars, bursting with savage ferocity on the Islamic world. Without delay Islam turned aside the force of the onslaught, swallowed it up, and assimilated it. Yet, this was not accomplished without causing in the spirit of Islam itself a profound upheaval in which the practices and traditions of this religion were forcibly modified.

Nonetheless in spite of the humiliation of the state by the Tartar onslaught, the Islamic community continued powerful and loyal to its ideals, and constant in the fundamentals of its religion, no matter how far it may have wandered from them in a few purely official aspects.

We must also bear in mind here that the Roman Empire, the building and growth of which had occupied almost a thousand years, was cut off and feli into pieces in a single century, as a result of the incursions of the Huns and Goths; nothing was left of it except a few scattered traces.

However, the Islamic state remained in occupation of a wide territory, although its building had occupied little more than half a century, and though it had to contend with a number of internal struggles between ruling families, as well as the external attacks of the Tartars, and others. Such factors demonstrate the intense vitality of Islam, in that it was able to meet these circumstances.

As we trace the development further, in the West we find the war in Spain, and in the East the disaster of the Crusades. In the first of these Islam was worsted, in the second it was victorious. But from that time to this it has had to contend with ferocious enemies of the same spirit as the Crusaders, enemies both open and hidden.

But the final overthrow of Islam took place only in the present age, when Europe conquered the world, and when the dark shadow of colonization spread over the whole Islamic world, East and West alike. Europe mustered all its forces to extinguish the spirit of Islam, it revived the inheritance of the Crusaders--hatred, and it employed all the materialistic and intellectual powers at its disposal. With these it sought to break down the internal resistance of the Islamic community and to divorce it gradually over a long period from the teachings and the heritage of its religious faith.

When we speak of the hatred of Islam, born of the Crusading spirit, which is latent in the European mind, we must not let ourselves be deceived by appearances, nor can we let their hypocrisy blind us to the fact that they deny to us any freedom of religion. They say, indeed, that Europe is not as unshakably Christian today as it was at the time of the Crusades and that there is nothing today to warrant hostility to Islam, as there was in those days. This is entirely false and inaccurate. General Allen by was no more than typical of the mind of all Europe, when, entering Jerusalem during the First World War, he said:

"Only now have the Crusades come to an end."

Similarly, the Governor of Sudan was no more than typical of the European mind when he placed all governmental power at the disposal of missionaries in the Southern Sudan, while forbidding any Muslim trader even to enter the country. It happened once that a certain official was stationed for a rather long time in South, and so asked for a transfer to the North; it was not granted. He then bethought himself to try lifting up his voice in the Muslim call to prayer; that single act sufficed to ensure his transfer the following day. And England is, of all the European countries, the most tolerant and patient and skilful in reconciling questions of religion.

People sometimes wonder how this obstinate spirit of resistance to Islam can persist so strongly and to such a pitch in a Europe which has discarded Christianity, and where the exhortations of preacher and monk no longer fill European ears as they did in the age of the Crusades. But this fact ceases to be surprising when we take account two facts:

> "The enmity which the Crusaders stirred up was not confined to the clangour of arms, but was, before all else and above everything, an intellectual enmity. The European mind was poisoned by the slurs which the Crusaders' leaders cast on Islam as they spoke of it to their ignorant Western compatriots. It was in that age that there grew up in Europe the ridiculous idea that Islam was a religion of unbridled passion and violent sensuality, that it consisted merely of formal observances, and that it had no teaching of purity or of regeneration of heart. And this idea had remained as it started. It was in this age also that the Messenger, Muhammad, was contemptuously known as

'*My Dog,'*[7] (Mahound).

"This loathing spread space. The ignorant mass of Crusaders had dependents in many places throughout Europe; and the process was hastened by the Spanish Christians in their war to deliver their country from 'the yoke of the idolaters".

But the downfall of Muslim Spain was to require many centuries before it was completed; when this protracted struggle and the constraint which it involved grew too great, a hostility to Islam started to take root in Europe, and ultimately became permanent.

Finally, it took the form of a complete extirpation of Islam throughout Spain after a conflict which reached a pitch of ferocity and bitterness hitherto unknown. The cries of joy which all over Europe greeted this event were unfortunately uttered in ignorance of the consequences which would arise; for the result was that science and learning were blotted out, and in their place came the ignorance and the barbarity of the Middle Ages.

But before the echoes of these happenings in Spain had died away, there took place a third event of immense significance, which was to hasten the breaking of the ties between the Western world and Islam. This was the fall of Constantinople to the Turks. Europe had always looked to Byzantium as a relic of the glory of ancient Greece and Rome, and had regarded it as the fortress of Europe against Asiatic barbarism. In the centuries which followed, and which were filled with wars, the hostility of Europe to Islam was no longer a question of merely academic importance; it was now a question of political import also. And this fact further increased the violence of that hostility.

In addition to all this, Europe derived great profit from this cleavage. The Renaissance or rebirth of European arts and sciences in the widest sense arose particularly from an Islamic and Arab source; in most cases it can be traced back to material contacts between the East and the West. Europe profited more than did the Muslim world, but it did not acknowledge the gift, because it was blinded by its loathing of Islam. Or, more correctly, the reverse is true, that loathing increased with the passage of time, until it was second nature.

At this point loathing swamped all understanding whenever the word 'Muslim' was mentioned; it entered into all their thoughts until it came to form a permanent part of the thinking of every European, man or woman. And still stranger than this is the fact that this feeling continued to flourish even after all the movements of intellectual exchange. Then followed the age of the Reformation, during which Europe was divided into various sects, each continually employed in arming itself against every other; yet hostility to Islam was the common feature of all of them.

This in turn was followed by an age when religious feeling started to subside, but the hostility to Islam continued unabated. One of the clearest proofs of this is that French philosopher and poet, Voltaire, was one of the bitterest critics of Christianity and of the Church in the eighteenth century; yet, he was at the same time violently hostile to Islam and to its Messenger. A few score years later came the age in which Western scholars commenced to study foreign learning and to regard it with a measure of sympathy.

All matters connected with Islam the traditional dislike began to creep in under a form of partisan spirit which was not conducive to academic study. Thus, the gulf which history had dug between Europe and the Islamic world remained still unbridged. Dislike of Islam thus became a fundamental part of European thinking; and the fact that the first Orientalists of the modern age were Christian missionaries who were working in Muslim territory meant that the picture which they formed of the teachings and the history of Islam was distorted; for it was founded on an axiomatic conception that Europeans were superior to 'idolaters'.

Despite the fact that Oriental studies have now been liberated from missionary influence, this intellectual bias had persisted, although any mistaken view can no longer claim the excuse of ill-informed religious zeal. Hence, the attacks made by Orientalists upon Islam betray an inherited characteristic, and a peculiarity of nature; they are based on an impression created by the Crusades, and shaped by all the mental influences of these on the early Europeans. But it will immediately be asked:

> How does it happen that an ancient antipathy such as this, which was originally religious in its basis, and which in the period of its birth owed its inception to the spiritual mastery of the Christian Church, can persist in Europe in an age when religious convictions are no more than a matter of antiquarian interest?

There is never anything surprising in such a situation; for it is well known to psychology that men may lose all the religious beliefs which they held in their youth, and at the same time retain some of their personal idiosyncrasies, even those which formerly centered upon the very religious beliefs which they have now discarded. It is these idiosyncrasies which provide the intellectual motivation for every act of such men. This is the state which obtains in Europe regarding Islam.

Despite the fact that the religious convictions which gave rise to European hostility to Islam have now lost their power and been replaced by a more materialistic form of life, yet the ancient antipathy itself still remains as a vital element to pour a secret poison into the European mind. So far as the strength of this antipathy is concerned, it undoubtedly varies from one individual to another, but that it exists is indisputable. The spirit of the Crusades, though perhaps in a milder form, still hangs over Europe: and that civilization in its dealings with the Islamic world still occupies a position which bears clear traces of the early Crusader spirit."[8]

European imperial interests can never forget that the spirit of Islam is firmly opposed to the spread of imperialism. Such an opposition must either be crushed or at least diverted. No weight need be attached to the contention of gullible or mercenary writers that religion is of no concern to Europeans, that the source of European power is not religious, and that the only thing about the Muslim world which Europe fears is its material power. Fundamentally, religion is a spiritual power which is always effective for the provision of material powers.

Islam is essentially different from Christianity; it encourages the fostering of material powers, it enjoins self-defence and defencive war, and it warns the weaklings who tamely submit that theirs will be an evil fate in this world and in the next.

> "Prepare for them as much as you can in the way of forces and cavalry, with which you may overcome Allah's enemies and your own."[9]
>
> "Do not take unbelievers for your friends in preference to Believers."[10]
>
> "So let those fight in the way of Allah who would exchange the life of this world for that of the next."[11]

"Do not grow weary or grieve now that you have the upper hand, if you are true Believers..., etc."[12]

Spiritual and Material Powers of Islam

Islam is at once a spiritual power and an incentive to material power; it is at once a form of opposition in itself, and an incentive to a still more forcible opposition. Therefore, European imperialism cannot but be hostile to such a religion. The only difference lies in the fact that the form of that hostility varies according to the imperialistic methods of each nation, and according to local conditions. Thus, for example, France declared open war on Islam in the Western Arab world, under the name of "Protecting the Berbers," or some such phrase. But England took a more devious and tortuous road to the same end in Egypt, that of education.

Its aim was to encourage the growth of a general frame of mind which would despise the bases of Islamic life, and even of Eastern life. When this was accomplished there would be a generation educated into this frame of mind, ready to go out into the schools and educational offices to imbue the coming generations with the same ideas.

These would set a fashion in manners and customs which would ultimately lead to the permanent establishment of the desired frame of mind, and would emphasize the difference between the basic elements of Islamic education and the policies of the Education Ministry. Thus, England could dispense with open hostilities as a means of opposition to religious convictions. And this objective was actually ascribed by a large and influential party to a desire to establish a pan-Egyptian mentality. In the Southern Sudan, again, there was no call for such guile; the position there was simply that which we have already described in speaking of the Christian missionaries and the Muslim merchants.

Thus, each imperialist state has proceeded by one means or another to oppose and to throttle Islam since the last century, and even before that. And that they still proceed to do essentially the same thing in concert is obvious from the position taken up by the United Nations on the question of Indonesia and Holland, on that of Kashmir, India and Pakistan, and on that of Hyderabad, India and the Nizam. Finally the same thing is supremely evident in the position of the United Nations on Palestine.

There are those who hold that it is the financial influence of the Jews in the United States and elsewhere which has governed the policy of the West. There are those who say that it is English ambition and Anglo-Saxon guile which are responsible for the present position. And there are those who believe that it is the antipathy between East and West which is responsible. All these opinions overlook one vital element in the question, to which all other elements are subordinate, the Crusader spirit which runs in the blood of all occidentals.

It is this which colours all their thinking, which is responsible for their imperialistic fear of the spirit of Islam, and for their efforts to crush Arab strength. For the instincts and the interests of all occidentals are bound up together in the crushing of that strength. This is the common factor which links together Communist Russia and Plutocratic America.

The truly remarkable thing is that the spirit of Islam has survived all these attacks which have been launched against it from the earliest period of its life right up to the present. It has persisted, in spite of sudden assaults and the effect which these have had on its life; it had lasted out, in spite of the modern conquest by Western civilization with its material and educational weapons, from which some Muslims have borrowed the means of breaking down and destroying Islam at the direction of imperialistic powers.

Despite all these things, the spirit of Islam has remained essentially sound, and its inner force had left clear imprints on the course of human life in the broadest sense. Islam has left its marks on the forms and objectives of civil government throughout fourteenth centuries to the present day. There is no political or military institution in the world that owes something to Islam; and this has been true even in those ages when the Muslim world has been weak and divided, when it has seen its spiritual, social, and economic life disturbed.

But the period of obscurity and weakness is now at an end, and the tide of Islam has commenced to rise. In East and West alike the Arab world is gaining unity, and two great Islamic blocs have made an appearance in Pakistan and Indonesia. These are portents which cannot be overlooked, significant of the underlying vitality of Islam. They are significant also of the massive resources of Islam, sufficient to bring about a complete renewal of Islamic life. Such a renewal need not be based merely on wishful thinking or on good fortune; rather it may be based on actual concrete facts which are apparent to the sight.

I personally, quite apart from the religious faith, have an absolute belief in the possibility of a renewal of Islamic life within the Muslim world. I believe in the soundness of Islam as a world-wide, rather than a local, system for the future. I have no desire to take refuge in vain speculation, but I do believe this to be not only possible, but even easy.

Not that there will not be various and vast difficulties; there will also be great tasks which must be accomplished before the complete renewal of Islamic life can take place with any facility within Muslim society. The assessment of these vast obstacles, and the inspiration to undertake the tasks involved is something which is necessitated by any true understanding of the immensity of the goal at which we are aiming, and of the weight of responsibility awaiting any man who aims at that goal. It is something which is necessitated also by an understanding of the importance of public opinion in such vast undertakings.

But, it is not enough for any one man to issue a ringing call for hope to become actuality, and expectation reality. The results and the consequences must be assessed, and the man who exhorts others must equally offer to them the same vast effort which he demands of them.

In the very nature of the case, the wide divergence between existing political theory and the spirit of Islam, which has arisen over a long period and has hence become deep-seated, will make it a matter of some difficulty to return to a theory which is truly based on that spirit. For the machinery of the state and of society, the foundations of life in all its aspects, the spiritual and intellectual background are all so build up on specific bases that they are difficult to change without the application of vast energy over a long time. And the longer the time, the greater the difficulty, and the greater the need for yet vaster and longer enduring effort.

The time factor is linked up with another consideration in the present age. We do no live only in this world, but we cannot live in isolation from it. Thus, our interests and our needs are interwoven with this present world, which is governed by a certain form of civilization, involving an outlook completely contradictory to that of Islam. This we shall see later. In one respect this fact will slow down our progress along the path of renewing the true Islamic form of life, and in another respect, it will lay additional responsibilities upon us.

The importance of this last consideration is enhanced by the fact that this Western world with which our interests are interwoven is at the present moment stronger than we; we do not have today the control over it, or the strength equal to its strength, that we had in the first age of Islam. At the same time, it is hostile to us, and in particular hostile to our religion. Therefore, it will not permit us to produce a new Islamic system, or to renew a truly Islamic form of life, however great the effort we put forth. This result we could hope for only if we had control of the Western world, if our strength were comparable to its, or if it were honest with us and with our religion to which we seek to return.

But all this does not mean that return to the Islamic system is impossible. All that it means is that this is a great and difficult task, requiring unremitting effort. Above all it demands courage to believe in it, boldness to face the inevitable results, patience to endure the hard work demanded, and faith to believe that this is necessary for Islamic society and for mankind as a whole. It demands the fostering of a new mentality, whose task will not be simply to elevate the existing state of things, but rather to produce a new and perfect state.

This is our task. We have already seen the foundations on which the system must be built; thus, we can now balance the profits which we shall enjoy if we return to it against the labours and sacrifices which we must make in order to realize it. When our faith in these profits reaches the point at which they outweigh the sacrifices, then let us settle the matter, make up our kinds, and leave the result with Allah.

Perhaps one valuable aspect of the present situation might be pointed out here. The great Western civilization has led the world into two global wars within a quarter of a century; after the second of these it has led it to a complete division into two blocs, an eastern and a western, and to the constant threat of a third war.

It has brought about a state of hostility in every quarter, it has produced starvation and destitution and adversity throughout three parts of the world. It should be pointed out also that the social fabric of the whole world today is in that state of insecurity and instability where it must look for new foundations and search for some spiritual means of restoring to man his faith in the principles of humanity.

We must not, however, read more than is legitimate into this readiness of the Western world to accept the foundations of our Islamic civilization; this is another matter. Although it may be it noted that such a man as Bernard Shaw says that the West had already started to turn in this direction, and even prophesied that it well come to it eventually, in these words:

> "I forecast that the religion of Muhammad will be accepted in Europe in the near future, for it has already started to gain some acceptance. The priests of the Middle Ages insisted on portraying Islam in the darkest colours, either out of ignorance, or from criminal bigotry; but they were led to excess by their hatred of Muhammad and his religion; indeed they held him to be the anti-Christ. For myself I find it preferable to call Muhammad the savior of mankind, and I believe that if such a man were given authority over the modern world, he would succeed in solving its problems and giving it peace and happiness. And how great is the world's need of these things."

Western Perspective of Islam

There were some impartial thinkers in the nineteenth century who discovered how much value there is in the religion of Muhammad. Among them were Carlyle, Goethe, and Gibbon. From this fact, there has arisen a salutary change in the attitude of Europe towards Islam. Thus, Europe has seen a great advance in the past years of the twentieth century, and has even started to respect the faith of Muhammad.

It may be that in the century that lies ahead, Europe will make further progress, and will acknowledge the contribution of this faith towards a solution of its problems. Many among may own nation and among all European nations already belong to the religion of Muhammad, a fact which enables us to say that the conversion of Europe to Islam has already begun.[13]

But so far as we can see Shaw's prophecy is still no more than a prophecy--if, indeed, it is not intended to drug the senses of Muslims and to make them content to wait idly for Europe to embrace their faith. But, however, this may be, we must at least wait until time has proved such a statement, for two principal reasons:

1. There is this deep-seated and inherited hostility toIslam in the very European nature itself. This is at present augmented by the opposition of imperialistic interests to the very existence of our faith, as being an obstacle in their path.
2. European culture is rooted in material foundations, and the influence of intellectual and spiritual interests are very weak; such has been the case from the time ofRoman civilization to the present day. This matter requires detailed consideration, and a full treatment, rather than merely a brief mention. So, we must here make an extended study of this important question: Is it possible for Islamic and Western civilizations to work together in partnership? And if so, then what are the limits of that partnership?

We have already asserted at the beginning of this book that Europe was never at any time truly Christian, because by its very nature its people had to fight over their meagre territories. Thus, the tolerant principles of Christianity could gain no footing in such a stubborn ground. In addition to this, Christianity is essentially an asceticism, a refusal to live, or to take an interest in, a practical worldly life. To these two factors we must now add a third, to which we have already made a passing reference.

This factor was the existence of the Roman Empire, and its position to thwart the path of Christianity, together with the permanent influence of that empire on the bases of European civilization even today. And that despite the infusion of Christianity which the Roman Empire received in its last days.

We may quote here some passages from*Islam at the Crossroads*, which we find completely satisfactory: The doctrine on which the Roman Empire was founded was to destroy by force, or to exploit other people for the sole benefit of the mother country. In order to indulge this privileged body the Romans saw nothing wrong in their violence and nothing humiliating in their oppression.

The famous Roman justice was a justice for Romans only. It is apparent that such a tendency as this is possible only on the basis of a materialistic ideal, which is wholly devoted to wordly life and civilization--though it may be an ideal promoted and shaped by a philosophical taste.

In any case it was far removed from any appreciation of spiritual values. The Romans did not really understand religion; their traditional Gods were only variant forms of the Greek myths which, as being mere shades, were never believed to have any connection with social affairs, and which were never permitted to interfere in any way with the real business of life. Their duty was to speak in metre through the agency of their attendant priests, when questions were asked of them; but no one ever expected them to enunciate laws for the guidance of mankind.

Such was the soil in which modern Western civilization grew up, though during the period of its growth it undoubtedly came under many other influences. Thus, in the very nature of the case, it changed and thereby modified the legacy which it had received from Rome in more than one way. Nevertheless the fact remains that all that is truly great in the modern West, whether of life or nature, owes its origin to Roman civilization. Hence, since, the intellectual and social environment of ancient Rome was always secular rather than religious--and that no exhypothesi, but in actual fact--so the same environment persists in the modern West.

The European mind has neither possible argument against the complete futility of religion nor will it ever admit the need for such an argument. For modern European thinking in general leaves the absolute outside its scheme of practical considerations--although-- it does tolerate religion, and even at times may assert that it is a social virtue. Western civilization does not irrevocably disown God, but it can see no place and no significance for Him in its present intellectual system. It has made a virtue out of a philosophical inability on the part of man, that is to say, out of his inability to take a comprehensive view of the whole field of life.

European, modern Europe tends to attach the greatest practical importance to the values deriving from the experimental sciences, or at least from those sciences from which may be expected some perceptible influence of human social relationships. And because the question of the existence of God does not fall into either of these categories, the European mind tends to drop the concept of God out of the sphere of practical considerations. A question emerges here:

> "How is this tendency to be reconciled with Christian thought? Is not Christianity a faith founded on the Absolute, as is Islam? And is it not ostensibly the spiritual background of Western civilization? There is no doubt that all these things are true. But there could not be any greater mistake than to imagine that Western civilization is the outcome of Christianity. The true philosophical basis of the Western system is to be sought in the ancient Roman view of life as a matter of advantage, quite independent of absolute values."

It is a view which can be summarized thus: Because we have no specific knowledge, either in the way of practical experience, or in that of proof, about the fundamentals of human life, or about its destiny after physical death; therefore, it is best for us to confine our powers to those material and mental fields which are accessible to us, rather than let ourselves to be tied down to metaphysical and moral questions arising from claims which can have no intellectual proofs.

Such an argument as this which is characteristic of modern Western civilization, will certainly not find acceptance in Christian thought, as it will not in Islam or in any other religion, simply because it is essentially religious. Thus, to try to establish a causal relationship between Christianity and modern Western civilization, is a gross historical error.

Christianity may indeed have played a very small part in the rise of intellectual materialism which today dominates modern Western civilization, but the truth is that the growth of this spirit had been the product of Europe's prolonged struggle against the Christian Church, and against its supervision of life. In its general aspect Christianity today is a purely spiritual thing, as was the case with the Roman deities, which were neither permitted nor expected to exert any real influence on society.

No doubt there are in the West individuals who are still prepared to judge and to think on a religious basis, prepared to fight a last ditch action to reconcile their beliefs with the spirit of their civilization; but they cannot be more than isolated cases. To Europe as a whole it is a matter of indifference whether the political system is 'democratic or fascist, plutocratic or bolshevist, technical or intellectual.'

Europe knows but one necessary religion--the worship of material prosperity; the only belief that it holds is that there is but one goal in life--the making of that life easier and easier. It is, as the definition has it in significant terms, an escape from the tyranny of nature.' The shrines of such a culture are huge factories and cinemas, chemical laboratories and dance-halls and power stations. The priests of such a worship are bankers and mathematicians, cinema stars and scientists and aviators.

The inevitable result of this state of affairs is that man strives to gain power a pleasure; this brings into being quarrelsome societies, all armed to the teeth and intent on mutual destruction whenever their conflicting interests come into active opposition. On the intellectual side, the upshot has been the evolution of a humanism with a moral philosophy confined to purely scientific questions, in which the highest criterion of good or evil is whether or not any given thing represents material progress.

The sum and substance of all this is that the present-day European conscience is not ready to accept the spirit of Islam, or to seek in it a solution of human problems. But even so, it is not impossible that even this may take place after a number of other changes and developments in the West, and after the Islamic world itself has entered upon a clearly defined and independent renewal of Islamic life. In this, the West may find philosophical realities and practical truths which will attract its attention and balance its thinking. But it is my personal belief that many generations must elapse before the West will be able to appreciate the spirit of Islam in any real sense.

Again, the substance of this argument is that the mode of the Muslim doctrine that work must serve moral ends, cannot be reconciled with the mode of the modern Western doctrine that morals must serve some material advantage. We must reckon with this fact, and hence we must work to establish a sound form of Islamic life; this cannot be achieved by the importation of elements borrowed from abroad, since such elements will not fit into the texture of our native beliefs.

The Muslim world will have to admit defeat on the first occasion on which it seeks to renew its own life by borrowing Western ways of thought, life and custom. Such an experiment can only result in the suffocation of that very form of life which it seeks to revive; for from the very first step the Muslim world will be departing from its own true and natural path.

This path involves a belief based on Islam that the moral element is fundamental to the structure of life; it regards work as a means to moral ends, and it will not make material advantage the highest aim of morals. We have already seen in an earlier chapter of this book that Islam satisfies all the highest aims of life, among them the moral consciousness. We have also seen that Islam's supreme virtue is that it preserves the unity of life, and that it makes no distinction between the means and the ends. It will not lend its authority to any idea that there is an opposition between material and spiritual in the substance of life or in the nature of the universe or of mankind; rather it emphasized that the whole of life is a unity which must make an orderly progress towards the highest objectives.

Islam, then, enunciates for men a complete theory of life. This theory is always liable to growth by development or by adaptation; it is not open to change or to adulteration, either in its fundamentals or in its general aims. Therefore, in order that this complete theory may bear its full natural fruits, it is necessary to make a complete application of it. Otherwise, even the slightest change in its fundamentals or its aims will produce a disorder, because it will no longer be in conformity with the Islamic conception of life.

The continual growth of this universal theory by development or by adaptation is a natural product of the nature of Islam; it is encouraged by Islam, the institutions of which are adapted to recognize it. Analogy, interpretation, and the wide powers entrusted to the head of the state --all these are living methods of ensuring growth through development and adaptation, in order to keep pace with life and to meet its needs as they emerge. But there is one thing which must be kept in mind: these developments must not pass out with the roots of the fundamental Islamic theory, nor must they be allowed to serve any foreign aim; they must not betray the spirit of Islam or give allegiance to any other spirit in preference to it.

The criterion by which we may accept or reject any development is first to compare it with the basic theory and the general spirit of Islam. Anything that is in agreement with this theory and this spirit we may accept, and anything which is contrary to these we must reject. Thus, we may profit by all the fruits of human labour within the bounds of our basic philosophy of the universe, man and life; we need raise no barriers between ourselves and human endeavour, nor need we stand in isolation from the continuous business of living.

Above all we must be firmly convinced of the value of faith and enthusiasm; we have a scheme of life greater than any possessed by the followers of any religion or school or civilization which has yet been born. And that is to say the least of it.

No renaissance of Islamic life can be effected purely by law or statute, or by the establishment of a social system on the basis of the Islamic philosophy. Such a step is only one of the two pillars on which Islam must always stand in its construction of life. The other is the production of a state of mind imbued with the Islamic theory of life, to give permanence to external forces leading to this form of life, and to give coherence to all the social, religious and civil legislations.

Social justice is an integral part of this Islamic life. It cannot be realized unless this form of life is first realized, and it cannot have any guaranteed permanence unless this form of life is built up on solid foundations. It is similar in this to all other social systems; it must have the support of public belief and confidence in its merits. Failing this, its foundations will be purely spiritual, and its establishment will depend on the force of religious and social legislation; these are too weak to sustain it, in which case it may easily miscarry.

Hence, Islamic legislation is more akin to ecclesiastical ordinance because it depends on religious belief. Thus, we must always keep in mind the necessity for a renaissance of our religious faith; we must cleanse it of all accretions, such as alterations and interpretations and ambiguities; only thus can it be a support for the necessary social legislation which will establish a sound form of Islamic life. This form of life will depend upon legislation and exhortation, those twin fundamental methods of Islam towards the achievement of all aims.

We must, then, establish our Islamic theory in individuals and societies, at the same time as we set up the Islamic legislation to regulate life. And the natural method of establishing that philosophy is by education.

But how can we possibly induce Islamic theory by education? For educational methods and modes of thought are essentially Western and essentially inimical to the Islamic philosophy itself; first, because they stand on a materialistic basis which is contrary to the Islamic theory of life; and second, because opposition to Islam is a fundamental part of their nature, no matter whether such opposition is manifest or concealed in various forms.

As we have already maintained, we shall advertise our defeat the first time that we adopt a Western theory of life as the means of reviving our Islamic theory. So, primarily, we must avoid the ways of Western thought; rather we must choose the ways of native Islamic thought, in order to ensure pure results.

The import of these words is not that we should adopt a position of isolationism in regard to thought, education, and science; all these are a common heritage of all the peoples of the world, in which we among the foremost have a fundamental part. We shall continue to take our rightful share in the furtherance of these things, even if it should become apparent that we are far removed from the influence which they exert. For the only true and permanent form of cooperation is that between all the nations of the Earth.

Isolation from human life, then, is not our aim; rather what we seek is to build up a characteristically Islamic theory of life, and to renew that form of life now, when it is apparent even to some of the more enlightened occidentals that the philosophy of materialistic Western civilization is a danger to the continued existence of man.

It breeds in human nature a ceaseless anxiety, a perpetual rivalry, a continual strife, and a weakening of human ties to the breaking point. And this is spite of all the triumphs of science which could have tended to human happiness and peace and content, had it not been that the bases of the Western philosophy of life were purely materialistic and hence unsuitable to men along the path to perfection.

As long as our aim is the building up of this Islamic theory along these lines, we must make a distinction between things which we may profitably accept, and those which we may profitably reject, out of Western society. Only thus may we complete the building of an Islamic society out of sound materials which will produce a structure secure against cooperation and opposition alike, against both borrowing and giving.

From another point of view we must ensure to the theory of life which we establish a safeguard in the form of a period of fostering...fostering, that is, in our own minds rather than in its own essence. For Islamic life in itself is a strong and definite thing when in does not stand in awe of any other Western form. Rather, it is we who need to be fostered and nurtured, as we are living on a strange diet hence we must be on our guard while we are engaged in the establishment of our new system.

In the case of the pure sciences and their applied results of all kinds, we must not hesitate to utilize all things in the sphere of material life; our use of them should be unhampered and unconditional, unhesitating and unimpeded.

Similarly, we must be careful to derive the fullest profit from other things also; from philosophy, which is the intellectual treatment of the universe and life; from literature which is the emotional treatment of these things; from history, which is a factual treatment, and from legislation, which is a treatment of the relationships between individuals and societies.

It will do us no harm to make use of the pure sciences in all the spheres of life; but on the other hand, it will do us harm to account these as the sum total of life; for such a view involves a philosophy which is not ours. It tends to establish a conception of the universe and of life which is at variance with the Islamic conception of those things; ultimately, it would led us along a path which is not that of Islam. It is this path which has produced the present ailments of mankind, and which is responsible for their present troubles.

It is sometimes objected that even if this be so, the pure sciences themselves cannot be held responsible, because essentially they cannot be divorced from the method of Western thought. The experimental method rests on the basis of a definite philosophy which is neither intellectual nor spiritual; if this had never established itself in favour, science would never have followed the course which lately it has taken.

In the same way, science can never remain in isolation from philosophy, nor can it be content to be influenced by philosophy without in turn influencing it. For philosophy benefits by the experimental results of science, and is influenced by it in aim and method.

Thus, a study of pure science involves a study of philosophy, which is influenced by that science, and which in turn exerts an influence on it. All this is over and above the fact that the applied results of science must influence all material life, methods of gaining a living, and the division of wealth. All this will in due time produce new forms of society based on a new philosophy, or at least based on a theory of life which must be influenced by these developments in the course of life.

All this is very true. But what must be there is no possibility of living in isolation from science and its products, though the harm that it does may be greater than the good. There is no such thing in this life as an unmixed blessing or an unalloyed evil. Thus, Islam does not oppose science, or the utilization of science; there is nothing contrary to the spirit of Islam in culling the fruits of science from all the sources of the world.

But while we may acknowledge the universal influences of philosophy and culture, history and law, together with all their consequences in the way of educational methods and modes of thought and logic, we must set all of this in its proper place on a spiritual Islamic foundation. We must hold to the guiding principle that all the results and material consequences of science do not essentially affect our universal philosophy of life and custom.

When we mention educational methods we might well bear in mind here that these are indivisible and inseparable from the general philosophy of the community. Thus, when we borrow Western methods of education, systems of training and curricula, we borrow also a general scheme of philosophy and a mode of thought which underlies these methods and systems and curricula, whether we like it or not.

There is a belief that these are questions of pure 'pedagogy', and therefore universal and identical throughout all countries. This is a naive and shortsighted belief, encouraged by the delusion of the psychologists, who give an undue weight to their own subject; despite the difference between psychology and philosophy, such men believe that they can master their own subject, and through it can answer the philosophical questions of education also.

That claim is one thing, but the actual fact is quite another. Psychology may perhaps be a pure science to be studied in the laboratory. But the treatment of its results and the use to which these are put, such as educational techniques and curricula--all these things are still influenced by the general philosophy of life, still accept the dictation of that philosophy, and still form an integral part of it.

Moreover, the very fact that psychology is ruled by the laboratory is one of the influences exerted by experimental philosophy, or by the experimental method. It is this same method which in later years has governed all materialistic Western thought. The only type of independence which psychology can expect from the philosophy which is its mentor is that superficial independence which cannot influence the final result.

For an example, we may look to the American curriculum, their methods of education and instruction. these are more akin to vocational training than to any system of thorough and systematic study; they have as their objective the promotion of technical skill based on theoretical principles. The reason for this tendency is to be sought in the philosophy of pragmatism, founded by Charles Pierce in 1878 which was advanced by William James and applied by John Dewey, the modern educational philosopher. This school of thought represents a reversal of the accepted terms of thought and study: bare ideas and theoretical principles are abandoned, as is the study of things according to their logical class and nature. According to Pragmatism all study should be confined to the practical effects and result of objects.

According to Charles Pierce of Pragmatism the idea is no more than a secondary product of some act or activity; it is not in itself a reality. For example, I may have the 'idea' of the horn of an automobile passing in the street; this 'idea' gains no meaning by my study of its nature, its origin, and the method of its production. It may be a reality or it may be a figment of imagination; it may be produced by the ear and the nervous system, or it may be produced by the horn, whether, the automobile is turning right or left, and whether a path must be cleared for the vehicle and its driver. It means only:

> "I am about to change the direction of my vehicle and to proceed in a different direction. Hence, Pragmatism argues that the idea is secondary to the act, or the product of certain conditioning circumstances. This is the first step along the path of Pragmatism in which all the remaining steps must follow."[14]

It has been the rise of this theory or this method of thought which has produced the educational techniques of America. It has been responsible for a teaching curriculum and a system which will encourage the mind to take this view of things and to rationalize life along this line. Also, it is this which has given American life its most characteristic mark, which has directed it towards technical production, and which has to a large extent diverted it from academic and theoretical education.

Accordingly, we must reckon with this general philosophy of life; if we borrow educational techniques, teaching systems, and curricula, this philosophy underlines all of them. This philosophy shapes and forms them, assisted by the results of pure psychology. Such an influence is inevitable, though this same science in its methods and in its results is itself influenced by that very philosophy.

From the theoretical point of view, then, our method of establishing an independent Islamic scheme of thought is to proceed readily but cautiously in the matter of borrowing such a philosophy along with its concomitants, such as educational techniques, teaching systems and curricula, literature, history and law. But we shall deal now with all these subjects together.

Universe and Mankind

So far as the study of philosophy is concerned, we have already indicated the universal theory of Islam on the universe, life and mankind. this is essentially different from the nature of other universal philosophies which have originated in the West from the days of the Greeks to the present. This is not the place to discuss this difference, and it will suffice to recognize merely that there does exist a radical divergence.[15]

A petition of peculiar importance was once addressed to the Azhar University concerning a matter which was not favourably regarded in this quarter. It requested that study be directed to this universal Islamic theory of life and that a full and clear treatment of it be given in modern terms and applications; also that it be compared with other schools of philosophy. But the Azhar, instead of responding to this petition, continued to teach in its Faculty of Theology what it called the errors of Islamic philosophy, taken from the writings of Ibn-Sina and Ibn-Rushd.

This is, of course, a reversion to Greek philosophy, which has no real connection with the universal philosophy of Islam. Thus, in effect the petition sent to the governors of the Azhar was neglected, and a spiritual and intellectual defeat was acknowledged in our primary seat of learning, a defeat for the Islamic theory of life.

If, then, we are to establish a sound Islamic theory of the universe, life and mankind, it is essential that Western philosophies and their moral corollaries should not be studied at all in our secondary schools, and that they should be studied in the university only after at least two years in the department of philosophy. And by the very nature of the case they should not be studied in the Azhar colleges until the very end of the course. In every centre of study such Western philosophies should be preceded by a course in pure Islamic thought, as distinct from the so-called "Islamic philosophy," in order to emphasize the true Islamic viewpoint.

Thus, the minds and thoughts of the students will assimilate the native bases of the spirit of Islam, together with its ideas on the universe, life and mankind, good and evil, work and reward, and all the other philosophic aspects of pure Islamic belief. This having been assured, we may in the later years of university study proceed to give some account of the other philosophies; these would include Greek philosophy and its opposition to Islamic, modern European and American philosophy; these should be compared in every case with Islamic philosophy.

In this way, we can ensure that the student's mind and conscience will not be too much influenced; we can ensure also a minimum influence on student's ideas and thoughts, because by then they will be equipped for critical appreciation. They will have the requisite knowledge to reject all that does not agree with the fundamental modes of thought of a Muslim people. Under these circumstances their new knowledge will not harm, but will rather benefit students; for it will be purely academic knowledge, largely independent of any influence on their conscience or on their conception and understanding of life and its requirements.

We have already given one example of pragmatism in its view of things. But in this example, there was no indication of the dangers inherent in that philosophy or in its method; so we must now follow out this philosophy in its further results, in order to note the dangerous influences of its intellectual system on any a nation which follows such modern of thought.

Most people believe in God. This is an idea which logically may be either false or true. Intellectual theory says:

> "If God really exists, then His existence must be logically demonstrable. Pragmatism on the other hand attacks the problem from a different angle, and lays the emphasis on a different aspect. In its view the truth of the idea of God does not depend on logical necessity; it depends solely on the profit of this idea to our well-ordered life, in our daily activity and on our experiences. If the idea tends to produce a profit in life, then it is sound and therefore true. Hence, God does exist. Apart from this test, pragmatism claims, in the first place we cannot judge this idea; and in the second place we cannot trust our own judgement."[6]

The Islamic line of thought differs to a greater or lesser extent from that of pure intellectual theory, insofar as it does not entrust the whole question to human logic alone, but relies also upon revelation. But it is in complete opposition to pragmatism; for when we follow out its logic to a conclusion we find that the idea of God must disappear if the outward benefits of material life are not forthcoming.

The idea of God loses its existence because it cannot control its instruments and set the machinery in motion. In consequence, material profit becomes the sole criterion, not only of the acceptance or the rejection of things, but also of existence or non-existence. This implies a state of affairs in which man loses all nobility, where he is neither more nor less than an instrument.

Policies in this world cannot be divorced from such philosophies. Thus perhaps, we are not far from the truth when we say that the policy of the United State on the Palestine question and its stand in the United Nations on the question of Egypt were merely the results of its intellectual background of pragmatism-- in conjunction, of course, with other factors.

The idea of right and justice had little effective place in materialistic American life; and hence it had little chance of permanent acknowledgement in international policies. This idea is perhaps the most satisfactory comment on these puzzling policies. What we do not want is to establish such an intellectual background as this, in our Islamic society. We must therefore be cautious about the study of Western philosophy until we have first established in adolescent minds a firm, strong, and clear pattern of thought which is founded on the universal Islamic theory.

Similarly, we must be cautious about borrowing educational techniques, curricula, and systems of teaching; for all of these are ruled by the general field of philosophy in their native lands; they subserve the aims which that philosophy assigns to them, whether immediate or remote.

Moral Philosophy of Life

Literature is the emotional response to life. It issues from the same well-spring whence flow in any culture all the philosophies, the religious beliefs, the experiments and the influences Literature is the most important factor in the establishment of a moral philosophy of life, and in the production of any specific influence on the human mind. Hence, we must exercise care in the choice of Western literature which we make available to our youth, alike in their Arabic and their foreign studies.

It is not necessary to take this as meaning that our youth are to be prohibited from reading European literature; what we have in mind here is simply a process of choice and selection. For in this literature, there are elements, the spirit of which is at one with the spirit of Islam. By this, we do not mean that such books 'encourage goodness and-reprobate wickedness' for literature is no preacher to exhort and to direct. Rather, we mean that such books have a view of life which is spiritual and moral, rather than materialistic, and that they acknowledge the spiritual values of life.

This type of literature agrees in spirit with the general teachings of our Islamic theory; it can therefore do no harm to the moral consciousness of our youth, nor can it upset their emotional and mental development at a dangerous stage. This dangerous stage lasts at least until the third year of university work, if not until the time of graduation.

There is no harm, but rather great benefit, in having private reading include all types of the literatures of the world, without restraint or exception. But the prime aim of a process of choice and selection is to safeguard the period of adolescence from being debilitated and led astray.

History is a branch of literature; but it is one which has its own characteristics, and which therefore had also its peculiar dangers. For history is a presentation of the events of life, and it is necessarily influenced by the materialistic background of the West. Even if it is by intellectual theory that it is influenced, it will still ignore the spiritual powers and their effect on the course of events, together with the spiritual explanation of facts. It will give its own interpretations, designed to establish a philosophy of life independent of the spirit and unconnected with moral aims. Here, it is opposed to Islamic theory.

Beyond this, historians,who have been for the most part Europeans, have made the history of Europe the focal point of world history. In view of the nature of man this is excusable, and we have borne it with patience as a characteristically Western and European delusion. Yet, if our youth are to study history in this spirit and by this method, then they will finish with two false beliefs:

1. That spiritual factors have no influence on the course of events in time, or at least that any such influence is very weak.
2. That Europe is the mistress of historical events, and that the influence of the East and of Islam is exiguous.

Both these ideas have harmful and dangerous results; they establish a false general idea of life, of the world, and of events, and they endanger our patriotic pride and our pride in Islam, which is so necessary in face of the sweeping pride of Europe. In order to guard our youth from this evil we must take the two following steps:

1. We must begin by putting general world history, as Islam views it, in perspective, in the form of events and happenings. We must not be concerned solely with theEuropean point of view in this present dangerous fashion. In such a history we must give Europe its rightful place and no more, and we must emphasize the part played in world history by the East in general, and by Islam in particular.
2. We must change the present curriculum of history teaching in our schools and colleges. We must start by teaching primarily the history of Islam throughout the Muslim world, and by expounding it from the Islamic point of view. It is not enough to teach our children the history of Islam as written by Western authors, or as expounded by Western philosophies. When their minds are filled with the history of their own countries, then we can give them the world history as written by ourselves, to form the next stage of study. And when they have completed that,then we can give them in successive stages the remainder of the developments of history.

The study of law is similarly influenced by the Western point of view, by Western philosophy, history, law, and society. For law is a reflection of society, or is produced by it; and society is the offspring of all these factors.

In order to build up a sound Islamic doctrine, we must teach Islamic law in a broad general way before beginning to teach any specific legal system. The teaching of Islamic law must be firmly in the control of Muslim professors, and the Western point of view must not be allowed to obtrude, except in the later stages. Similarly, the study of law in general must not be opened up till that same later stage.

It is one of the requirements of Islamic life that the religious law shall occupy a paramount position; and that very fact will make necessary such a study of Islamic law as we have indicated. The great necessity which faces our professors of Islamic law in this field is to follow the authoritative path traced out by the Imams and their students at the time of the first growth of Islamic law.

When we have disposed of this theoretical question of the objective, we are still confronted by that of the specific constitutional enactments which will ensure a sound form of Islamic life and which will guarantee social justice to all. In this question, it is not possible to take a stand purely on the form of the original Islamic life; rather we must utilize all possible and permissible means which fall within the general principles and the broad foundations of Islam. Nor must we be afraid to use also all the discoveries which man has made in the way of social legislation and systems, so long as the principles of these do not run counter to the principles of Islam, and so long as they are not opposed to its theory of life and mankind.

We must include these in our legislation so long as they conduce to the true welfare of society, or so long as they ward off any impending evil. In the two principles of 'public interest' and 'blocking of means' we have two clear Islamic principles which give wide powers to the temporal ruler to ensure the general welfare at all times and in all places. Before we go on to deal with the application of these two principles it might be well to quote a short passage in explanation of them.[17]

Public Interest as Enunciated by Islamic Thought

Any welfare measure which has no specific detailed authority to support it is known as a measure of public interest. The question of whether or not it is a root of jurisprudence is a matter of dispute among the jurisconsults. Al-Qarafi has argued that all the jurisconsults have used it or have admitted it as a proof at one time or another, even though in lecturing most of them deny it the status of a root. He says in regard to this point:

> "Other people loudly deny the validity of public interest. But when the case is closely examined, they are found to refer to the word in its absolute sense. They do not trouble to take any account of the evidence offered by the reference of the term in its synonyms and contexts; they hold that it means merely convenience, and that such is the sole meaning of the phrase, public interest."[18]

No matter whether this claim is true or false, it is certain that the validity of any measure of welfare which lacks a specific validating authority is a matter on which the ulema may well disagree. And even if public interest is not one of the accepted roots of jurisprudence, at least it had the status of a custom, as Al-Qarafi indicates. The opinions of the ulema in this matter can be divided into four main views, as follows![19]

1. The Shafi'ites and those who share their opinions do not believe in any form of public interest whose validity is unsupported by legal evidence; for they only admit legal precedents and the treatment of these by analogy, based on the existence of a solid connection between the root and its derivatives, that is to say, between a case governed by a precedent and another analogous to it. If we follow Al-Qarafi we must admit that it is strange that they should deny public interest while they admit analogy.
2. The Hanafites and others of similar opinions maintain the principles of preference and analogy, but their interpretation of preference is sometimes almost indistinguishable from public interest. A fair estimate would say that in their system they make a greater use of interest than do the Shafi'ites, But even so, the extent to which they do use it is negligible, and hence we cannot say that this principle is one of the roots of their system; not, at least, on any grounds of the use which they make of it in itself.
3. There are those who attach an excessive importance to public interest, even to the point of making it stronger than precedent in their dealings with cases; they regard it as a form of precedent, or rather, as a form of consensus. Thus where the ulema are agreed on a point turning on precedent, but some aspect of that point runs counter to public interest, then the validity of the latter is the stronger. This applies also to specific cases, as Al-Tufi has maintained.
4. There are those who hold a middle course, which is the soundest of all. Here, validity is granted to public interest, but it is not derived from precedent, which is held to be entirely different. To this view most of the Malikite rites adhere.

Malik held that public interest was an independent root of the system of jurisprudence, but that it was a derived, rather than an original root; and that so, for the following reasons:

1. The Companions of Allah's Messenger found that ques tions arose after his death which had not been apparent during his lifetime. Thus, they collected the noble *Qur'an* in book form. This had not been done in the time of the Messenger, but now such a collection was in the public interest; for they feared that the *Qur'an* might be forgotten because of the deaths of those who had memorized it. Umar saw such men dying in numbers during the Wars of Apostasy, and, fearing that through their death the *Qur'an* might pass from memory, he advised Abu-Bakr to have it collected in book form. to this the Companions gladly assented.
2. After the death of Allah's Messenger his Companions agreed that the punishment for wine-drinking should be eighty lashes. Their reason for this was the public interest or general inference; for they saw that drinking tended to produce lying and the slandering of chaste women because of the wild talk in which drinkers indulged.
3. The orthodox Caliphs agreed upon imposing conscription on craftsmen, although the root principle was that the exercise of their craft was a matter of good faith. But it was found that unless they were conscripted they would neglect the care of the people's belongings and wealth. There was great need of craftsmen, and therefore, it was in the public interest to conscript them, that they might perform the duties which they had. Thus Ali, when he prescribed the conscription, said: 'The people's inter ests cannot be served otherwise.'
4. Umar ibn-al-Khattab used to claim half of the wealth of those governor whom he suspected of having increased their resources by extortion. This also was a form of public interest, because to his mind it was in the interests of the governors to prevent them capitalizing on their power to amass money and heap up illegal plunder.
5. It is told of Ali that he poured out on the ground milk which had been adulterated with water, as a lesson to the man who had done it. This act also was akin to public interest, to show that people were not to adulterate goods.
6. There is tradition that Umar put a whole community to death for the murder of one man, for which they had been jointly responsible. This he did because the public inte-

> rest demanded it. There was no precedent for the case, but the public interest demanded that the case be considered as one of premeditated murder of a sacrosanct individual. To let the murder pass unavenged would have been to deny the root principle of 'an eye for an eye', while to choose one out of the many who had a hand in the business would have made the whole matter ridiculous. For the man chosen would know that in his case it was not a case of retaliation, Or if it were said that this was an anonymous murder, a killing without a killer, on the grounds that every single individual could not be said to be the murderer, then the guilty party was the community itself. The whole of a community can commit a murder in exactly the same way as an individual criminal. And murder can be charged against a community just as it can against a single person, and the members of the community stand in the same relation to the act of murder as does an individual. Hence, the community furthers the public interest when it prevents bloodshed and guards communal life."

Role of the Imams in Delineation of Public Interest

Another general aspect of public interest is the power which is granted to the Imam to levy upon the rich whatever toll he thinks that the circumstance warrants. This he can do when the public treasury is empty, or when the army has extraordinary needs, while there are no funds to meet those needs. Toll may be levied until the treasury is replenished, or until the needs are sufficiently met.

Further, the Imam has the duty of instituting this levy at times of bountiful harvest and plentiful crops, so that the rich will not be overburdened by the fact that it is they alone who pay it. The public interest here lies in the fact that if a just Imam did not do this, his power would be in vain, and wealthy establishments would provide an incentive to civil war, and to attacks by envious persons. It is sometimes said that the Imam, instead of enforcing the provisions of the levy, borrows money for the public treasury. To this Al-Shatibi retorted that:

> "Borrowing in times of need is allowed only when the treasury has the prospect of more revenue. Otherwise, or alternatively when the revenue is too small to be sufficient,

then recourse must be had to the principle of a levy."

A means is that which leads to an end, and to 'block the means' is to remove it. The sense of the phrase is that anything which conduces to a forbidden end is itself forbidden, while anything conducive to a desirable end is itself desirable. Thus, for example, adultery is forbidden, and, therefore, to admire the charms of a strange woman is also forbidden, as being a means towards adultery.

On the other side, attendance at prayers is compulsory, and therefore an effort to attend prayers is also compulsory, as is leaving one's business to make that effort. To make the pilgrimage is compulsory; therefore an effort to visit the Sacred House and to perform the other rites of pilgrimage is also compulsory.

The fundamental reason for the validity of 'blocking the means' is a realization of the repercussions and final results of all actions. If they are conducive to those public interests which constitute the aims and objectives of the dealings of man with man, then they are as desirable as those aims themselves. But if they are not equally desirable, or if their results might be evil, then they are forbidden just as evil is forbidden, even though the means may be somewhat less objectionable.

In considering the results of actions, the matter of interest is not the purpose or the objective of the agent; rather, it is the result and outcome of his action. The individual will be rewarded or punished for his intention in the next world; but in this world, it is according to its result and outcome that an action is good or bad, desirable or undesirable. For this world must take its stand on the welfare of mankind, on judgement and justice, and these things require a scrutiny of results and outcomes rather than of estimable aims and worthy intentions. A man who out of a sincere love for the worthy intentions and for the worship of Allah reviles idols has gained the approval of Allah by the formulation of his purpose; and yet, he has forbidden such reviling in cases where it would result in the rage of the idolaters, who would then revile Allah the Great, Himself. So, His exalted words run:

> "And do not revile those who invoke deities other than Allah, lest in response they revile Allah without knowledge."[20]

In this noble prohibition, regard is had to thc actual consequences, rather than to the commendable religious aim. Hence, it appears that in cases which tend towards crime or evil, the veto is directed not towards the aim itself, which is sincere, but towards the consequences which will arise; thus an act may be forbidden because of its consequences, even though Allah may be aware that the intention underlying it is sincere.

Sometimes also a man may seek an evil end through a legal act, in which case he is guilty in his own conscience and in the sight of Allah. But no man may take measures against him, nor may any legal penalties be invoked upon him. Such is the case of man who cuts the price of his goods in order to injure a business rival. This is undoubtedly a legal act; yet, it is a means towards a crime, that on injuring another.

This crime is the man's object, but in spite of that his action cannot be punished by the power of the law, nor does it fall under any penalty which the law of the land can impose. His action, from the point of view of intention, is a means to evil, but externally it is a means to public and private benefit. Undoubtedly the seller benefits by selling, by the circulation of his goods, and by the goodwill which he gains; equally certainly the public benefits by the cut in price, by which a general lowering of prices is encouraged.

The principle of blocking the means had regard not only to individual aims and intentions, as we have seen, but also to the encouragement of public welfare and to the prevention of public evil. Thus, it must take account of the consequences along with the intention, or even of the consequences alone.

The principle of 'means' is firmly established in the *Qur'an* and the *Sunna*. In the former, there is the verse: "And do not revile those who invoke Gods other than Allah, lest in response they revile Allah without knowledge." Of this it is related that the idolaters said that they were content to have their Gods reviled if they in turn could revile Muhammad's God. Thus again: "O you who believe, do not say *Ra'ina;* say *Unzurna* and hearken. This was because the Muslims used the former word with good intention, but the Jews took it as implying a derogatory sense to the Prophet."[21]

In the *Sunna* there are many stories of the Prophet and many decisions of his Companions. Among them is that of his refusal to kill the hypocrites, lest the unbelievers should have a pretext for saying that Muhammad killed his Companions.

There is also the story that the Prophet forbade a man who had loaned money to accept a gift from the debtor, unless the gift was counted as part repayment of the loan. The reason was simply that the gift was a means of postponing payment, and was therefore a form of interest. For the lender would get his money back and extra also in the form of the gift. We have also the account of the Prophet's having forbidden that men's hands should be cut off in time of war; the purpose was to stop this practice leading to an illegal treatment of fighting men which would inevitably ensue.

Similarly, laws should not be intermitted in times of war, lest freedom become licence; the two are closely related. And there is the account of the earliest Believers, both Emigrants and Helpers, having on their death-beds appointed their divorced wives as their heirs; this they did because there was a suspicion of a plot to debar such wives from inheriting. It was not even certain that such a plot existed, but divorce was a 'means' which might have produced injustices.

Again, the Prophet forbade monopolies, saying: 'Only sinners hold monopolies.' For a monopoly is a means to oppress the people in all things which are considered to be essential. But there is no law against a monopoly in any article which cannot injure the people by being withheld, such as cosmetics and the life; for these things do not come under the heading of necessities.

The Prophet also forbade any man who had given alms to buy them back, even though, he might see them displayed for sale in the market. Thus, he sought to check the means to recover what had been given to Allah, even by purchase. Thus, anyone who gives alms is forbidden to repossess them by purchase, and is yet more stringently forbidden to repossess them by other means. To permit repossession by purchase might be a means of cheating the poor; the rich out of his wealth would give alms to the poor, and might then buy them back from him at less than their value. The poor man, on the other hand, would see some profit to himself, and thus his conscience would not oppose the sale.

Thus, there are many indications of this principle, deriving from the Messenger and his Companions.*Ibn-Qiyam* has collected some ninety such examples from actual occurrences, in all of which the principle of blocking the means is clearly illustrated.

> "Means are counted to be half of the legal principles of Islam."

These two principles, that of public interest and that of blocking the means, both run back to a common root, that of ensuring the welfare of society. They are integrally connected with the established laws of Islam and with its general purposes. It is these two principles which can guide us to wards the legislation necessary to ensure a sound form of Islamic life and to include in its scope a comprehensive social justice.

This principle must be our concern in a general work dealing with social justice in Islam; yet, it is desirable to mention some of the things which Islam is able to ensure in this sphere for the present and the future. We must also deal with the legislation necessary to produce these things, so that it may be used as a pattern for analogous treatment in other cases. We cannot deal with all possible developments but these may be safely left to the dictation of circumstances times and conditions.

Laws Governing the Poor-tax

This tax was a compulsory duty in Islam, levied on all possessions according to a sliding scale of one-tenth, one-twentieth, and one-fortieth. In all cases, it represented a very small fraction, and hence, it is but natural that the question should arise: How could such a small sum be of assistance to all the Muslim poor? To answer this question we must consider the following facts:

1. The small amount of capital on which the tax had to be paid made the greater part of the community liable to it. The exemption value for the poor-tax was fixed at six pounds, which meant that practically all the population had to pay the tax; thus the income from it was relatively great.
2. Disbursements from the tax money were confined to specifically limited classes of people. For their livelihood the great majority had to rely on work, which has always been reckoned by Islam to be the primary source of a living.

3. Most important of all, the livelihood of the very poor did not depend solely upon this source of income. There were also the vast sums acquired as booty during the war days, sums which lasted for more than half a cen tury. In this booty all the fighting men shared, and most of them were of the poor classes. They received four-fifths of the booty, while the other fifth was turned into a charitable foundation for the benefit of all classes of necessitous persons, relatives, orphans, the destitute, and the wayfarer. And when Umar resolved not to take the booty away from the conquered countries, but to leave it for the benefit of the native peoples, he instituted the land-tax in its place, as this later on was sufficient to provide for all the poor.

Today, the last primary source of revenue is no longer available, and the poor-tax in itself is not sufficient. Therefore, we must consider alternative sources to take the place of booty and plunder, in order to provide an ample living for the generality of men.

Before we consider new sources we must first exhaust the poor-tax as a source in itself. It is a compulsory duty, and it must be paid if the community is justifiably to be described as Islamic. For the payment of the poor-tax is a spiritual duty as well as financial one. Again, we must consider the source of the poor-tax as including all types of property, some of which are not at present included because they were not familiar in the early days of Islam.

That is to say, we must bear in mind those forms of wealth which are liable to the poor-tax but which are not mentioned in the *Qur'an* except generally in the verse:

> "O you who have believed, expend of the goods which you have acquired, and of that which We have provided for you from the Earth. And do not propose any evil in thus expending it; for you got it yourselves only by connivance."[22]

The fact that the poor-tax was prescribed as a duty only upon such types of property as were familiar in the time of the Prophet does not prevent its being prescribed today as a duty on all that is known as Property or wealth, and on all that produces an income. It may not be of difference that such things may not be the kind on which the tax was originally imposed.

Similarly, we can control the outlets for the tax money, just as Umar exercised the same control when he stopped payments designed to convert unbelievers. It must not be given in any form of money to those who are eligible for it; rather it must be given to them in the basic form of goods or services, or it must be used to buy for them some part of their basic necessities. The source of their livelihood must be fixed and unconnected with any kind of temporary or haphazard charity; for these things are not in accord with the needs of modern life.

But in any case such detailed considerations have no place in this book. The scope of our thinking here is the broad field of the promotion of social justice and equity, as the Muslim world gives its attention to a renaissance of the true Islamic life.

Laws Governing the Mutual Responsibility of Society

The Prophet said: "Any household which suffers a man to remain hungry among them is outside the protection of Allah, the Blessed and the Exalted." In this brief sentence, he emphasized the principle of mutual responsibility in society, a principle which most of us must recognize from the precedents and the examples provided by our study of the *Qur'an*. This principle was authoritatively imposed on both the individual and the social conscience. Today the law must again enforce it as an essential root of Islam. This means that the law can enforce that which Umar intended to enforce:

> "If I had known earlier what I now know, I would have taken the excess of their wealth from the rich and given it to the poor."

Thus, the law can impose taxes, the only limit of which is the establishment of equality in the social sphere, the removal of crime and oppression from the community in general, and the ample provision of food and drink, clothing and housing, medical treatment and skill for every single individual in the country. It does not matter how much tax is placed upon capital so long as the latter is not thereby made incapable of work and of reasonable increase; this condition must be observed because the steady turning of the wheels of labour brings other benefits which cannot be overlooked.

Thus, the law can put into the hands of the poor with perfect justification a stretch of funded property which they may use without paying any basic rent, or at a nominal rent, that they may from it obtain a means of life. For this constitutes a source of livelihood and is the only means of work within their power. By this act the law will fulfill the Messenger's words:

> "Anyone of you may permit to his brother the use of his land as gift, without exacting for it any agreed rent."

The law may also with justification fix the wage of the factory or the farm worker at a stipulated proportion of the production or of the harvest. The lowest limit of this wage must be a competence to cover food and drink and clothing, and medicine and medical care to a certain extent. The standard is to be taken as that of a moderate living, determined by the proportion of the inhabitants of the country to its general wealth.

Laws Governing General Taxation

Every individual in the Muslim community has the duty of taking a share in the general expenses of the state according to his ability. We have already noticed the opinion of the Imam Malik on what may be done when the treasury is empty, or when the needs of the army are increased; the law has the power according to need to levy a toll on the wealth of the rich. Similar to the needs of the army are the other needs of the state, such as improvements in public services, irrigation of waste lands, the education of the people, and the medical treatment of the sick.

All these things are communal duties which must be met and satisfied just as much as the needs of the army; they must be preserved as strongly as frontiers and defence posts must be guarded. This is particularly true today when wars make demands on all the resources and services of the belligerent nations. In modern war everyone may be said to be in the army, and thus should be capable of taking responsibility in time of peace.

Laws Governing Public Resources

Monopolies on the necessities of life are forbidden by Islam. A monopoly on food is forbidden, for example, since Islam has always asserted the communal ownership of water, pasturage, and fire, as being the primary needs of life. But the needs of life are not unchangeable, varying as they do from age to age. Consequently, the preservation of this general Islamic principle demands what is known today as the nationalization of natural resources.

It is essential not to have in the hands of private individuals or companies the resources of water, light, heat, electricity, coal and oil, or the resources of public transport and public food supplying, and other such things. For private ownership gives the power of monopoly, imposes upon the general public he will of the monopolists, and permits them to indulge in that disgraceful exploitation which we witness today.

The head of the state has the power to make all these things state-owned, and to fix prices and costs of them so that they can get it at equitable rates without excessive prices. By these means the Islamic aims for the checking of monopolies can be realized.

Laws Governing the Public Interest and the Blocking of Means

Everything which tends to advance the public welfare or to retard oppression of the public is a duty laid upon the law, and everything which tends towards a prohibited end is itself prohibited. The application of these established principles of Islam lays on the law today following duties:

1. The taking of excessive wealth out of the hands of bloated capitalists. The fact that such excessive wealth is in their possession tends towards a number of crimes. In the first place, it tends to produce that luxury which is forbidden by Islam. Luxury is a relative matter, which can be defined only in terms of the general condition in each age and country. The permanent rule is that luxury shall not increase beyond the mean struck by the national wealth in proportion to the population. One result of luxury is the iniquitous rise in prices which springs from the fact that one section of the populace has an unlimited power to buy, while the goods available for sale are not equal to the demand. Another result is the rise of social vices, springing from the fact that some people possess more money than they need; to dispose this, they look for illegal outlets and seek sensual and corrupt pleasures; through these, their morals and their standards are degraded, and on the other hand their victims are the needy men and women who always exist in an unbalanced society.
2. The removal of extreme poverty, because it results in the

way of crime and evil. These results include a great number of social evils which can only exist in surroundings of privation and destitution, theft, infamy, and moral degradation, a general atmosphere of corruption. This is over and above the vast differences which are set between those who have and those who have not, the hatreds and the social disturbances which the law must prevent before they occur by removing their causes. If it be asked how this extreme poverty is to be removed, it is by the ample provision of work for every able-bodied man, and by the provision of an adequate wage, by social security for all who are disabled, and by speedy relief. This is the method in general outline; the specific applications are easy once the general aim is established.

3. The struggle against disease and ignorance: Because of their evil effect on the individual and the community these weaken the general strength of the community and afford a footing to its enemies. This condition is forbidden, as is any factor which leads to it. Nothing can oppose disease and ignorance successfully except a rise in living standards and in general wealth; but the laws of charity and such other things are only a palliative to soothe the sore, not to heal it. The real treatment is that every individual should be possessed of private means for medical and educational purposes. Or alternatively that medical care and education should be provided free to every individual in the country on a common basis and to a common level. The rich must not be able, by money, to get more than the poor in schools or hospitals.

Laws Governing Legacies

When there are present at the division of the estate relatives, orphans and poor people, give them a provision out of it and speak to them fair.[23] Thus runs the *Qur'anic* precept. It clearly means that out of every estate there must be a share for relatives, orphans and the poor. The law has the power of disposal according to the nature of the case; it may change the beneficiaries, or it may leave them unchanged. So, Umar did in the case of paying out money to convert others to Islam. The law also has the power to apply the regulations according to the needs of the estate or according to those of the community.

We must remember that the meaning of being 'present' can legitimately be extended to cover virtual presence, that is to say, existence. In every community, there are orphans and poor, and there is no necessity for them to be present in person when an estate is being divided; they are already present in time and space. So by the power of the law all duties must be enforced which are not enforced by the power of conscience.

Laws Governing Mutual Help and Usury

Islam rooted out usury, and fought it in all its forms and appearances; hence, it is impossible for any form of Islamic life to exist on an economic basis which includes the principles of usury. We have already discussed the causes which made Islam unable to countenance usury, but they may be summed up by saying that it is the negation of the spirit of mutual help and friendliness. If usury obtains, then it is to the benefit of the capitalist who can thus increase his wealth without working and without the risk of loss.

The national economy must be set on a basis of mutual help rather than of usury. All the faults which can be alleged against the later system have been summed up to justify its rejection by Maulana Muhammad Ali in his book, *Islam and the New World Order*, from which we may quote the following passage:

> "It is objected that to forbid interest on money will hinder business and commercial transactions, and will hinder the accomplishment of important domestic projects. We may grant the truth of this, but on the other side we have the far greater advantage that to proscribe interest will prevent world wars, which can only end in misery, and which are kindled and inflamed only by loans and debts governed by interest. And if we examine the facts of the case, we shall find that from the very first, trade followed its natural course and spread over more and more widely! Wider limits were brought within the Islamic sphere. So that today the Islamic states are still among the greatest of the old-established countries of the civilized world."

This prohibition of usury cannot in any sense be reconciled with the conditions of the new world which materialistic Western civilization is bringing into being. The social system most required is that practical system which Islam today has in mind, which was successfully applied in practice by Islam, at its inception, centuries ago.

As for the capital sums, without which business cannot be carried on, there was little difference between the gains which they made under the Islamic system and those which they made by ordinary lending; for the Islamic system was in effect one of partnership between capital and labour. Such a partnership is not impossible, for the Islamic system holds that capital and labour should share together in all profit and loss; whereas the result of paying a steady rate of interest is that, capital makes a continual profit, even when labour had to work at a loss.

It is sometimes objected that the partnership of capital and labour in both profits and losses is not practicable, because it means that regular accounts have to be kept, since this is one of the necessities of trade; and further, because trading records have to be available for the assessing of taxes which have to be paid. But all the share-issuing companies which take part in trading on a large scale have to keep accounts.

Indeed this partnership system is more to the public advantage than that of giving all the dividends to capital; for it is the latter system which produces most of the evils of capitalism, and which is the source of the oppression of the workers. And the loans which are floated by governments or companies to carry out immense projects such as railroads or canals or such things have done no more than prove this point.

But since the system of state banking depends on the principle of mutual help, which is approved by the Islamic social system, it must be of great benefit to mankind.

This is a general statement, the particular details of which are too lengthy for a book dealing with general ideas. At the same time, there can be no harm in giving an example as a guide to the general objective which we have in mind. Suppose, the state decrees the abolition of interest on funds in banks, companies, public enterprises, and private loans, what will happen then?

What will happen will be that capitalists will find themselves unable to increase their wealth except by two general methods. First, they may put it to some profitable use themselves in manufacture or trade or agriculture. Or second, they may put it to a profitable and helpful use by investing it in share-issuing companies, where the share values may rise or fall. Both these methods are sanctioned by Islam, and neither of them will work the slightest injury to economic life.

It is sometimes feared that the rich will refrain from depositing their money in the banks, which generally finance the large public projects. This is an imaginary danger which gains currency among us because we are familiar only with European methods of using money.

In Europe, the primary natural impulse is to make money increase; this can be accomplished only by using it for some means of exploitation, and so, this natural impulse is a guarantee that money will not be kept out of circulation. But when he desired to take in handsome large project to justify what is known as the great ear of production, we have the power to create legislation covering various kinds of industry; this legislation enacts that no new enterprise may be set up except on the basis of capital over such and such a sum. On that capital sums flow in to take up shares and to become liable to profit and loss on the market.

Thus, there is no more need for banks, except for the issuing of currency. If other banks wish to make a profit, then they must only with permission-in some profit-seeking enterprise, where the shares are liable to fluctuation in the open market. But the system will not stop the flow of capital, either domestic or foreign; for the greater proportion of capital wealth is not deposited in banks, but is put out to profit in enterprises.

At for insurance companies, it may be that their basis is Islamic, inasmuch as the funds which are deposited with them are liable to profit and loss, to fall or rise. Funds deposited in these companies are put to work in profit-seeking enterprises, subject to fluctuation. Everytime a beneficiary receives more than he has paid in, the amount of the company's loss is deducted from the remainder of the depositors in proportion to the funds which they have invested. Thus insurance companies' members form a body united for mutual help; in effect they pay out of their own pockets to support any unfortunate one of their number, when need arises.

They have a form of security from which they can benefit in time of hardship or need. This can be applied also to savings banks and similar institutions, all of which rest on the basis of mutual help in one way or another, and from which funds are employed in profit-seeking enterprises, always liable to fluctuation. Such institutions have no fixed rate of interest, and hence our economic system here can be free from the taint of usury; hence also all capital is compelled to work as the only method of achieving profit and increase.

Laws Governing Gambling

Gambling is a dishonest practice, both in act and in spirit, for it represents an effort to make money without working. In addition, it produces enmity and hatred among its adherents, and gives rise to laxity and insecurity in the fabric of society. There are many forms of gambling, of which lotteries are but one. It is not any spirit of charity which prompts people to buy lottery tickets, not is it any desire to assist works of healing and charity. It is merely the desire to gain more money without working. This is at once practically and spiritually dishonest, as we have said; it hinders and retards the feelings of mercy. There is no need to mention the disgraceful foreign race-meetings which draw their immense crowds; this is merely the outcome of luxury, and the corrupting result of luxury loving natures with their aversion to virtue and their love of vice, with their avarice except when money is lavished on sensual pleasures and coarse enjoyment.

We must halt the practice of gambling altogether, with its green tables, its tempting lottery tickets, and its late hours. Islamic life had need of none of these things, and Islam will never admit that relations between man and man should ever stand on such a basis, or that charity should spring from such impure desires.

Laws Governing Prostitution

Prostitution is the Product of spiritual degradation and material destitution, sometimes together and sometimes separately. Islam prohibits illegal sexual intercourse in all its forms, and the most degraded of these is prostitution. Lewdness is the poison characteristic of an unbalanced community, for the two factors which produce prostitution are excessive wealth and humiliating necessity. It was once said:

> "A well-born woman cannot feed from her own breasts because she is hungry; but she may do so if she is in danger of death."

We must not expose people on the one hand to the trials of need, and on the other to the temptations of wealth and other things, and then expect them to be models of self-control and virtue. The principle of blocking the means, demands that the law gives attention to check this thing at its root. The laws affecting prostitution must be established without delay.

Laws Governing Alcohol

The nature of these laws needs no discussion. Alcohol is undeniably forbidden, and the Islamic community can never countenance its use. It is closely related to prostitution in most cases, and is especially allied to it socially; similarly, it is related to luxury and to the destitution which arises from luxury. For luxury produces a spiritual weakness and a need for inhibiting thought and vital activity by means of some intoxicant. Whereas the life, the work, and the watchfulness which Islam prescribes can never be reconciled with alcohol or with any other drug.

Islam forms a plastic social system, capable of adaptation to all times and all circumstances; it is preserved by its general spiritual and principles. Its duty is to ensure a form of life which will be virtuous, sound, productive, and strong; to ensure a comprehensive social justice based on all the foundations of human nature, and aiming at giving every man his due. But it must never stand in the way of fruitful individualism, nor must it permit that individualism to become a harmful egotism.

The Islamic theory of life is the finest that the world has known because it brings together the material and the spiritual elements of life, making out of them a unity directed towards the highest standards and aimed at patterns which can be actually achieved. It does not envisage objectives which are woven only of the imagination.

But the perplexed and disturbed world, fearful and cautious, can only be brought to Islam and to peace, can only be given complete security and justice, when it returns to this perfect social system, under the will of Allah.

References

1. *The Holy Quar'an*, Sura, 5:48. Cf, supra, p. 10.
2. A *fatwa* is the decision of a Mufti, based on the Islamic law.--Trans.
3. The Qarmatians, thus named from Qarmat, the dwarf, which was

the nickname of the original leader, were Islam 'ilis' who raised a dangerous rebellion in Iraq and Syria during the reign of Al-Muktafi. They were defeated in the province in 901 A.D. [288 A.H], but their fierce risings continued to trouble the Abbasids for at least fifty years.--Trans.

4. Alphonse Gouilly, *L'Islam devant le Monde Moderne*.-Trans.
5. H.A.R. Gibb: *Whither Islam*? p. 379.-Trans.
6. From Prof. Hasan Habashi: *The First Crusade*.
7. This takes place through equating the form *Mahomed* and the form ''Mohound.'' ''Ma'' whichis the first person possessive pronoun, my, and 'hound' from the German ''hand'' a dog. This is a play on words between the forms ''Mahumad'' and ''Mahund''--From Leopold Weiss: *Islam at the Crossroads*. This work was originally written by Muhammad Asad, and published by Ashraf, 1937, Lahore. It was translated into English in 1938 by Weiss, and thence retranslated into Arabic by Umar Farrukj.--Trans.
8. *Ibid*.
9. Sura, 8:62.
10. Sura, 4:143.
11. Sura, 4:76.
12. Sura, 3:133.
13. Quoted from Haikal's *'Life of Muhammad'*, where he quotes from an article in the magazine *Nur al-Islam*, No. 40, p. 5720, dated 1934 A.D. [1353 A.H].
14. Jacob Fahm, *Pragmatism, or the Philosophy of Means*.
15. The present author hopes in the near future to produce for the Arab reader a complete study on *The Islamic Doctrine of the Universe, Life, and Mankind*.
16. Jacob Fahm, *op. cit*.
17. Quoted from *The Iman Malik* by Prof. Muhammad Abu Zuhra Professor of the *Shari's* in the Faculty of Law in the Fu'ad al-Awwal University.
18. Public interest'' is an arbitrary but convenient translation for a phrase which means literally a measure of welfare for society which lacks a precedent in the primary authorities--Trans.
19. Reference is made here to three of the four schools into which Muslim jurisprudence is divided; these are the Shaf'ite, the Hanafite, the Malikite, and the Hanbalite schools. The roots by which the system of jurisprudence is governed, being also mentioned here, may be said to include: *nass* or precedent, drawn from the *Qur'an* or the *Sunna*; these two authorities are in theory the sole root of jurisprudence (*fiqh*); *Ijma'* or concensus of opinion; *qiyas* or analogy. Other principles in use but more dubious of acceptance are *ray*, or independent critical opinion and, *istihsan*, or preference. Vd. Lammens; *Islam* p. 82ff.--Trans.

20. Sura, 6:108-Trans.
21. Sura, 2: 98. Baidawi in his commentary on this verse gives the explanation that the Jews of Arabia took the form *ra'ina*, look at us, or better, pay attention to us, as connected with a similar word meaning 'evil'. Muhammad, therefore, disliking their ridicule, prescribed the use of the word, which was to be replaced by another which did not lend itself to such paranomasis. Vd. Jeffery, *Foreign Vocabulary of the Qur'an* 136, and Palmer: *Koran*, 13. --Trans.
22. Sura, 2:269-270.
23. Tradition No. 2541 in Prof. Ahmad Muhammad Shakir: Musnad, iv, published by Dar al-Ma 'arif. (The *isnad*, or chain of transmit ting authorities, which has been omitted in the body of the trans lated text, follows tradition. It runs as follows: Related by Ahmad on the authority of Affan, from Humad ibn-Zaid on the authority of Amr ibn Dinar, who quoted it from Tawus, who had it from Abdullah Ibn Abbas.- Trans.

Bibliography

Primary Sources

Abbas Khan Sarwani, *Tuhfa-i Akbar Shahi,* Dacca, 1964.

Abdu'i-Baqi Nihawandi Khwaja, *Ma'asir-i Rahimi,* Calcutta, 1910-1931.

Abdu'i-Hamid Lahori, *Padshah-nama,* Calcutta, 1866-72.

Abdu'i-Karim Khwaja, *Bayan-i Waqi',* Lahore, 1970.

Abdu'i-Latif, *Ahmad-nama, I.O.*, 3964.

Abdu'i-Qadir Bada'uni, *Muntakhab u't-tawarikh,* Calcutta, 1864-69, Vol. I, English tr. by G.S.A. Ranking, Calcutta, 1895-99, Vol. II, W. H. Lowe, Calcutta, 1884-98; Vol. III, T.W. Haig Vd., Calcutta, 1899-1925.

Abdu'l-Qadir Khan, Ja'isi, *Tarikh Imad al-Mulk,* Vol. VIII, Bankipur, 615.

Abdu'r-Razzaq Ishaq Samarqandi, *Matla'i sa 'dain wa-majma'-i, Bahrain,* Ivanow, 81, Oriental College Magazine, Lahore, 1933.

Abdu'i-Fazi 'Allami, Shaikh, *Akbar-nama,* Calcutta, 1873-87, English tr. by H. Beveridge, Calcutta, 1897-1921.

A'in-i-Akbari, Lucknow, 1892, English tr. Vol. I, by H. Blochmann, 2nd rev. edn. by D.C. Phillott, Calcutta, 1939; Vols. II and III tr. by H.S. Jarrett and revised by J.N. Sarkar, Calcutta, 1948.

Muktabat-i'Allami, Delhi, 1846.

Abdu's-Sattar B. Qasim Lahori, *Samratu'I-Falasifa,* Rampur MS.

Abu Nu'aim al-Isfahani, *Hilyat al-awliya',* 10 vols., Cairo, 1351-57/1932-38.

Abu Talib al-Makki, *Qut al-qulab,* 2 vols., Cairo, 1306/1888-89.

Abu' i-Faiz Kamalu'd-Din Muhammad Ihsan, *Rauztu'I-Qayyumiyya,* Ivanow, Curzon, 82.

Ahmad, B. Muhammad Baqir al-Isfahani, *Mir'at al-ahwal-i-Jahan-nama,* Rieu, I, 385a.

Ahmad Tattavi, *Tarikh-i-alfi,* Rieu, I, 119a, Ethe, 110.

Akhtar, Wahid, Khwaja Mir Dard, *Tasawwufaursha'iri,* Aligarh, 1971.

Ali Muhammad Khan, *Mir'at-i Ahmadi,* Baroda, 1927-28, 1930.

Amin Ahmad Razi, *Haft iqlim,* Tehran, n.d.

Amir, Shah Khan, *Amir u'i-Rawayat,* Saharanpur, n.d.

Amir Khwurd, *Siyar al-auliya fimahabbat u'i-Haqq jall wa'ala,* 1302/1885.

Anonymous, *A'ina-i haqq-nama,* India Office, D.P., 259b.

Ansari, Muhammad Riza, *Bani-i dars-i Nizami,* Lucknow, 1973.

Aqil Khan Razi, *Waqi'at-i'alamgiri,* Aligarh, 1946.

Arif Qandahari, Muhammad, *Tarikh-i Akbari,* Rampur, 1962.

Asad Beg Qazwini, *Halat-i Asad Beg,* Rieu, III, 979b.

Aurangzib, *Adabi-i'Alamgiri,* Lahore, 1972.

Ruqa'at, Kanpur, 1879.

Kalimat-i Tayyibat, Bibilotheque Nationale, Paris.

Azad, Mir Ghulam Ali, *Yad-ibayza',* Bankipur, VIII, 691.

Sarw-i Azad, Lahore, 1913.

Khizana-a'Amira, Kanpur, 1900.

Ma'asiru'i-Kiram, Lahore, 1971.

Subhat'u i-Marjan, Bombay, 1903.

Azad, Mawlana Abu'i-Kalam, *Tazkira,* Lahore, n.d.

Azar, Hajji Lutf Ali Beg, *Atash-Kada,* Bombay, 1277/1860.

Aziau'r-Rahman, Mawlana Mufti, *Tazkira-i Masha' ik-i Deoband,* Bijnor, 1950.

Babur, Zahir u'd-Din Muhammad, *Babur-nama,* Turkish text, Leiden and London 1905, English tr., A.S. Beveridge, London, 1921, reprint, Delhi, 1972.

Badakhshi, Hajji Muhammad Amin, *Manoqib-i Hazrat,* Author's Personal Collection.

Barnawi, 'Ala'u'd-Din Muhammad Chishti, *Chishtiyya-i bihishtiyya or Firdawsiyya-if Qudsiyya,* Punjab University, Lahore MS.

Bashiru'd-Din Ahmad, Waqi'-at-i daru'i hukumat-i -Dihli, Delhi, 1337/1918-1919.

Waqi'at-i Mumlikat-i Bijapur, Agra, 1915.

Faramini-i Salatin, Delhi, 1944.

Bayazid Biyat, *Tazkira-i Humayuna wa Akbar,* Calcutta, 1941.

Bhim Sen, *Dilkusha,* Rieu, I, 271a.
Bhupat Ray, *Insha'-i Roshan-Kalam,* Aligarh MS.
Chand, Shaikh, *Sawda,* Delhi, 1940.
Chandrabhan Barahman, *Char Chaman-i Barahman,* Rieu, 838b.
Munsh'at, Lucknow, 1885.
Chaturman Kayath Sakesena, Ray, *Chahar-Gulshan or Akhbar Clnawadir,* Bodleian, 264, English tr. of topographical and Statistical portions by Jadunath Sarkar, Calcutta, 1901.
Chekhovich, O.D., *Samarqand Documents,* Moscow, 1974.
Danishmand Khan, *Ni'mat Khan-i 'Ali, Ruz-nama-i waqa't' ayyamidarjuljihad,* Haydarabad, Kanpur, 1901.
Jang-nama, Kanpur, 1279/1862-63.
Bahadur-Shah-nama, Rieu, II, 745a.
Ni'mat-i'uzma, Ivanow, Curzon, 337.
Farid, B. Shaikh Ma'ruf Bhakkari, *Zakhiratu'l-khawanin,* 3 vols., Karachi, 1961-74.
Fazlu'llah al-Amin B. Ruzbihan, *Sulukue-muluk,* Tashkent MS., English tr. by M. Aslam, Islamabad, 1976.
Miliman-nama-i Bukhara, Tehran, n.d.
Fayzi Sirhindi, Shaikh Ilahdab, *Akbar-nama,* Ethe, 289.
Firishta, M. Qasim Hindu-Shah,Astarabadi, *Gulshan-i Ibrahimi,* Lucknow, n.d.
Gardizi, Fath 'Ali Hussaini, Tajkira-i 'Ali-i Hussaini Gardizi, Aurangabad, n.d.
Ghaziu'd Din Khan Firuz-jang, *'Imadud-Mulk, Manaqib-i Fakhriyya,* I. O., D.P., 728, Delhi, 1315/ 1897.
Ghulam Husain B. Hidayat 'Ali Khan, *Tarikh-i Muhammad-Shahi,* Asafiya MS.
Ghulam Husain Khan Jawhar, *Gulzar-i Asafiya,* Bombay, 1308/ 1891.
Tarikh-i Dil-afruz, Asafiya MS.
Ghulam Husayn Khan Tabataba'i, *Siyar al-muta' Ahkirin,* Lucknow, 1282/1866.
Ghulam Murtaza, *Basatinu'i-Salatin,* Hyderabad, Deccan, 1310/ 1892-1893.
Ghulam Sharafu'd-Din, *Ganj-i Fayyazi*, Cambridge University MS.
Gilani, Manazir Ahsan, *Tazkira-i hazrat Shah Waliu'llah,* Hyderabad-Deccan, 1946.
Gulbadan Begam, *Humaun-nama,* London, 1902.
Hasan Beg Rumlu, *Ahsanu't-tawarikh,* Baroda, 1931.

Haydar, Sayyid Kamalu'd-Din, *Tarikh-iAwadh,* Rieu, III, 962b.

Haydar Malik, *Tarikh-i Kashmir,* Ethe, 2846.

Ibn Jubayr, *Rihla, Beirut,* 1389/1959.

Ikram, Shaikh Muhammad, *Ab-i kawsar,* Lahore, 1975.

Rud-i Kawsar, Lahore, 1975.

Mauj-i Kawsar, Lahore, 1975.

Ishwar Das Nagar, *Futuhat-i'Alamgiri,* Rieu, I, 269a.

Iskandar Beg Munshi, *Tarikhi-i 'alam-aray-i 'Abbasi,* Tehran, 1350/1971.

Jahangir, the Emperor, *Tuzuk-i Jahangiri,* Ghazipur and Aligarh, 1863-1864, English tr. by A. Rogers, ed. by H. Beveridge, London. 1909-1914, reprinted, New Delhi, 1978.

Jawhar Aftabchi, *Tazkiratu'i-waqi'at,* Rieu, I, 246a.

Jur'at, Mir Hashim Musawi Khan, *Munshat-i Musawi Khan,* State Archives, Hyderabad, Deccan, MS.

Karl Jahn, *Rashid u'd-Din's History of India,* the Hague, 1965.

Kashifi, Husain B. 'Ali Wa'iz, *Rawzat ush-shuhada,* Kanpur, 1891.

Mawahib-i 'Aliya, Lucknow, 1888.

Khafi Khan, Muhammad Hashim, *Muntakhabu'l-lubab,* Calcutta, 1850-1874.

Khaliq, Anjum, *Mirza Muhammad Rafi Sauda,* Aligarh, 1966.

Mirza Jan-i-Janan ke Khutut, Delhi, 1962.

Khwaja M. A'zam Dida-mari, *Woqi'at-Kashmir,* Lahore, 1303/1885-1986.

Khwurshah B. Qubad al-Husaini, *Tarikhi-i ilchi-i Nizam-Shah,* Rieu, Supp., 32.

Lal Ram, *Tuhfatu'i-Hind,* Rieu, 1, 236a.

Lutf, 'Ali, Mirza, *Gulshan-i Hind,* Delhi, 1960.

Mir'Alam, Abu'l-Qasim B. Raziu'd-Din al-Musawi, *Hadiqatu'i-Alam,* Ethe, 465.

Mir, M. Amin Bukhari, *Ubaydullah-nama,* Tashkent MS.

Mir, Sayyid Muhammad Sha'ir, *Tabsirata'i-nazirin,* Rieu, III, 963b.

Mirza, Haydar Dughlat, *Tarikh-i Rashidi,* Riew, I, 164b, English tr. by E. Denison Ross, London, 1898.

Mirza, Muhammad B. Mu'tamad Khan, *Tarikh-i Muhammadi,* Rampur MS.

Muhammad Aslam, *Farhtu'i-Nazirin,* John Ryland Library, Manchester MS.

Muhammad Baga, *Shaikh, Mir'atu'i-'Alam* Rieu, I, 1256.

Mir'at-i-Jahan-Nama, Rampur MS.

Muhammad Kazim Munishi, *'Alamgir-Nama,* Calcutta, 1865-73.

Muhammad Murad, B. Shaikh Shihabud-Din, *A history of Aurangzeb's Successors,* Bodleian, 262.

Muhammad Sadiq Khan and Abu'i-Fazl Ma'muri, *Shahjahan-nama,* Rieu, I, 262.

Muhammad Salih Manbo Lahori, *'Amal-i Salikh,* Calcutta, 1912-36.

Murtaza Husain, *Hadiqat al-Aqalim,* Lucknow, 1881.

Mushtaqi Shaikh Rizaqullah, *Waqi'at-i Mushtaqi,* Rieu, II, 820b.

Musta'id Khan, Muhammad Sharif B. Dust M., *iqbal-Nama-i Jahan giri,* III, Lucknow, 1870, **Allahabad,** 1931.

Mawdudi, Mawlana Abu'l-' Ala', *Tajdid wa Ihya'i-Din,* Lahore, 1953.

Mazhar Baqa, *Usul-i fiqh aur Shah Waliu'llah,* Islamabad, 1973.

Mihr, Ghulam Rasul, *Saiyid Ahmad Shahid,* Lahore, n.d.

Mirza'Ali Lutf, *Gulshan-i Hind,* Hyderabad-Deccan, 1906.

Mufti Muhammad Ghulam Sarwar, *Hadiqatu'i-Auliya',* 2nd edn., 1976.

Muhammad Ihsanu'llah Gorakhpuri, *Sawanih 'umri Hazrat Mujaddid Alf-i Sani,* Rampur, 1926.

Muhammad Iqbal Mujaddidi, *Ahwal Wa asar-i 'Abdu'llah Khweshgi Qasuri,* Lahore, 1972.

Muhammad Latif, *Auliya'-i Lahore,* Lahore, 1962.

Muhammad Miyan, *Ulama-i Hind ka Shandar Mazi,* 4 vols., Delhi, 1957-60.

Muhammad Qasim, Nanawtawi, *Qibla-nama',* Deoband, 1969.

Muhammad Tayyib, *Daru'i-'ulu Deoband,* Karachi, 1972.

Mujibu'i-Hasan, *Sufiyya-i Wududi,* Delhi, 1366/1946.

Nami, Mir M. Ma'sum, *Tarikh-i Sind,* Poona, 1938.

Nadwi, Saiyid Abu'i-Hasan 'Ali, *Sirat Saiyid Ahmad Shahid,* Karachi, 1974-75.

Naqawi, Sayyid Ghulam 'Ali Khan, *'Imadus-sa'adat,* Lucknow, 1864.

Nawwab Dargah Quli Khan Salarjang, *Muraqqa'i Delhi,* Hyderabad-Deccan, n.d.

Ni'matullah B. Habibullah al-Harawi, *Tarikh-i Khan-Jahani wa Makhzan-i Afghani,* Dacca, 1960.

Nisyani, Mir Tahir Muhammad, *Tarikh-i Tahiri,* Hyderabad, Sind, 1964.

Nizami, K. A., *Shah Waliu'llah ke Siyasi Maktubat,* Aligarh, 1950.

Hayat-i Shaikh 'Abdu'l-Haqq Muhaddis Dihlawi, Delhi, 1953.

Tarikh-i Masha-ikh-i Chishti, Delhi, 1953.

Nizamu'd-Din Ahmad, Khwaja, *Tabaqat-i Akbar Shahi*, Calcutta, 1913, 1927, 1931.

Nizamu'i-Mulk Tusi, *Siyasat-nama,* Tehran 1320/1902-3, English tr. H. Darke, The book of Government, London, 1960.

Nu'mani, Muhammad Manzur al-Furqan, *Mujaddid-i Alf-i Sani nambar*, Bareilly, 1357/1937.

Tazkira-i Imam-i Rabbani Mujaddid-i Alf-i Sani, Lucknow, n.d.

Nur Ahmad, Chishti, *Tahqiqat-i Chishti,* Lahore, 1964.

Yadgar-i Chishti, Lahore, 1975.

Nuru'i-Haqq al-Mashriqi al-Dihlawi al-Bukhari, *Zûbadatu't-tawarikh,* Rieu, I, 224b.

Qalqashandi, *Subhu'l-A'sha*, 14 Vols., Cairo, 1914-28.

Qazi, Jawid, *Afkar-i Shah Waliu'llah,* Lahore, 1977.

Barr-i Saghir men Muslim Fikr ka irtiqa', Lahore, 1977.

Qazwini, Mirza Muhammad Amin, *Badshah-nama,* Rieu, I, 258b.

Quddusi, Fijazu'l-Haqq, *Tazkira-i Sufiya' i-Sind,* Karachi, 1959.

Tazkira-i Sufiya'-i Panjab, Karachi, 1962.

Tazkira-i Sufiya'-Bangal, Lahore, 1965.

Tazkira-i Sufiya'-Sarhad, Lahore, 1966.

Quraishi, 'Abdu'l-Razzaq, *Mirza Mazhar Jan-i Janan aur unka Kalam,* Bombay, 1961.

Makatib-i mirza Mazhar, Bombay, 1966.

Rafi'u'd-Din Ibrahim Shirazi, *Tazkiratu'l-Muluk,* Rieu, I, 316a.

Rahim Bakksh Dihlawi, *Hayat-i W'ali*, 2nd edn., Lahore, 1972.

Hayat-i Tayyiba, Lahore, 1976.

Rashidu'd-Din Fazlu'llah, *Jamit'u't-tawarikh,* Tehran, 1338S.H/1970, English tr. by J.E. Boyle, New York and London, 1971.

Sadiq Sadiqi, Mirza Muhammad, *Subh-i-Sadiq,* VI, Bankipur, 471-4.

Shah-Nawaz Khan, Nawwab 'Abd al-Rahman, *Mir'at-i aftab-nama,* Aligarh, MS.

Shahid, Muhammad Isma'il, *Taqwiyat al-Iman wa Tazkirat al-Ikhwan.*

Kalam-i Shah isma'il Shahid, Lalitpur, 1974.

Shakir Khan, *Tarikh-i Shakir-Khani,* Rieu, I, 279b.

Shamsu'r-Rahman, *Shah Waliu'llah ke 'Umarani Nazariye,* Lahore, 1968.

Shirani, Mazhar Mahmud ed., *Maqalat-i Hafiz Mohmud Shirani,* 6 Vols., Lahore, 1966-72.

Sikandar, B.M. Manjhu, *Mir'at-i Sikandari,* Bombay, 1890.

Sujan Ray Bhandari, *Munshi, Khulasatu't Tawarikh,* Delhi, 1918.

Syed Ahmad Khan, Sir,*Tazkira-i ahl-i Delhi*, Karachi, 1955.

Tahmas Khan, *Tahmas-nama*, Rieu, III, 980b.

Talish, Shihabu'd-Din Ahmad, *Fathiya-i 'ibriya*, Bodleian, 240.

Thaneswari, Muhammad Ja'far, *Hayat-i Saiyid Ahmad Shahid*, Karachi, 1968.

Maktubat-i Saiyid Ahmad Shahid, Lahore, 1969.

Tattawi, Mir 'Ali Sher Qani,'*Tuhfatu'l -kiram*, hyderabad, Sind, 1971.

Ubaydu'llah Sindhi, *Shah Waliu'llah aur unka Falsafa*, 3rd edn., Lahore, 1946.

Shah Waliu'llah aur unki Siyasi Tahrik, 2nd edn., Lahore, 1945.

Tasawwuf ke Adab wa Ashghal Lahore, 1946.

Wali, Mir Abu Turab,*Tarikh-Gujarat*, Calcutta, 1909.

Wali'ullah Dihlawi, Shah, *Tafhimat-i Ilahiyya*, Hydrabad, Sind, 1970.

Iqd al-jidd fi Bayan Ahkam al-ijtihad Wa't-taqlid, Delhi, 310/1892.

Sarf-i Mir, Delhi, n.d.

Al-musaffa, Delhi, n.d.

Al-insaf fi bayan-i Sabab al-ikhtalaf, Delhi, 1935.

Sharh Tarajama Ba'z abwab Bukhari, Hyderabad-Deccan, 1949.

Risala-i danishmandi, Lucknow, 1894, at the margin of the Wasiyatnama.

Husn u'l-'aqida, Delhi, n.d.

Maktubat, ma' Manaqib-i Bukhari wa Fazilat-i Ibu Taymiyya, Delhi, n.d.

Al-Muqaddimt al-swnniya fi'l-intisar li-i firaqa al-Sanniya, Asafiya MS.

Al-durr al-samin, Delhi, n.d.

Al-irshad ila muhimumat 'ilm al-isnad, Lahore, n.d.

Maktubat, Rampur MS.

Warid, Muhammad Shafi,*Mir'at -i-waridat*, Bodleian, 424.

Tarikh-i Chaghatay, Rieu, III, 924b.

Yusuf Mirak B. Amir Abu' i-Qasim Namkin in Bhakkari,*Mazhar-i Shahjahani*, Hyderabad Sind, 1962.

Yusuf Salim Chishti,*Anwar-i Mujaddidi*, Lahore, 1961.

Zahiru'd-Din, Saiyid Ahmad,*Kamalat-i 'Azizi*, Karachi, 1972.

Zaidpuri, Ghulam Husain Khan Salim,*Riyazu's -Salatin*, Calcutta, 1902-1904.

Zawwar husain Shah, Saiyid,*Hazrat Mujaddidi Alf-i Sani,* Karachi 1972.

Zubaidi, Sayyid, Murtaza, *Ithaf al-sadat at-Muttaqin,* 10 vols., Cairo, 1311/1893-94.

Secondary Sources

Afifi Abu'l-'Ala, *The Mystical Philosophy of Muhiy'd Din Ibnu'l 'Arabi,* Cambridge, 1939.

Ahmad, Aziz, *Studes in Islamic Culture in the Indian Environment,* Oxford, 1964.

Anawati, G.C. and Gardet, Louis,*Mystique Musulmane,* paris, 1961.

Arberry, A.J.,*The doctrines of the Sufis, tr., of Kalabadhi's Kitab alta, Aruf,* Cambridge, 1935.

An Introduction to the History of Sufism, London, 1942.

*Pages from the Kitab al--luma,*London, 1947.

*Sufism: An Account of the Mystics of Islam,*London, 1950

(ed.),*The Mystical poems of Ibn al-Farid,* Dublin, 1956.

Classical Persian Literature, London, 1958.

The Ruba'iyat of Jalalu'd-Din Rumi, London, 1959.

(tr.), *Discourses of Rumi,*London, 1961.

Tales from the Matnawi, London, 1963.

Mare Tales from the Mathnawi, London, 1963.

Muslim Saints and Mystics, London 1964.

Aspects of Islamic Civilization, Ann Arbor, 1963.

Mystical Poems of Rumi, Chicago, 1968.

(ed.), *Religion in the Middle East,* 2 vols., Cambridge, 1969.

A Sufi Martyr, London, 1969.

Arnold, Sir Thomas,*The Preaching of Islam,* reprint, Lahore, 1956.

Arnold, Sir Thomas,*The Calilhate, rev. edn.,*London, 1965.

Athar 'Ali, *Mughal Nobility under Aurangzeb,* Bombay, 1968.

Bagley, R.R.C. (tr.)*Ghazali's Book of Counselffor Kings,*Oxford, 1964.

Basham, A. L.ed.,*A Cultural History of India,* Oxford, 1975.

Boyle, J. A. ed.,*The Cambridge History of Iran,*Cambridge, 1968.

Browne, E.G.,*A Literary History of Persia,* 4 vols., reprint, Cambridge, 1957.

Burckhardit, Titus,*Introduction to Sufi Doctrines,* Lahore 1959.

Burton, Sir Richard,*Sind and Races that Inhabit the Valley of the*

Indus, London, 1851.

Calverley, Edwin Elliot,*Worship in Islam, being a translation with Commentary and introduction of al-Ghazzali's book the Ihya' on the Worship,* Madras, 1925.

Corbin, H,*Avicenna and the Visionary Recital, tr.*,W. Trash, New York and London, 1960.

Confessions Extatiques de Mir Damad', Melanges Louis Massing non, I, France 1965, pp. 331-78.

Imagination Creatrice Et priere Ereatrice dans le Soufisme di'ibn 'Arabi', Eranos Jahrbuch, XXV, 1956, pp. 122-240.

Divine Epiphany and Spiritual Rebirth in Ismailian Gnosis', Man and Transformation, New York and London, 1964, pp. 69-160.

Etude preliminaire pour le'Livre reunissant les deux sagesses', de Nasir-e Khosraw, Tehran and Paris, 1953.

L'ismaelisme et le symbole de la Croix', La Table Ronde, Paris, December, 1957, pp. 122-34.

*Les Motifis Zoroastriens dans la philosophie de Sohrawardi,*Tehran, 1946.

Recherches sur l' hermeneutique lutherienne' in Annuaire de l' Ecole des Hautes Etudfs *Section des Sciences Religieuses, Paris,* 1939, pp.99--102.

Terre celeste et Corpus de resurrection: de I'Iran mazdeen a l'Iran Shi'ite, Paris, 1961.

*Histoire de la Philosophie islamique,*Paris, 1964.

*ed., Opera Metaphysica et Mystica,*vol. I, Istanbul, 1945,' Vol.II, Tehran, 1952.

Czaplicka, M.A.,*The Turks of Central Asia in History and the Present Day,* reprint, Amsterdam, 1973.

Dawud, Rahbar,*God of Justice,*Leiden, 1960.

De Laet, Description of India and Fragment of Indian History, tr., J.S. Hoyland and annotated by S.N., *The Political Systems of Empire,* New York, 1963.

Faris, Nabith A.,*The Book of Knowledge, tr.,* of a chapter of Ghazali's Ihya', Lahore, 1962.

*The Foundations of the Articles of Faith,*tr., of a chapter of Ghazali's Ihya', Lahore, 1963.

The Mysteries of Alms, tr., of a chapter of Ghazali's Ihya', Beirut, 1966.

Faruqi, Bhrhan Ahmad, *The Mujaddid's Concption of Tauhid,* Lahore, 1940.

Faruqi, Ziya'u-i Hasan *The Deoband School and the Demand for Pakistan*, Bombay, 1963.

Field, Cland H., *Al-Ghazali: The Alchemy of Happiness*, London, 1910.

Mystics and Saints of Islam, London, 1910.

Foster, W., *The English Factories in India*, 13 vols., Oxford, 1906-27.

Francois Bernier, *Travels in the Mogul Empire*, 1656-58, tr, *A. Constable*, ed. V.A. Smith, London, 1916.

Friedmann, Johanan, *Shaykh Ahmad Sirhindi: An outline of his thought and a study of his image in the eyes of posterity* Montreal, 1971.

Frykenberg, R.E. (ed.) *Land Control and Social Structure in Indian History*, Wisconsin, 1969.

Gairdner, W.H. Temple *Al-Ghazzali's Mishkatu'l-anwar, The niche for lights*, London, 1915.

Gibb, H.A.R, *Islamic Society and the West*, London, 1960.

Gilsenan, Mechael, *Saint and Sufi in Modern Egypt: An essay inthe Sociology of Religion*, Oxford, 1973.

Halepota, A.J, *Philosophy of Shah Waliu'llah*, Lahore, n.d.

Haq. M. Anwaru'l, *The Faith Movement of Mawlana Muhammad Ilyas*, London. 1972.

Haqq, En'amul, *Muslim Bengali Literature*, Karachi, 1957.

Hasan, Ibn, *The Central Structure of the Mughal Empire*, reprint, New Delhi, 1980.

Hasrat, B.J., *Dara Shikuh: Life and Works*, reprinted, New Delhi, 1982.

Hodgson, G.S. *The Order of Assassin*, The Hague, 1955.

Holt, P.M., Lambton, A.K.S. and Lewis, B *The Cambridge History of Islam*, Cambridge, 1970.

Husaini, S.A. Q., *The Pantheistic Monism of Ibn al-'Arabi*, Lahore, 1970.

Ikbal 'Ali Shah, Sardar, *Islamic Sufism*, London, 1933.

Ikram, S.M., *Muslim Civilization in India*, New York.

The Cultural Heritage of Pakistan, Karachi, 1955.

Iqbal, Sir Muhammad *The Development of Metaphysics in Persia*, reprint, Lahore, 1964.

Six Lectures on the Reconstruction of Religious Thought in Islam, Lahore, 1930.

Irfan Habib, *The Agrarian System of Mughal India*, Bombay, 1963.

Irvine, W., *Later Mughals*, reprint, New Delhi, 1971.

Izutsu, Toshihido, *A Comprehensive Study of the Key Philosophical Concepts of Sufism and Taoism, Tokyo, 1966-67.*
Ethico-religous Concepts in the Quran, McGill,. 1966.
Ja'far Sharif, *Islam in India, or the Qamun-i Islam*, tr., by G.A. Herklots, ed., by W. Crooke, Oxford, 1921, reprinted, New Delhi, 1972.
Jalbani, G. N, *Teachings of Shah Waliyullah of Delhi*, 2nd edn., Lahore, 1973.
Khaja Khan, *Studies in Tasawwuf*, Madras, 1923.
Khushwant Singh, *A History of the Sikhs*, Vol., 1469-1839, Princeton, 1963.
Lewis, Bernard, *Islam*, New York, 1974.
Luckner, R.C, *The Bhagavad-Gita*, Oxford, 1969.
Landau, R., *The Philosophy of the Ibn'Arabi*, London, 1959.
Lings, Martin, *A Sufi Saint of the Twentieth Century*, 2nd edn., London, 1971.
McCarthy, R.I, *The Theology of al-Ash'ari*, Beirut, 1953.
MacDonald, D.B., *The Religious Attitude and Life in Islam*, Beirut, 1965.
Manucci, N., *Storia do Mogor*, 1653-1708, tr. W. Irvine, London, 1907-8, reprint, New Delhi, 1980.
Massignon, L., *La passion d'al-husayn Ibn Mansour al-Hallaj, 2 vols.*, Paris, 1922.
Essai sur les origines de lexique technique de la mystique musulmane, Paris, 1928.
Mayne, P., *Saints of Sind*, London, 1965.
Meer Hassan Ali, *Observations on the Musulmauns of India*, 2 vols., London, 1832.
Mir Valiuddin, *Love of God*, Hyderabad-Deccan, 1968.
Mohaghegh, Mahdi and Landolt, *Collected Papers on Islamic Philosophy and Mysticism*, Tehran, 1971.
Mohan Singh Diwana, *An Introduction to Punjabi Literature*, Amritsar, 1951.
Shikh Mysticism, Amritsar, 1964.
Mohiuddin Ahmad, *Saiyid Ahmad Shahid*, Lucknow, 1975.
Mole Marigan, Les Mystiques Musulmans, Paris, 1965.
Monserrate, Fr.A., *Commentary*, tr. J.S. Holyland and annotated by S.N. Banerjee, Cuttack, 1922.
Moreland, W.H, *India at the Death of Akbar*, London, 1920.
Moreland, W.H. *From Akbar to Aurangzeb*, London, 1923, reprint, New Delhi, 1972.

Mujeeb, M.,*The Indian Muslims,* London, 1969.

Nageeb al-attas, Syed, *The Mysticism of Hazmali Fansuri*, Kuala Lumpur, 1970.

Raniri and the Wajudiyyah of 17th Century Acheh, Singapore, 1966.

Some Aspects of Sufism as Understood and Practised among the Malays, ed.by S. Gordon, Singapore, 1963.

Preliminary Statement`on a General theory of the Islamization of the Malay-Indonesian Archipelago, Kuala Lumpur, 1969.

The Origin of Malay Sha'ir, Kuala Lumpur, 1968.

Concluding Postscript to the Origin of the Malay Sha'ir, Kualampur, 1971.

Nasr, Seyyed H., *Three Muslim Sages,* Cambridge, Mass., 1964.

An Introduction to Islamic Cosmological Doctrines, Cambridge, Mass.,1964.

Science and Civilization in Islam, Cambridge, Mass., 1966.

Ideas and Realities of Islam, London, 1966.

Sufi Essays, London, 1972.

ed.,Isma'ili Contributions to Islamic Culture, Tehran, 1977.

Nicholson, R.A.,*The Mysteries of Islam*, London, 1914.

Studies in Islamic Mysticism,1921, reprint, Cambridge,1967.

The Idea of Personality in Sufism, Cambridge, 1923.

A Literary History of the Arabs, Cambridge, 1930.

Tales of Mystic Meaning, London, 1931.

A Persian Forerunner of Dante, Tocoyn-on-Sea, 1944.

Rumi, Poet and Mystic, London, 1950.

ed. and tr.*Selected Poems from the Divan-i Shams-i Tabriz*, 1898, reprinted, Cambridge, 1961.

Nyberg, H. S., *Kleinere Schrifteu des Iban 'Arabi*, Leiden, 1919.

Padwick, C.E., *Muslim Devotions*, London, 1960.

Palamer, E. H., *Oririental Mysticism: A treatise on the Sufistic and Unitaian Theosophy of the Persians*, 1867, reprint, London, 1969.

Petersen,E.L., *'Ali and Mu'awiya in early Arabic Traditions*, Copenhagen, 1964.

Philips, E.C.ed., *Politics and Society in India*, London, 1963.

Qanungo, K.R., *Dara Shikoh*, Calcutta, 1935.

Qureshi, I.H., *The Administration of the Sultanate of Delhi*, Kara-

chi, 1944, reprinted, New Delhi, 1971.
The Muslim Community of the Indo-Pakistan Subcontinent, The Hague, 1962.
The Administration of the Mughul Empire, Karachi, 1966.
Rafiqi, A.Q. *Sufism in Kashmir,* Delhi, 1977.
Raverty, H.G., *Selections from the Poetry of the Afghans,* London, 1862.
Richards, J. F. *Mughal Administration in Golkonda,* Oxford, 1975.
Riazu'l Islam, *Indo-Persian Relations,* Tehran/Lahore, 1970.
Rizvi, S.A.A., *Muslim Revivalist Movements in Northern India in the Sixteenth and Seventeenth Centuries,* Agra, 1965.
Religious and Intellectual History of the Muslims in Akbar's Reign, Delhi, 1975.
A History of Sufism in India, Vol. I, Delhi, 1978
Shah Wali Allah and His Times, Canberra, 1980
Shah 'Abd al-Aziz, Canberra, 1982.
V.J.A. Flynn *Fathpur-Sikri,* Bombay, 1975.
Rosenthal, E.I.J., *Political Thought in Medieval Islam, reprint,* Cambridge, 1962.
Russel, Ralph and Khurshidu'l Islam *There Mughal Poets,* Cambridge, Mass., 1968.
Sadarangani, H.I, *Persian Poets of Sind,* Karachi, 1956.
Sadiq, M., *A History of Urdu Poetry,* London, 1964.
Saksena, B.P., *History of Shahjahan of Dihli,* Allahabad, 1958.
Saksena, R.B., *A History of Urdu Literature,* Alllahabad, 1927.
Saran, P., *Provincial Government of the Mughals,* Allahabad, 1941.
Studies in Medieval Indian History, Delhi, 1952.
Schacht, J., *The Origin of Muhammadan Jurisprudence,* Oxford, 1950.
Schimmel, A., *Islamic Literatures of India, Sindhi Literature, Classical Urdu Literature, in J. Gonda, History of Indian Literature,* Wiesbaden, 1973-75.
Gobriel's Wing, Leiden, 1963.
Mystical Dimensions of Islam, Chape Hill, 1975.
Pain and Grace, Leiden, 1976.
The Triumphal, Sum, London, 1978.
Sharif, M.M, *A History of Muslim Philosophy,* 2 Vols., Wlesbaden.
Sharma, R.S. and Jha, V. ed. *Indian Society: Historical Probings,* Delhi, 1974.
Sharma, S.R., *Mughal Government and Administration,* Bombay,

1951.
The Religious Policy of the Mughal Emperors, 2nd edn., London, 1962.

Shehadi, F., *Ghazali's Unique Unknowable God,* Leiden, 1964.

Shejwalker, T.S., *Panipat: 1761,* Poona, 1946.

Shemesh, A.B., *Taxation in Islam,* Leiden, 1958, 1965.

Sherwani, H.K., *The Bahmanis of the Deccan,* Hyderabad-Deccan, *1953.*
Muhàmmad Quli Qutb Shah, Bombay, 1968.
Cultural Trends in Medieval India, Bombay, 1968.

Siddiqi, M.Z., *Hadith Literature,* Calcutta, 1961.

Smith, M., Rabi'a *The Mystic and her Fellow Saints in Islam,* Cambridege, 1929.
An early Mystic of Baghdad, Cambridge, 1920.
Studies in early Mysticism in the Near and Middle East, London, 1931.
Al-Ghazali: the Mystic, London, 1944.
The Sufi Path of Love, London, 1954.
Readings from the Mystics of Islam, London, 1950.

Sorley, H.T., *Shah 'Abdu' i Latif of Bhit: His Poetry, Life and Times, 1940,* reprint, Oxford, 1966.

Spear, P., *Twilight of the Mughals,* 2nd edn., Cambridge, 1969, reprint, New Delhi, 1970.

Storey, C.A., *Persian Literature, a Bibliographical Survey,* London, 1927-58.

Subhan, J. A, *Sufism: Its Saints and Shrines,* 2nd edn., Lucknow, 1960.

Sufi, G.M.D., Kashmir, Lahore, 1940-9.

Tarachand, *Influence of Islam on Indian Culture,* 2nd edn., Allahabad, 1963.
Society and state in the Muhal Period. Delhi, 1961.

Tavernier, Jean-Baptiste, *Travels in India,* 1640-67, tr. V. Ball, ed. and revised by W. Crooke, London, 1925, reprinted, New Delhi, 1977.

Temple, R. C., *Legends of the Punjab* London, 1893-1901.

Thevenot, Jean de., *Relation dei'Indostan, 1666-67,* by Lovell, edn. by S.N.Sen, *The Indian Travels of Thevenat and Careri,* New Delhi, 1949.

Thomas, R. C, *Legends of the Punjab,* London, 1893-1901.

Thomas, W.F., *Mutual Influence of Muhammedans and Hindus in India,* Cambridge, 1892.

Titus, M.,*Indian Islam*, Milford, 1930, reprinted, New Delhi, 1979.

Tod, J.,*Annals and Antiquities of Rajasthan,* Oxford, 1920.

Trimingham. J.S.,*The Sufi Orders in Islam,* Oxford, 1971.

Tripathi, R.P.,*Some aspects of Muslim Administration,* 2nd edn., Allahabad, 1959.

Tritton, A.S.,*The Caliphs and their non-Mulim Subjects,* Oxford, 1930.

Underhill, E.,*Mysticism: A Study in the Nature and Development of Man's Spiritual Consciousness*, Paperback, New York, 1956.

Vaudeville, Charlotte, *Kabir,* Vol. I., Oxford, 1974.

Wahed Husain, *Administration of Justice during the Muslim Rule in India*, reprint, Delhi, 1977.

Waheed Mirza, *The Life and Works of Amir Khusrau,* Calcutta, 1935.

Walker, B., *Hindu World,* London, 1968.

Wang Gungwu, ed., *Self and Biography,* Sydney, 1974.

Watanmal, L., *The Life of Shah 'Abdul Latif,* Hyderabad, Sind, 1889.

Watt, M., *The Faith and Practice of Al-Ghazali*, London, 1953.

Muslim Intellectual: A Study of al-Ghazali, Edinburgh, 1963.

Whitting, C.E.J., *Al-Fakhri,* London, 1947.

Wolfson, H.A., *The Philosophy of the Kalam,* London, 1976.

Ysuf Hussain, *L'Inde Mystique au Moyen Age,* Paris, 1929.

Glimpses of Medieval Indian Culture, 2nd edn., Bombay, 1959.

Yusuf Iblish and Peter Lambron Wilson, *Traditional Modes of Contemplation and Action,* Tehran, 1977.

Zaehner, R.C, *Hindu and Muslim Mysticism,* London, 1960.

Ziadah, N.A.,*Sanusiyah: A Study of a Revivalist Movement in Islam,* Leiden, 1958.

Zubaid Ahmad, *The Contribution of Indo-Pakistan to Arabi Literature,* 2nd edn., Lahore, 1968.

[illegible] Sanskrit Literature, Indology [illegible]

Index